Civic Education in Ten Countries

An Empirical Study

Judith V. Torney, A. N. Oppenheim
and Russell F. Farnen

With a Contribution by
John R. Schwille

and a Foreword by
Torsten Husén

A Halsted Press Book
John Wiley & Sons
New York – London – Sydney – Toronto

Almqvist & Wiksell International
Stockholm, Sweden

First published by
Almqvist & Wiksell International
Stockholm, Sweden
ISBN 91-2200034-8

Library of Congress Cataloging in Publication Data
Torney, Judith V
Civic education in ten countries.

(International studies in evaluation; 6) "A Halsted Press book."

Bibliography: p.
1. Political socialization. 2. Civics—Study and teaching. I. Oppenheim,
Abraham Naftali, 1924—joint author. II. Farnen, Russell F., joint author.
III. Title. IV. Series.

JA76.T67   323.6'5'072   75-42147

ISBN 0-470-14989-2

Design Dick Hallström

Printed in Sweden by
Almqvist & Wiksell, Uppsala 1975

Contents

Foreword

When the International Association for the Evaluation of Educational Achievement (IEA), after the completion of its Mathematics Survey, decided to cover a number of other subject areas it courageously decided to include Civic Education. This study represented a new challenge to IEA and called both conceptually and methodologically for approaches which differed from those in subject areas like Science or English as a Foreign Language, where the main emphasis was on the study of cognitive outcomes. It was clear from the outset that one had to focus a study of Civic Education on both affective and cognitive aspects of political socialization, a process that occurs both inside and outside the school even in countries where Civic Education does not appear as part of the formal curriculum. The first task of the International Civic Education Committee was to analyze the domain of subject matter which could be considered civic education in each of the participating countries. This developed into a research endeavour in its own right. The next very demanding task was to construct instruments by means of which the more or less elusive outcomes of civic education could be assessed. The particular importance attached to the measurement of attitudes called for pioneering ventures in devising new types of instruments. "How Society Works" is one example. Since a detailed report on these endeavors could not easily be accommodated within an overall report of the entire project, Professors Oppenheim and Torney undertook to write up a separate report on instrument construction which was included in the IEA Monograph Series. (Oppenheim, A. N. and Torney, Judith. Stockholm: Almqvist & Wiksell International and New York: John Wiley, 1974.)

Irrespective of whether Civic Education is a separate school subject or not, schools purport to teach children values and attitudes as well as the factual knowledge and skills they traditionally are expected to impart. The overall social organization of the school, the student–teacher relationship and the work practices in the classroom convey certain values and attitudes. The study of how these outcomes are

11

related to factors, such as home background and teaching practices, is limited by the fact that the sources of information about the independent variables have been questionnaires administered to students, teachers, and school principals. Certainly, additional sources of information, such as direct classroom observations, student and parent interviews, and an analysis of student mass media exposure, would have been most welcome. But there is a limit to the amount of resources that can be employed in a survey conducted on relatively large nationally representative samples. On the basis of the data collected, the study stands out as an empirical landmark in the research on civic education and political socialization.

The present report addresses itself to the following issues in civic education. First, it sets out to define the subject area cross-nationally. Second, it deals with methodological problems encountered in cross-national assessment of civics achievement and attitudes among students. Third, it conveys a detailed picture of student knowledge in civics and of attitudes such as support of democratic values, support of the national government, and interest/participation in civic affairs at three age levels. Fourth, an attempt has been made to assess the relative impact of home and school on the acquisition of civic knowledge and attitudes. Fifth, particular analyses have been conducted in order to relate selected characteristics of the schools and the national political systems to the affective and cognitive outcomes of civic education. Finally, the place of a comparative study of civic education in the research on political socialization is considered.

As expected, striking differences between countries could be observed in cognitive achievement and political attitudes. However, the factor pattern of civic attitudes turned out to be strikingly similar across countries. Thus, the same three attitudinal factors mentioned in the foregoing paragraph were obtained in all countries. A consistent pattern of similarity also emerged from the regression analyses, which is an additional indication of the validity of the instruments employed. As is often the case in pioneering research, the present study in some instances raises more questions than it answers. In other instances, it has mapped out the terrain and prepared for further research.

The first draft of the present report was prepared by the authors listed on the title page. When all the chapters were available, it became evident that the material was too abundant to be accommodated in one single volume. As mentioned earlier, it was then decided to present the analyses of the curricula and instrument development separately and to limit the exposition here to a short summary. Professor Torney kindly agreed to serve as the coordinator of the entire volume; in addition to writing a considerable part of the report, she made revisions of the work of her co-authors and prepared material to tie together different parts of the volume.

The Civic Education Survey, as well as the studies conducted in other subject areas, is an outcome of collective efforts where many researchers at both the national and international level have been involved. It is, therefore, not easy to acknowledge contributions of single individuals. However, in the first place I should like to thank the members of the International Civic Education Committee, which under the chairmanship of Professor Russell F. Farnen, prepared the study. The names of the committee members are listed opposite the title page. Furthermore, thanks are due to Dr. T. Neville Postlethwaite and his successor as Executive Director of the project, Mr. Roy W. Phillipps. The former was closely involved in the instrument construction and data collection, whereas the latter took a major part in the coordination of the data analyses and the editing of the volume. I would also like to thank Mrs. Clotye Larsson and Mrs. Shirley Isgaard of IEA International who, in various ways, contributed to the preparation of the manuscript for the printer, and Mr. Robert Liljefors, Technical Officer at the Swedish National Center for IEA, for his skillful assistance with the reading of the proofs.

I should like to express our deep gratitude to the authors of this report, who had to carry a heavy burden in this venturesome project. From a wealth of data they have distilled many thought-provoking findings which have strong implications for policy makers, curriculum developers and classroom teachers interested in the inculcation and development of attitudes relevant to today's society. Further research of much of the unreported data is still desirable and to this end IEA has established a well documented Data Bank which is accessible in Stockholm and a number of other centers around the world. I hope that research workers will take the opportunity to work further on this unique data set. Thanks are also due to Dr. John R. Schwille not only for his contribution of a chapter to this volume but for his conscientious work, together with the Stockholm Data Bank team, in making the Bank a working reality.

The present report, as with other studies within the framework of the Six Subject Survey, has been brought to a successful completion

13

thanks to the financial support that IEA has obtained from various sources. The international operational costs have been met by generous grants from the Bank of Sweden Tercentenary Fund, the US Office of Education, the Ford Foundation, the Stiftung Volkswagenwerk, the Leverhulme Trust and UNESCO. The Swedish Government has, through the Office of the Chancellor of the Swedish Universities, provided data processing time. The University of Stockholm has been serving as the host of the IEA International Secretariat since 1969. Since 1971, when the Institute for the Study of International Problems in Education was established, the project has been accommodated on its premises. Finally, the publication of this report has been made possible by a grant from the Bank of Sweden Tercentenary Fund.

Stockholm, Institute for the Study of
International Problems in Education, 1975

Torsten Husén
Chairman of IEA

Authors' Preface

At every stage of the IEA Civic Education Project we have depended upon the competence and dedication of a large group of persons with diverse skills. The International Civic Education Committee, under the chairmanship of Russell Farnen, first met in the fall of 1966; at that time its membership included Dr. Aldo Fabi of Italy, Mrs. Charity James of England, Dr. Sixten Marklund of Sweden, Dr. Mohamed Mashayekhi of Iran, and Dr. Franklin Patterson of the United States. At later meetings Mr. Leslie Smith replaced Mrs. James as the English representative. Dr. Judith Torney of the United States and Dr. A. N. Oppenheim of England joined the committee in 1967 to provide additional expertise in the measurement and analysis of attitudinal outcomes of civic education. The international committee was also assisted at various phases by Mr. Kai Lehtonen (Finland), Dr. Wolfgang Hilligen (Federal Republic of Germany), Dr. Arieh Lewy (Israel), Dr. John Raven (Ireland), Dr. Sjaak Sandbergen (The Netherlands), Mr. David Francis (New Zealand), Mr. Kimmo Leimu (Finland), Dr. Mahmud Mansour (Iran), Dr. Aldo Visalberghi (Italy), Dr. Luigi Meschieri (Italy), and Mr. Henry Macintosh (England). Each of the national committee members who advised their international committee representatives as well as the National Technical Officers in each of the participating countries also have the gratitude of the authors.

The major responsibility for the design of many aspects of the Civic Education study as well as for the day-to-day administration was most ably performed by Dr. T. Neville Postlethwaite during his tenure as Executive Director of IEA. His comments on the manuscript after he had taken a position at IIEP in Paris were also most helpful to us. Mr. Roy W. Phillipps, the Executive Director from 1972 through 1974, facilitated the analysis and writing of this final report in every way possible. Members of all the IEA Committees owe a tremendous debt to these two Executive Directors as well as to the members of the IEA Council and the Chairman, Professor Torsten Husén, who has graciously provided a Foreword to this volume.

The inauguration of the IEA Spencer Fellowship program in 1972 invigorated the organization with bright young scholars interested in comparative education research. Dr. John R. Schwille ably coordinated the civics' regression analysis, first as a Spencer Fellow then as the Senior Research Officer on the IEA Data Bank Project. We are pleased to include in this report his chapter on the Cognitive Civic Education regressions. Mr. Dean Nielsen, an IEA Spencer Fellow for 1974–5, has made an important contribution to this work by revising portions of the manuscript, preparing the bibliography, and working on supplementary materials.

Those responsible for the computer work over five years have included individuals in several locations with special responsibility for Civic Education analyses: Mr. Mats Carlid and Miss Birgit Cedheim in Stockholm; Mr. Paul Barbuto and Mr. Kevin Doyle in New York; Mr. Larry Koranda and Mr. Tony Kay in Chicago. No acknowledgement would be complete without reference to Mr. Gilbert Peaker's advice and inspiration. Secretarial and editorial assistance was also provided by an international group. In Stockholm the office and editorial staff working on this volume included Mrs. Shirley Isgaard, Mrs. Clotye Larsson, Miss Stella Jones, Miss Stella McDowell, Miss Wendy Fryer, Mrs. Miyoko Forssell, Miss Marit Prestegaard, Mrs. Jackie Ahlström and Mr. Johan Klintberger. They were all much appreciated by visiting authors and committee members. As authors in dispersion we relied upon Miss Joyce Rozwadowski at the University of Illinois at Chicago Circle, and Miss Clare Legget at the London School of Economics. Our colleges and universities have each provided supplementary funds for additional analysis, which are gratefully acknowledged.

Our acknowledgements would not be complete without reference to those who participated with us in discussion of the project and reacted to preliminary versions of this report: Dr. Jeffrey Bulcock, Dr. Ingemar Fagerlind, Mr. Frank Litton, Mrs. Anne Vollmar, and Dr. David Walker. Finally we are grateful to our families who coped with the stresses and strains of everyday life while we were travelling for "the project."

We wish for those who work in future comparative education research the same vision of the contribution of the IEA subject area surveys which kept us continually challenged.

Judith V. Torney
University of Illinois at Chicago Circle

A. N. Oppenheim   *Russell F. Farnen*
London School of Economics   Madison College, Virginia

Summary

This study is concerned with the political education of young people in 10 nations. In each of these countries the schools carry out a systematic teaching program aimed at producing well-informed, democratically active young citizens. The study was designed to show how and to what extent these objectives are being achieved, and what other influences besides the school (such as the family, the mass media or friends) are important.

The research began in 1967 with a careful study of reports and materials on Civic Education obtained from the countries taking part. From this it became obvious that civic education involves not only factual *knowledge*, but also the teaching of democratic *attitudes* (such as tolerance, support for civil liberties, etc.). Extensive pilot work (Oppenheim and Torney, 1974), led to the construction of a set of classroom administered questionnaires covering factual knowledge, civic attitudes, perception and understanding of political processes, as well as background information. In 1971 these were answered by more than 30 000 10-year-olds, 14-year-olds and pre-university students, and by their teachers, in the following countries: Federal Republic of Germany, Finland, Iran, Ireland, Israel, Italy, the Netherlands, New Zealand, Sweden, and the United States of America. (The Iranian data were later withdrawn from international analysis.) In each country, the student respondents were a representative sample of the school population at each of the three age-levels. The results were submitted to a number of complex statistical analyses, to bring out similarities and differences between the political education in different countries; to show some of the influence processes at work; and to compare the results at different age-levels.

Political socialization is a complex process, and its outcomes are subtle and varied. Knowledge and awareness of political processes interact with civic attitudes and democratic ideals under the influence of parents, teachers, friends, the mass media and personal experience in the minds of young people whose capacity for understanding develops very gradually. The study attempts to chart these processes, and to disentangle some of the major and minor influences at work.

What kind of citizens do these countries bring up? The widely-held objective of producing loyal, informed, critical and actively participating democratic citizens was *not* successfully attained in any of the countries in this study. In some, there was a nationalistic pattern of strong support for the central government but below-average support for democratic values (for example, Israel, the United States); in others, there was strong support for democratic values, but below-average support for the central government (for example the Federal Republic of Germany, the Netherlands); and there were other combinations of outcomes. It may be that there is some inherent incompatibility in trying to foster both patriotism and such democratic values as freedom to criticize the government, equal rights for all citizens, tolerance of diversity, and freedom of the mass media.

While the students' responses from different countries varied considerably, the underlying influencing processes were remarkably similar—despite differences in régime, school system, social structure, and so on. Many expectations about important influences were *not* borne out; for example, there were few differences between the responses, on average, by boys and by girls, or by children from different social backgrounds; adolescent rebelliousness was not an important factor, and participation in civics-related activities did not seem to be very important. Indeed, some of the findings were *contrary* to expectation: for example, "traditional" schools with a strong emphasis on memorizing facts produced students who tended to be *less* knowledgeable and informed about politics; and students who reported frequent participation in patriotic rituals were both less knowledgeable and less democratic in their outlook. On the whole, the results showed that specific classroom practices were less important than what is often called the "classroom climate": more knowledgeable, less authoritarian, and more interested students came from schools where they were encouraged to have free discussion and to express their opinion in class. But students who reported having frequent political discussions with teachers were not necessarily more democratic in their attitudes.

Disentangling cause-and-effect was difficult. Students who were interested in radio or television programs dealing with civics-related topics were also more knowledgeable and more democratic on the scales—but which came first? Did these programs arouse student interest, or did they become interested in such programs because of what they learned at school? Or both, at different times, perhaps? Caution must therefore be used in translating these findings into action.

The students' mental development is of crucial importance. Their intelligence and their command of language are both relevant to their grasp of political attitudes and principles. Their understanding of the way society operates goes through a series of stages, from "sheltered" to "sophisticated"—and sometimes to "cynical." A young child tends to see things in concrete, personal terms; thus, he can understand the basic functions of the Police, but not yet those of Political Parties or of Labor Unions. As he grows older, he becomes more aware of broad political disagreement among adults, and also of such problems as oppression and class bias. Now he can begin to perceive and to understand the functions of many social institutions concerned with adult conflict. Eventually, he outgrows the "harmonious" view of society, and in some countries (for example, the Federal Republic of Germany) he may come to reject many political institutions.

All these findings have many broad implications, but there are some results which have particular relevance to teachers and to parents.

IMPLICATIONS FOR TEACHERS

The use of printed drill in class, the stress on factual aspects of the subject matter, and the engagement of the student in various patriotic rituals (such as flag raising ceremonies) have, if anything, a counter-productive effect in civic education.

The acquisition of knowledge does not correlate highly with support for democratic values, and even less as children get older. It is therefore unwise to assume that the knowledgeable student will automatically support democratic values. Neither does knowledge of civics correlate highly with various measures of political participation.

The students' home background and general vocabulary level are related more strongly to the acquisition of factual knowledge than to democratic values or to political interests. A school where students come from lower socio-economic strata, for example, does not face severe handicaps in developing democratic ideals.

The development of a classroom climate or atmosphere where students are encouraged to express their own opinions seems to foster several important outcomes of civic education.

Pre-adolescents often find it difficult to understand the purpose of political institutions because they have not yet discovered that different groups of adults may disagree about public policy. They tend to perceive adult society as monolithic and omniscient, and consequently see no reason for pressure groups, political parties, or institutions which serve as arenas where conflicts can be resolved or adjudicated. Schools need to address this issue.

IMPLICATIONS FOR PARENTS

The present study is primarily school-oriented; it is seriously deficient in data about the home, and no parent interviews could be carried out. From the students some basic data have been obtained, however, such as parental occupation and education, family size, and also some information on how the child and the parent interact. For example, are young people aware of the political views held by their parents and, if so, do they agree with them? To a slight extent, more political discussion and awareness in the home correlate with more democratic attitudes in the child—but children tend to agree less with their parents as they grow older.

Such home attributes as "bookishness," parental education, and family size would seem to have relatively little impact; position in society, as indicated by parental occupation, did not make a substantial difference, though the relationship was stronger in some countries than in others. It is widely assumed that sex roles are primarily developed within the family, but few differences were found on the scales between boys and girls. Rebelliousness, or rejection of non-political parental values, also made little difference to civic attitudes.

In terms of leisure-time activities, there was no evidence that doing things such as helping in a political campaign or other civic activities had any formative influence. However, children with an interest in civics-related radio or television programs tended to be both more knowledgeable and more democratic—though the cause-and-effect relationship is unclear.

In general, peer-group behavior has only a slight impact on civic education. However, the tendency to settle disagreements within the group by taking a vote did correlate with some democratic attitudes.

CONCLUSION

Nations place great faith in the ability of social institutions, especially schools, to prepare young people for citizenship. This faith is only justified in part, because influences outside the school may also be important, and because sometimes the effects of the school are contrary to what was intended; more importantly, this study shows that nowhere has the system proved fully capable of producing the ideal goal of a well-informed citizenry, with democratic attitudes and values, supportive of government policies, and interested in taking part in civic affairs. Perhaps a hierarchical organization such as the School is not the right setting for inculcating democratic values (certainly school alone cannot accomplish this task). Perhaps there is an inherent contradiction among these four components of the democratic ideal. Perhaps nationalism or some other ideology distorts the pattern. Perhaps the basic objectives of democratic civic education should be questioned. Clearly the introduction of a new course here, or a different requirement for teachers there, is unlikely to produce a ready solution. This study shows that a basic reconsideration is needed of what can be expected of political education in democracy.

Chapter 1

Background of Civic Education Project

The decision to include Civic Education in the Six Subject Survey conducted by the International Association for the Evaluation of Educational Achievement (IEA) is an indication of an increasing awareness that it is insufficient for citizens in a society to know how to read and write, to perform mathematical operations and to understand physical facts. They should also be capable of understanding social realities and must hold attitudes toward each other and toward social and political institutions which allow society to function. To phrase it in another way, citizens should be capable of exercising the fundamental freedoms which are guaranteed to them, willing to grant these rights to others, and prepared to cope with future social and political events whose character cannot be predicted.

In addition to recognizing the importance of the development of political attitudes, civic behavior, and knowledge of society, the inclusion of Civic Education in this international survey indicates a willingness to test the frequent assumption that only parents and the home exert strong or important influences upon a child's political attitudes. Recognition of the importance of parental influence upon personality development in the early years and of the cumulative effect of childhood experience seems in some cases to have obscured the importance of socialization processes which influence attitude development at all ages and in many settings. During childhood and adolescence a large portion of that socialization occurs in educational institutions. It is therefore an especially significant step that an organization with particular competence in assessing school inputs has conducted this major survey of the outcomes of Civic Education. Also significant is the scope of the project which tested more than 30 000 students at three age levels, as well as 5 000 of their teachers in 1 300 schools in 10 countries.

One of the major aims of IEA has been to assess the influence of input variables which display only limited variability within a single nation but considerable variability if different nations are examined. IEA was uniquely equipped to assess the influence of societal factors as well as school inputs upon civic knowledge and attitudes in countries which vary in their governmental structures as well as in their educational systems.

Another major aim of IEA is to assist the analyst of educational policy who seeks information on the results of various alternative courses of budgetary and political action. This study may be thought of as assessing naturally occurring experiments in educational practice in civics. The data make it possible to observe the effect of many educational practices embedded in a variety of national policy orientations. Comparative research in the attitudinal and cognitive outcomes of schooling makes a major contribution to educational policy studies.

A third aim of IEA is to provide information to teachers who want to know whether one method ought to be preferred over another or whether the style of interaction within the classroom may be as important as the content or thoroughness of a presentation. Although survey data cannot do justice to the vital interaction within the classroom, it can suggest a variety of possibilities for further consideration and evaluation.

These three aims are common to the purpose and framework of all the IEA subject area surveys.

THE STUDY OF CIVIC EDUCATION

Any field of study needs to be examined from more than one point of view—particularly when the field is so broadly defined. The traditional view of "citizenship training" has a long history traced back to Plato and Aristotle. Moving closer to our own time, in the early 1930's Charles Merriam (1931) conducted an eight-nation study of citizenship focussing particularly on the growth of political loyalty and patriotism. However, the purpose here is not to demonstrate that concern for Civic Education is a historical phenomenon of interest to philosophers or political scientists, but that it is a contemporary problem which should be of interest to all citizens. Of course, some citizens are more likely to be interested in the results of a study of civic education than are others—teachers of social studies or history more interested than teachers of mathematics; members of school advisory boards more than recreation district boards; officials in national ministries or offices of education more than those in ministries of defense; political scientists more than chemists. When the streets become unsafe because of crime, when corrupt political leaders are re-elected because of voter apathy, when fundamental rights are regularly violated because of public indifference, the impact of the failure of Civic Education in pre-adulthood extends to every member of the society.

A second major aspect of this study is the current body of research on political socialization, political learning, and the acquisition of political attitudes by children and adolescents. Political socialization research has most frequently been performed by political scientists seeking to understand the sources of citizen support for the political system or by psychologists and sociologists seeking to trace commonalities in the development of attitudes toward elements of the social or governmental system. Previous studies of political socialization have only occasionally included measures of civic knowledge as part of the test battery; the affective or attitudinal outcomes of civic education have been more extensively researched. These attitudinal outcomes have been measured by scales indexing a sense of political efficacy, cynicism about politics, perception of citizen duty, value placed upon elections, and interest in political issues, to mention only a few. Political socialization research is usually less concerned with the "oughts" of education or character training than is research in Civic Education or citizenship education. It has in particular been concerned with the role of the family, the media, and the peer group as well as the school. During the past few years, as a subdiscipline of political science, this research has developed empirical indices, conceptual frames of reference, and bodies of generalizations about the political orientation of youth. Although the background of research available in 1969 was of some importance in formulating the IEA Civic Education study, it was not fully sufficient as a framework because of the paucity of information about school inputs.

A third aspect of the Civic Education study comes from social and developmental psychology which has provided techniques for the measurement of attitudes and conceptualizations of the cognitive development of children. The cross-national data collected by the IEA Civic Education study is particularly important for the light it sheds upon basic processes of attitudinal development which characterize children in a variety of cultural settings.

Political socialization research attempts to describe what is learned about political life, from whom, at what stage in life, under what mediating conditions, and with what effects for the individual (and the political system). There have been some attempts to provide a conceptual framework for understanding this socialization process. Dawson and Prewitt (1969) distinguished between direct and indirect forms of socialization. In a direct mode, the individual is presented with explicitly political learning experiences or stimuli. Being taught about citizenship in a civics classroom is an example of this mode. In the indirect mode, phenomena such as the transfer of predispositions from family or teacher to child are also included. Dawson and Prewitt also refer to the "apprenticeship mode," where the individual learns through practice in non-political organizations (such as the Girl Guides or Boy Scouts) how to cast votes and choose leaders, what respect for rules means, etc. Finally, they consider the "generalization mode" where individuals move from predispositions such as trusting human nature to being optimistic about politicians or politics in general.

Hess and Torney (1967) discuss four ways of conceptualizing the process of political socialization. Their first model is the Accumulation Model. This model is based on the implicit assumption that if children are exposed to symbols, ideas and attitudes, they will accumulate and absorb them and, presumably, express them when appropriate. This process certainly accounts for part of political socialization, for example, learning facts about the structure of the government, though it is insufficient to account for all of it. This model assumes that the teacher or parent has basic control of all relevant information and that the major information flow occurs in one direction only. The child's task is to be a passive recipient. Factors which are of little concern to this model are the organization of knowledge, previous learning, the readiness of the child to learn, and the mediation of other factors of the social milieu. This theory is comforting to some teachers and parents because it suggests a direct relationship between the amount of time spent, the effort expended, the punishment or reward used, and the learning achieved. Because the learning process is a complex one which is influenced by many characteristics of the child, this Accumulation Model cannot be relied upon exclusively.

The Accumulation Model also introduces a value problem because, as Cleary (1971) aptly points out, democratic values by their nature demand that one use a process other than indoctrination. Otherwise the contradiction between the value and the mode of transmission is extreme, e.g., "You will not be authoritarian because I tell you not to be."

A second model, most clearly applicable to acquisition of a political party allegiance, is the Identification Model. It assumes that the child copies behavior, particularly that of parents, in choosing superordinate labels (e.g., political party) which have a considerable effect upon issue orientation and candidate preference in adulthood. This model may operate even when the parent has no intention of transmitting his preference for political party or candidate to the child. Among political scientists with an interest in this field identification as the source of political attitudes is of great interest (Hyman, 1959; Hirsch, 1971; Dawson and Prewitt, 1969), in part because these researchers are interested in the continuity from generation to generation of political party membership.

The Identification Model does emphasize the groups to which one belongs and their influence upon attitudes. For the young child, the family is his most important primary group; so, it is the influence of parents that is designated in using the Identification Model. When a child enters elementary school, teachers become important as figures to be imitated; peers also become crucial reference groups. Every part of the experience which teachers and peers present to the child is available for his modeling including pieces of information or behavior which they intend for him to copy as well as other elements which are not perceived by the sources as material to be imitated.

A third model is the Role Transfer Model. It is in some respects the reciprocal of the Identification Model. Children rely on previous experience to guide their forming orientations toward the political and legal system, with which they have had little direct experience. For example, the child has had little experience with laws, a great deal of experience with rules. The generalization of expectations and behaviors from one situation to another often occurs without any direct reinforcement from agents of socialization. Children structure and sometimes distort information in accordance with these transferred role expectations. They may make assumptions based on very vague information. But it should be stressed that actual similarities among many levels of social authority (family, school, nation) make the Role Transfer Model particularly important. The

27

Identification Model focusses on the way a child copies the behavior of an authority (like a parent); the Role Transfer Model focusses on the way a child takes a role with which he is familiar (as a child in his home, as a pupil in his school) and transfers or generalizes role-appropriate behavior to the political system (as a citizen). Mutual expectations are important in the learning of many social roles and they are the basis of children's relation to the political system.

The Cognitive-Developmental Model stresses the older child's increasing ability to deal with abstract and complex aspects of the social world as his tendency to see things in a personalized and egocentric fashion declines. This is the model from among the four discussed which has the clearest developmental, age-related character. To understand attitude development, one must be aware of the ways in which thought processes of the 10-year-old differ from those of the 17-year-old; this includes the way in which the child transforms and misperceives information as well as the way he accurately stores and reproduces it. The child's capacity to reason, using certain levels of thought, has an influence upon his attitudes and therefore upon his socialization. When applied to the classroom, this point of view gives clues to obstacles children may experience in the socialization process. For example, the acceptance of the value of dissent in matters of public policy requires that individuals be able to perceive an ideal mode of government operation and contrast it with the realities of a given practical political situation.

These four models of socialization cannot be fully tested in a survey such as that reported here. The models nevertheless present the variety of processes which operate in home situations, school environments, and the society as a whole to influence the acquisition of civic knowledge and attitudes.

The present survey focusses most sharply on the varieties of Civic Education content, the sequence of political concept development, and the relative influence of various socializing agents, all in a cross-national perspective. A number of studies addressing these and related issues have appeared since 1969, when the IEA Civic Questionnaire was formalized. Although this study cannot fully explicate these problems and models, interpretation of the IEA data is enriched by previous attempts to provide a conceptual framework.

The Sequence of Political Concept Development

The design and integration of a survey of attitudes and information also requires knowledge of existing material concerning the sequence of political concept formation in children. The target populations for this survey (as in all IEA subject areas) included those students in school at age 10, age 14 and the pre-university year in secondary school. Most previous political socialization literature has also focussed upon this age span.

Childhood and adolescence are important periods for political learning. For example, Hess and Torney (1967) demonstrated considerable differences between the attitudes of children seven and 13 years old; attitudes of the older group were very similar to those of teachers. Andrain (1971) interrelated factual knowledge of different governmental levels and of the political regime with cognitive abilities, motivation and grade level. He concluded that "age and increased education, together with intelligence, provide those cognitive abilities necessary to comprehend and internalize knowledge about the complex political world and to process the diverse political stimuli which the child confronts increasingly as he or she matures."

Connell (1971) studied children aged 5–16 in Sydney, Australia through the use of interviews. His report identifies several stages of political attitude and concept development. For example, Australian children move from the intuitive thinking stage, where confusion and fantasy reign and attitudes are unstable, to primitive realism where the self is distinguished from the political world; in a third stage construction of the political order occurs and the perception of relationships among political actors is expanded at a fourth level of ideological thinking typified by use of abstract terms in political argument and conception of alternative courses of action.

Most studies have found that the child's initial attachments are to his political community, his nation, his tribe or some other basic polity. He learns, for instance, that he is a Swede or a New Zealander and that this makes him different in some respects from citizens of other systems who may speak a different language. His initial emotional reaction to the system is predominantly positive, but is not based on much information or reasoning. His feeling toward political or authoritative figures, such as the policeman, the mayor, the chancellor, the prime minister, the Shah, the president is usually one of trust.

Between the ages of 12 and 15 the youth's political image begins to take on greater depth, clarity and precision. He begins to associate issues and ideological orientations with political parties. His capacity to perceive and understand more abstract political symbols increases. The nation is no longer represented by the Queen, President or Prime Minister alone. Other political institutions have taken on greater salience and meaning. Students then begin to assess politics, government, office holders and political authority figures more realistically. The political system and political roles are still held in high esteem, but students exhibit somewhat more ideological concerns. They become capable of seeing the interrelationship between political roles of, for instance, the President or Prime Minister or Member of Parliament or Congressmen. The fast pace of such politicization between the ages of 11 and 13 brings the young adolescent to a stage in his political development which is not greatly different from that of many adults in his own political community.

Although it has not been conclusively demonstrated that middle childhood and early adolescence are critical periods for the development of political attitudes immutable to further influence (Torney and Morris, 1972), it can be argued that for most people certain consensual values are internalized during that period that are not likely to be significantly modified (Weissburg, 1974; Langton, 1969). Those who have investigated politicization among slightly older students pinpoint later adolescence as a time when an active phase of political participation is initiated.

The School in the Socialization Process

Opinions differ about the influence of the school in the development of political attitudes, skills and cognitions. In 1931, Merriam labeled the school as "the major instrument in the shaping of civic education" in eight Western nations, including the United States, the United Kingdom, Italy and Germany. He concluded that "In all the systems appraised in this study the school emerges as the heart of the civic education of the political community, and in all probability will continue to function increasingly in this role."

Even in more recent studies, claims about the importance of the school receive some support (Almond and Verba, 1963; Hess and Torney, 1967). However, the particular aspect of the school which has the major impact is still not clear. Some researchers in education argue that civics courses have no real importance and that school life as such (organization, teaching processes, student grouping, social climate, decision-making) is the only factor of real import. According to the latter position, having different types of school means having different types of Civic Education, regardless of the intent of their published curricula. For example, in Sweden a number of comparative studies have been made between the new comprehensive school system and the traditional parallel school structure. The student's self-evaluation, which is thought to be of importance for the development of a sense of political efficacy, was higher among comprehensive school students than among students in the *folkskola* and the *realskola* (Magnusson, 1960). In a corresponding study, students in the comprehensive system showed greater independence of adult authority than students in the traditional schools (Anderson, 1969). In other comparisons of this type, however, no significant differences were found. Ehman (1969) has concluded that teacher willingness to discuss controversial issues, together with the openness of the classroom did have an impact on political learning in the United States.

Debates about the *relative* impacts of home and school also abound in the political socialization literature. Weissburg (1974) summarizes this research. He concludes that even if the family is of considerably greater importance than the school in terms of amount of influence, in Western democratic societies the school system is viewed as an appropriate means to reshape social and political attitudes by prescribing political content while attempts to manipulate the family would be viewed as highly inappropriate.

In a most recent report of a study of high school seniors, their parents, teachers and principals conducted in 1965 in the United States Jennings and Niemi (1974) conclude the following:

> "Although the impact of parents on their offspring varied enormously across the range of political orientations, residues of that impact almost always remained when other relevant characteristics in the school and the larger environment were controlled statistically . . . (p. 327)."

On the other hand, they show that "the high school's influence, while not as strong across the board as that of the family, has independent strength in a number of areas..." (p. 328). With regard to the sum total influence of a variety of socialization agents in the United States, Jennings and Niemi report that even when a variety of family and school factors are considered, variations in the political dispositions of 18-year-olds cannot be fully accounted for. They list a variety of reasons for this, including the pluralism of socialization forces and the importance of the self as an independent and mediating influence. A multi-faceted approach to understanding the processes and outputs of Civic Education is clearly indicated.

31

Conclusion

Many of the findings reviewed here have been replicated in studies conducted in countries other than the United States. The process of political socialization in nations sharing western democratic orientations, values and institutions (the "Atlantic political community" nations) seems basically similar, despite varying practices of child rearing, schooling, communications, peer group relations, and political structures and institutions.

The study of Civic Education and political socialization undertaken here took some direction from some of the research reviewed above which was available at the time of instrument construction. A major contribution of the IEA Civic Education study to the field of political socialization could be to give estimates of the balance of home and school factors on a cross-national comparative basis and also to indicate the specific characteristics of the school (and to some extent the home and peer group) which are important for explaining the acquisition of civic knowledge and political attitudes.

A full understanding of the development and background of this study also requires a brief description of the process by which the study was designed.

BRIEF HISTORY OF THE CIVIC EDUCATION SURVEY

The first study of educational achievement by IEA dealt with mathematics performance in twelve countries (Husén, ed., 1967). In its later phases IEA has broadened its efforts to include six other subjects, namely, Science, Literature, Reading Comprehension, French as a Foreign Language, English as a Foreign Language and Civic Education. The decision on whether or not to participate in any given subject area was made at each national educational research center (National Center) in the 22 countries which held membership in the IEA Council.

Work on the IEA Civic Education project began in 1966 after Dr Birger Bromsjö of the University of Stockholm, School of Education delivered a paper indicating that a cross-national study of Civic Education was both important and feasible within the purposes, goals, and scope of IEA. The list of major content topics proposed by Bromsjö for testing "civics" included the following: problems of co-existence (small-group functions); purpose of society (rights and duties); working life (policy making); law and justice; economic problems; problems of democracy (propaganda analysis, political parties and organizations, public opinion); and international problems.

Subsequently an International Civic Education Committee was appointed, meeting first in Hamburg, Federal Republic of Germany in 1966. Each committee member came from a nation where the National Center had either decided to participate in the Civic Education study or was considering doing so. This allowed the Committee to develop an international perspective on the problem of defining the subject area. (Its membership over the several years of the project is listed opposite the title page of this volume.)

The survey of Civic Education definitions and practices began in late 1966 with a collection of national documents from England, the Federal Republic of Germany, Finland, Iran, Italy, Sweden, and the United States. A shorter working paper was received from Israel. Later Ireland, New Zealand, and the Netherlands joined the project, each producing a set of national documents on Civic Education. Some of the countries which were considering joining the survey withdrew at this stage, generally for financial reasons. In the present volume a full report is made on the data collected in all of the above countries except England and Iran. England, which contributed considerably to the first phase of the Civic Education survey, had to withdraw before the final testing. Since this country was a full contributor up to the field testing stage, it has been included in some reports dealing with the development of test instruments. Iran elected to withdraw from international analyses after field testing. Thus only a portion of the data collected there is included in this volume.

In sum, ten of the present twenty-two IEA member nations completed testing in Civic Education, including the Federal Republic of Germany, Finland, Iran, Ireland, Israel, Italy, the Netherlands, New Zealand, Sweden and the United States. All of these countries plus England contributed to the curriculum analysis and construction of the instruments.

Defining the Subject Area

Several possible names for this subject area were considered, such as Social Education, Political Studies, Political Socialization and Social Studies Education. When it was decided to use the term Civic Education this did not mean that the subject was to be studied only in terms of the content of a narrowly defined curriculum, however. The

Committee members recognized that construction of an international test could not begin without further information on how Civic Education was defined in different nations. This was the impetus for the curriculum survey in which each of the National Centers was asked to provide the Committee with certain materials and a national working paper summarizing the most important features of the following:

1. The major goals of Civic Education as seen in public laws or other statements.
2. The most important curricular statements relating to civic instruction up to and including the three student years which were to be examined (i.e., for students about 10, 14, and 18 years old).
3. Examples of Civic Education examinations.
4. Summary lists of texts used in civic instruction, tables of contents from representative textbooks, summary lists of other teaching materials such as films, recordings and newspapers.
5. Estimates of the amount of time students spend in studying civic education, number of students taking specific courses and training of Civic Education teachers.

After receiving this information from the National Centers the International Civic Education Committee met again in April of 1967. It was clear from the surveys of curriculum content in the participating nations that knowledge and analytical skills formed only part of the intended outcomes of the civics curriculum. Attitudes such as support for democratic values and institutions, support for civil liberties, a desire to participate actively in civic affairs, observance of the law, loyalty to country, acceptance of certain standards of moral conduct were also of great importance. This led to the decision to include civic attitudes as measured outcomes of Civic Education. Consequently two separate subcommittees were formed in order to develop international survey instruments for both the cognitive domain and the affective domain of Civic Education.

National Civic Education Goals and Curricula

A common core of Civic Education objectives and content was sought by examining national reports on goals (public laws, official statements, constitutions) and curriculum (teachers guides, textbooks, course syllabi). A summary of these goal and curriculum statements for each country is presented briefly here.

34

Federal Republic of Germany. Since West Germany is a Federal Republic it does not have a formal "national education system." Instead, each of the 11 states (*Länder*) sets its own educational objectives and establishes its own curriculum. However, in recent years national planning efforts have brought state ministers together in such a way that educational policy in the Federal Republic of Germany is becoming more uniform from state to state. The national report from the Federal Republic of Germany indicates that Civic Education is taught in schools throughout the country under the name of community studies (*"Gemeinshaftskunde"*), Citizenship Education (*"Staatsbürgerkunde"*) or political education (*"politische Bildung"*). In at least seven *Länder* the subjects to be taught are specified in the state constitution. They include the following information, values and skills: knowledge about democratic institutions, knowledge about the German economy and culture, and knowledge about Western Civilization, respect for the dignity of man, tolerance of others' opinions, patriotism, international peace and conciliation, "liberal democratic outlook," political responsibility, and skills for social action.

The methods for teaching these concepts and the sequencing of political education varies from state to state, but the information gathered from the state of Hessen shows a pattern which is becoming increasingly typical. Children between the ages of 10 and 11 years are taught information on government officials and organizations; they are instructed in current social realities, such as unemployment and strikes, and are given training in citizenship skills, such as electing a class spokesman. By the time the children are 14 years old in Hessen they are given more sophisticated information on such aspects of the national political system as political parties, unions and federal organizations, and taught about more abstract democratic values such as citizen rights, the value of criticism and the importance of rules and leadership. In addition, 14-year-olds are taught about international organizations and world interdependence. Youth in Hessen (as in the other *Länder*) who remain in school until the pre-university year are all expected to study for the *Abitur* or school leaving examination which includes two areas of political education. At this level they study topics which are both more general in scope (e.g., understanding of contemporary German politics, economics and culture) and more controversial (e.g., democratic and totalitarian policies from 1918–1941). International topics are also stressed at this level, including European unification and world decolonization. Finally, the national report indicates that there is general attention to citizen rights and responsibility for public service at this age level.

Finland. In Finland, Civic Education is based on a nationally adopted curriculum. According to the National Center report, historical study has been used to teach understanding of modern Finnish society and general social, economic and political life. In official statements much emphasis is placed on the concepts of tolerating and understanding others and on modern economic life, including personal enterprise and thrift. With respect to the actual Civics curriculum, students aged 11 to 15 years study topics such as the following: citizens' rights and obligations, the democratic state, the three branches of government, public finance and taxation, national defense, local government and political parties. Much study is also given to economic affairs (including the role of the state in the economy, economic terms and economic activities) and social affairs (including labor laws, social security, population, public health, criminality and emigration). At the pre-university year, students learn about the separation of powers principle, popular rule and parliamentarianism, foreign policy, the bureaucracy, local government, the military, religious liberty; they study in depth some of those topics introduced earlier in the schools. Economic, social and cultural topics are also discussed under concepts such as economic growth, communications processes, the monetary system, full employment, trade unions, labor law, the school system and the role of education in society.

Israel. Israel's Ministry of Education has defined the official civics program to be taught at different age levels and in different types of schools (vocational, agricultural and academic secondary schools). The Ministry requires that certain basic concepts be taught such as: citizenship; nationalism; the State of Israel; the Diaspora and Israel; the welfare state; the legislative, executive and judicial authorities in Israel; Israel and the developing nations; reparations agreements and compulsory service laws; religious minorities in the state; the World Jewish Congress; and the law of Jewish repatriation as citizens of Israel. The major goal of Civic Education is to prepare the student for successful integration into adult social and political life.

All schools in Israel follow the same curriculum in Civic Education. Civic Education as such is taught as a separate subject at age 12 and 17 only, but the development of governmental systems and social

36

conditions in foreign nations are major topics of study in history classes throughout all school years.

While the preliminary work was being done on the international civics study, Israel was developing a new national civics curriculum. By 1971 the National Department of Education had implemented a new curriculum at age 12 and was about to reform the curriculum for the 17-year-olds. The curriculum at both levels was organized to cover not only areas of cognitive competence, but also values and skills. However, since none of the respondents in the Israeli sample had been exposed to the new curriculum, a review of the traditional one is more appropriate.

The report on the curriculum for 12-year-olds reveals an emphasis on information about government offices and institutions. Topics emphasized at this level included the following: the individual and society, the nation and the state, civil rights and duties, elections, governmental structure, the army, the courts, the president and prime minister, the bureaucracy, local government and democracy. At the 17-year-old level the emphasis was still on formal or organizational aspects of the government, though there was also some emphasis on national and world problems. Topics of discussion at this level included the following: basic law and political parties; legislative bodies and processes; the executive (including the national bureaucracy) and judicial branches of government; internal and external security systems; employer and employee organizations; the international position of modern Israel; religion and the State; world Jewry; national and international economics; and current problems with immigration, minorities, villages and cities, youth and social services.

Italy. Italian goals for Civic Education were formulated by decrees from the Ministry of Education in 1955 (primary school reform) and in 1958 (secondary school reform) to be part of the course of study in history. Generally the aims of Civic Education are the development of interest in public life, active and responsible participation in it and endorsement of community values for the common good.

In Italy at the primary school level, the Civics curriculum emphasizes the family, one's basic rights and duties, love of country, the environment, the importance of occupations and work, national traditions and public respect, traffic education, and social institutions and organizations. Also discussed in history lessons are the Italian

Constitution, the structure of the state, and the principles of international cooperation. In addition, character and habit formation are stressed, with particular attention devoted to the development of personal responsibility and group solidarity. At the secondary level, the Italian Civic Education curriculum emphasizes training in the Constitution of the Republic; the development of democracy; the World Wars, the resistance and the fight for liberation; the concepts of liberty, justice, law, duty and rights; and certain other "spiritual" (religious or humanistic) values. At the pre-university level, Italian students study the history, structure, and "inspirational principles" of the Italian Republic; the guarantees and limits of freedom; social solidarity and the state; the history of social problems; the social organization of work; social assistance; the drafting and execution of laws; and international organizations.

Sweden. In its 1962 and 1964 statutes, the Swedish government determined that the purpose of civics instruction is to make students aware of modern society and of their educational and occupational opportunities, while serving to further their individual and social development. The National Board of Education has divided its regulations regarding Civic Education into different requirements for different age groups. For example, at the lower grades nature study and civics study are combined into a local studies program. At the intermediate and upper levels, social orientation or knowledge of society (*"samhällskunskap"*) is taught through topics in civics, history, and geography classes. Pupils are exposed to an expanding communities sequence—from their personal lives to the family, to the school, to the municipality, to the nation, and to the Nordic and international communities. According to the National Board, schools are generally to teach those skills which are necessary for pupils to become active, contributing members of a democratic society and a communal life.

The expanding sequence mentioned above is reflected in the curriculum at various age levels. Swedish pupils aged 10–12 years study three principal items, namely, how people live and work together, basic economic problems, and school life, and make study visits dealing with postal services, banking, telephones, and means of transport. Thirteen to 15-year-olds study societies and clubs, school life, occupations, social problems, local government, elections, racial problems, national governmental organization, taxation, basic economics, national defense and international cooperation. At the pre-university year, students in the humanities and social science concentrations (or tracks) study peoples of the world, the population of Sweden, the world economy, current trends in Sweden's economy, economic expansion, problems of education, principles of a market economy, price fixing and resource use, the economic balance of society, foreign trade, comparative economic policy, regional surveys, settlement patterns, town and country planning, the Constitution, politics and political theories, public opinion analysis, democracy and dictatorship, international relations, the international economy, and current social problems.

United States. Like the Federal Republic of Germany, the United States has a federal system of government which means that it has no formal national educational system. But also like the Federal Republic of Germany, the several states have developed rather similar educational goals, many of which are spelled out in state laws. For example, more than 40 out of 50 states require by law that instruction be given in the United States Constitution; more than 30 require a study of United States History and of the State Constitution; more than 20 require the study of state history, United States Government, education about proper respect for the flag; geography, instruction in patriotism and courses in civics; and between 16 and 18 specifically require instruction in the Declaration of Independence, local government, the principles of representative government, the duties of citizenship, democracy and American institutions. Somewhat fewer states oblige schools to teach about election laws, Communism, political parties, and economic principles. The majority of states require a course in Civic Education for 13- or 14-year-olds.

A review of curriculum materials from the first six grades in the various states typically shows a pattern where the following subjects predominate: "social studies," geography, history (particularly biographies of famous men) and local studies. Thereafter the curriculum pattern becomes more complicated and varied. Perhaps the best way to assess what is taught in the middle and pre-university school grades is to examine the content of several widely adopted texts. The examination of a representative cross section of ninth grade civics texts reveals the predominance of the following topics: the federal government and the Constitution, citizenship, personal and community needs and goals, government services, controls and finances, state and local government, national defense and international topics. At the pre-university year the texts examined devote most attention to the following topics: foundations and basic concepts of American Government (including the Constitution); the executive, legislative and judicial branches of government; political processes, organizations and participation; the national economy; foreign policy and national defense; territories and dependencies, state and local government; the study of "political science;" essentials of effective, democratic and responsible citizenship; and personal rights and liberties.

Other countries. As was mentioned earlier two countries, England and Iran, participated in the goals and curriculum analysis phase of the Civic Education project but did not enter the final stages of analysis. By contrast, three countries, Ireland, the Netherlands and New Zealand did enter into the final stages of the project, but were not included in the initial phases when national Civic Education goals and curricula were compared. As a result, the general themes chosen for concentrated examination may not have fully represented what is actually taught in the participating countries. The inclusion of Iran in this initial phase expands the international scope of the project even though full analysis of that data was not conducted.

The profile for Civic Education goals and curriculum in Iran is very similar to that of the "Western" countries. One theme lacking in its profile which is common in other countries is that of citizen rights. Themes which are present in its profile not mentioned by the other countries are the following: protection of public property, limits on social freedom, one-party government systems, uses of citizen's identity card, insurance and international diplomacy.

Summary of National Statements

This brief survey of national goals and curricula illustrates that Civic Education appears under various titles in different nations. In some it is treated as a separate subject, in others as a series of topics within other subjects such as history or geography. Nearly all nations teach basic facts about governmental organization, the nature of law, international affairs, the national economic system, the functions of education, voting procedures, electoral and political party processes, and individual freedom and social responsibility. Considerable cross-national variation was also observed. Certain nations (Italy, Iran, Israel, the United States) seem to stress national history, government structure, social conformity and civil obedience; others

40

emphasize social services and cooperation (Sweden), economic themes (Finland), or dissent toleration and conflict resolution (England, Federal Republic of Germany). Themes common in all countries, but receiving different degrees of emphasis were comparative government, modern political theory, war and peace and the use of inquiry and social science methods in solving social problems. Affective outcomes (democratic and citizenship values, political participation) were also common in all nations surveyed.

Variations among nations were also noted in the degree of uniformity of the Civic Education curriculum and in the time devoted to its study. Considerable regional variations occurs in the nations where there is no formal national education system (Federal Republic of Germany, United States, England). In other nations where national boards or departments make policy, considerable uniformity exists (Sweden, Finland, Israel). In two nations it was difficult to determine to what extent national guidelines for Civic Education were being applied in individual schools (Italy, Iran). With respect to the time factor, it is clear that considerable instructional time is devoted to Civic Education at all age levels in the Federal Republic of Germany, Sweden, Finland and the United States. In addition, this instruction appears to be sequenced in a relatively orderly manner. In the other countries (Italy, Iran, England, Israel before the reforms) relatively fewer hours were devoted to Civic Education instruction.

Having taken these national variations into consideration, the International Civic Education Committee arrived at a set of themes which were agreed upon as common to all participating nations. These were the following:

Cognitive Content:

1. Constitutional framework
2. Meaning of concepts related to citizenship, such as patriotism, duties, authority
3. Historical development of country
4. Governmental structure, organization, and institutions at different levels
5. Political processes including elections, political parties and voting
6. The legislative, executive, and judicial branches at different levels
7. The bureaucracy and civil service

8. Foreign affairs and international organizations
9. Government and the economy, including taxation
10. Government and social services, including welfare
11. Communication and mass media
12. The social sciences and methods of problem solving
13. Man as a social and interdependent animal

Affective Content:

1. Understanding rights and obligations: respect for others, tolerance, loyalty, belief in equality, respect for law, willingness to defend the homeland
2. Support for the democratic way of life: belief in freedom of the individual, right of citizens to express dissent, right to be represented; willingness to participate by voting
3. Appreciation of world interdependence and amity
4. Respect for government and for national tradition without ethnocentrism
5. Respect for diversity in moral and religious values, as well as respect for political opposition
6. Interest in current events and social problems at national and international level

Behavioral Content:

1. Willingness to obey the law, pay taxes, accept military obligations, participate in patriotic rituals
2. Participation in group decision-making by joining, leading, and voting in groups
3. Practicing tolerance and showing respect for others
4. Demonstrating logical and critical thinking ability in problem solving
5. Reading newspapers and learning from current sources of information such as radio, books, magazines, and television

The Research Instruments

Considerable further work was needed to devise items to measure the achievement of these objectives in the participating nations. The instrument development and pilot testing for cognitive and some behavioral content are summarized in Chapter 4 of this volume. The instrument development and pilot testing for the affective and some behavioral content is detailed in Oppenheim and Torney (1974) and is summarized in Chapter 7 of this volume. The political so-

42

cialization literature which had been published up to 1969 was also a source for the attitudinal measures.

In addition to measuring student outcomes in Civics, the gathering of extensive background information was required. The development of the questions specifically for the political background variables is briefly described in Chapter 7. General background information (family socioeconomic level, family participation in educational activities), general motivational information (Liking for school) and a measure of general verbal ability (Word Knowledge) were taken from the IEA General Stage 2 questionnaires. Previous IEA studies gave clear guidance as to the most efficient measures to include and, in the case of Home background and Type of school, the criterion-scaled values and weightings to be utilized. It was not possible to collect any information directly from parents.

There was also considerable similarity between the instruments administered to teachers of Civic Education and those administered to teachers in other IEA subject area surveys. These included measures of types of teaching methods and student evaluation used, number of years of training, and the like. There were also sets of questions specifically for Civic Education, including amount of social science study, perception of the appropriateness of discussing controversial topics in the classroom, membership in subject matter associations, conception of the "good citizen," and assessment of the importance of teaching about topics such as democracy, political history, social problems, international problems, local and national government and political parties.

School principals and administrators were asked to indicate at what grade students began the study of social studies or civics and who was involved in making decisions about textbooks, school regulations, syllabi, teaching methods, and so on. The National Centers were also asked to provide general information on political parties and voting statistics, mass media usage, and other factors useful for describing the political context in which the educational system was operating.

"Dry Run," Field Testing and Data Analysis

In May of 1970 a "Dry Run" was conducted, administering the cognitive and attitudinal civics instruments together for the first time. As a result it was found that the two types of measures worked well together, as well as independently. Consequently, a complete battery of achievement tests, attitudinal measures, and background questionnaires was submitted to the participating National Centers for their final approval. As a result, the following nations agreed to participate in full field testing at the population levels indicated below:

	Population		
	I (age 10)	II (age 14)	IV (pre-university)
Federal Republic of Germany	×	×	×
Finland		×	×
Iran		×	×
Ireland		×	×
Israel	×	×	
Italy	×	×	
Netherlands	×	×	×
New Zealand		×	×
Sweden			×
United States		×	×

The project proceeded to a full field testing in the ten nations in 1971. The statistical analysis (which followed the format used in other IEA subject areas) and write-up of the results continued through 1974. Throughout this process the various National Centers were involved in answering questions about national response patterns and reviewing the manuscripts of various chapters.

At one point in the design of the study an attempt was made to formulate a series of hypotheses. One problem with this procedure was that a distinction between dependent or outcome variables and independent or explanatory variables was of limited value, since a number of the scores could be conceptualized in either fashion. Our major guidelines for analysis were therefore the previous IEA studies which utilized between-country analysis (included here in Chapter 5 for cognitive measures and Chapters 9 and 11 for attitudinal measures) and between-student analysis (Chapter 6 for cognitive, and Chapter 10 for attitudinal measures). The other chapters describe the sampling and characteristics of respondents (Chapters 2 and 3), the construction of the instruments (Chapters 4, 7, and 8); and the conclusions (Chapter 12).

Conclusion

This chapter has introduced the aims and perspectives which were important in the development of the IEA Civic Education Survey, previous literature on the process of political socialization and the major activities of the International Civic Education Committee from 1966 to 1974. It has also summarized by country the results of an assessment of Civic Education goals and curricula. It is clear that all participating nations are engaged in some sort of civic and political education. While there are differences in Civic Education objectives from one country to another the International Committee was able to define the subject area in a way that was acceptable to all participating nations and was able to develop a set of themes which formed the basis for the construction of research instruments suitable for the cross-national assessment of cognitive and affective outcomes.

Chapter 2

Sampling and Procedures of the Civic Education Study

GENERAL SAMPLING AIMS AND PROCEDURES

The purpose of the IEA study of Civic Education was to assess and compare the relative impact of various characteristics of the school and of educational and other experiences upon the growth of information about and the development of attitudes toward governmental structure and process. Previous studies of political socialization, such as those described in Chapter 1, have used ingenious methods to investigate knowledge and attitudes. Some have compared the character of these predispositions in countries of divergent political backgrounds and have used information about the political or educational system to speculate about the sources of between-country differences in young people.

These studies, for all their carefully thought-out methods and diverse samples, have had one major factor standing in the way of making replicable estimates of the frequency of participation in Country X *versus* Country Y—their use of convenience samples. Some political socialization or Civic Education studies within the United States have used national random samples of students (Langton and Jennings, 1968) or tested a large number of children from a variety of national regions and community sizes (Hess and Torney, 1967). Some studies within a single country other than the United States (Weiler's (1971) study of German youth, Abramson's (1967) study of English secondary schools) have paid careful attention to sampling. However, cross-national investigations involving three or more countries have typically relied upon convenience samples (some adequate and representative of major societal groups—others mainly commended to the researchers by their availability). This is an understandable failing. Drawing a national probability sample of any country's adults or school children is an expensive enterprise. Doing this for more than one country requires a tremendous effort and specialized cooperation from within the country.

46

Because a major aim of IEA studies is to estimate population values in order to make fair comparisons between country's educational inputs and outputs as well as to estimate the percentage of explained variation attributable to different sources, sampling has played an important role in IEA studies. Although the more technical aspects of the sampling plans will be discussed in Peaker (1975), relevant details of the sampling execution in the Civic Education survey are important for interpretation of the findings.

Population Definitions

Age has been an important factor in many studies of political socialization and Civic Education, sometimes operationalized by interviewing children of specified ages, at other times by choosing students according to their school grade level. Most of the previously conducted IEA studies were less concerned with making statements about changes over age and more interested in assessing the impact of school variations at different points in the educational process.

The following target populations were defined for Civic Education, in the same manner as for the other subject areas in Stages 2 and 3 of IEA testing:

Population I—all students aged 10:00–10:11 years/months at the time of testing in full-time schooling. This is a point at which nearly all students can read but have not yet left a general teacher.

Population II—all students aged 14:00–14:11 in full-time schooling. This is the last point where more than 75% of an age group will still be in compulsory schooling in the majority of IEA member countries.

Population IV—all students in the pre-university grade or year in full-time schooling (in university-preparing programs or programs of the same length). These students varied in age both within and between countries.

Note that Population III was a group tested at the option of a National Center and the data were not included in the international analyses.

The Sample Populations as defined in each country differed in some respects from these target populations. In many countries students enrolled in classes for the retarded or handicapped were excluded. In countries where 14-year-olds are spread over several grade levels (due to retention in a grade, late school beginning, or other factors) the decision was made by the National Center to draw only those 14-year-olds who were in a specified number of adjacent grades rather than dipping down into lower grade levels. This is indicated in the specific sampling descriptions of countries which adopted this procedure. Students who dropped out of school previous to the age of 14 were not sampled. In the countries included in the Civic Education survey the percentage of the 14-year-old age cohort which is still in school ranges from 25 percent in Iran and 55 percent in Italy to more than 75 percent in the other countries tested. The figure is 99 percent for Finland, Sweden, New Zealand and the United States. Because it is presumed that national citizenship is a role for all students, in defining the sample populations no distinction was made between those who took Civic Education classes and those who did not take such subjects. Likewise, in choosing schools no distinction was made between those where Civic Education classes were offered and those whose formal curriculum did not include them.

Country Inclusion in Civic Education Study

The decision whether or not to administer the Civics Education tests in a country was taken by the research organization which was a member of IEA and designated as the National Center. This Center also took responsibility for the sampling and testing. Although 21 countries elected to participate in some phase of the Six Subject Survey conducted by IEA in 1970–72 (Science, Reading, Comprehension, Literature in the Mother Tongue—Stage 2; Civic Education, French as a Foreign Language, English as a Foreign Language—Stage 3) only 10 countries elected to participate in the final Civic Education portion of the research. England, which participated in early pilot phases of the work, did not test in the final field work because of funding problems. Iran, where data were collected in 1970–71, requested in 1973 that they be withdrawn from international analysis. The presentation of data from Iran is therefore confined to computation of median scale reliabilities (Chapter 8) which had been completed before the withdrawal was requested. Although considerable research indicates the importance of the years before 14 in the development of political and civic orientations, the National Centers declined in all but three countries to test national samples of 10-year-olds, preferring to devote their limited resources to older students. In addition, Israel tested a judgment sample of this younger group.

Detailed General Procedures for Sampling

One of the objectives of the research was to estimate national mean values of both input and outcome measures with the lowest possible errors of sampling. The use of stratified probability samples from the chosen population was the method used to accomplish this aim.

Typically two-stage stratified probability sampling was employed. In the first stage, schools were to be selected from a nationally stratified frame with a probability proportional to the size of their student body. In the second stage, students were to be selected randomly from within the chosen schools with a probability inversely proportional to the size of the school. From each school approximately equal numbers of students were to be drawn, with each student having the same non-zero chance of entering the sample. Sampling errors were to be reduced by stratifying the school by factors such as size of school, type of school, and region served by the school. The exact variables used in stratification and variations from these sampling procedures are described briefly for each country in the following section. In planning the sampling, one guiding principle was to keep the average number of students selected from each school to about 30 with as many schools as possible included, depending on the manpower and money available to carry out the survey.

In addition to this planned sampling of students, it was planned to sample general classroom teachers within the selected Population I schools (at least five teachers per school). Within the Population II and IV schools, teachers who taught Civic Education or any of the social studies (History, Political Science, Geography, Sociology or Economics) were to be sampled. This procedure of testing a sample of teachers in each school corresponded to the general decision by the IEA Technical Committee that no attempt would be made to link students to those particular teachers with whom they had studied, but rather that each school would be represented by a composite picture obtained from the responses of a number of teachers in the school. The principal or headmaster was to provide information about the general character of the school program in social studies, and information about school budget and facilities.

This was, in brief outline, the plan proposed in much greater detail to each National Center which had agreed to test in Stage 3.

The National Center in each country then provided the International Sampling Referee (Gilbert Peaker, C.B.E.) with their plans for sampling which, when amended and approved, were referred to as the Design Sample for each country. The National Technical Officer and his staff in each country then had the responsibility for drawing schools according to the sampling plan, and also drawing a list of replacements in the case of refusals. In most countries, schools were enumerated separately for each population. In a few countries the National Technical Officer began with the list of schools sampled for Stage 2 testing in Mother Tongue and Science and drew replacements as necessary for schools which no longer existed or which could not be included in Stage 3 for other reasons. In most countries new samples were drawn for stage 3. The next step was contacting schools which had been drawn, most of which were cooperative. However, in some countries where a substantial number of schools declined to participate, extensive use of the list of replacements was required.

After obtaining the cooperation of a school, the students were drawn from within that school by the procedure described earlier. The "notional date" referred to in the reports of testing was the date on which the students' ages were determined (e.g., countries testing students who were 14 as of March 1, 1971 would designate that as their notional date). The actual numbers of schools, teachers and students who answered the questionnaires and tests was the Executed Sample. There is not a perfect correspondence between Design and Executed Sample. In some cases the school census data, from which the sampling frame was designed, were out of date; other factors such as postal strikes, teacher strikes, floods and epidemics caused shortfall in some of the strata. The collection of all data from the Executed Sample completed the part of the research for which the National Centers had major responsibility.

At the IEA Data Processing Center in New York a screening was conducted for missing information and unusable protocols. If a principal had failed to fill out a questionnaire describing his school, or if no teacher had answered a teacher questionnaire, the entire school and all its students were dropped. This caused a further reduction in the number of schools, teachers and students, the resulting sample being called the Achieved Sample.

Table 2.1 reports the number of schools and students in the Achieved Sample in Civic Education for each country and population. Student weights per stratum were calculated to bring each

Table 2.1. *Achieved Sample Sizes for Schools, Teachers and Students by Country and Population*

Country	Population I			Population II			Population IV		
	Schls	Tchrs	Stds	Schls	Tchrs	Stds	Schls	Tchrs	Stds
FRG	36	178	1 083	45	218	1 317	44	254	1 188
Finland	—	—	—	72	302	2 401	73	333	2 358
Ireland	—	—	—	43	270	848	38	259	803
Israel	16	33	433	47	106	1 048	—	—	—
Italy	127	553	2 423	67	320	939	—	—	—
Netherlands	78	151	1 762	74	168	1 696	46	69	1 314
New Zealand	—	—	—	76	582	2 010	68	565	1 697
Sweden	—	—	—	—	—	—	88	418	1 867
United States	—	—	—	127	317	3 207	120	285	3 045

Note: The numbers recorded in this table are derived from the number of cases entering the final analyses. These are sometimes slightly different from the numbers in the samples and in the current IEA Data Bank. (The IEA Data Bank brings together all the data from the Six Subject survey. It is available from IEA at the University of Stockholm and a number of other centers throughout the world.)

country's Achieved Sample into correspondence with the Design Sample. For example, in order to correct for undersampling in a stratum, students in that stratum were given weights larger than 1.00; in order to correct for oversampling in a stratum, students in that stratum were given weights smaller than 1.00. The weights for all students in a country average out to exactly 1.00, meaning that the sum of weights is equivalent (within rounding errors) to the number of students tested. The weights for the aggregated teacher and school variables are the sum of the student weights in·that school. This weighted set of school, teacher, and student responses comprise the data which were analyzed. There are also some particulars of sampling and testing in the various countries that need to be noted.

Description of Sampling and Testing by Country

Federal Republic of Germany. In the Federal Republic of Germany testing was conducted in June of 1971 for Populations I and II; Population IV was tested in November 1971 because of a clash with other examination schedules. Population I was defined as 10-year-old students and Population II as 14-year-old students (not including those in private schools or schools for the retarded or handicapped— estimated as totaling less than 10 % of the age group). Population

IV was defined as all students in the last grade of the *Gymnasium* (excluding the 10% enrolled in private schools). Three stratification criteria were applied for Populations I and II: type of school (*Volksschule, Realschule, Gymnasium*); area (10 *Bundesländer* plus West Berlin); size of school (three categories). For Population IV only students in *Gymnasia* were included. Sampling in the Federal Republic suffered from three problems; the recent reorganization of the school system which was not always reflected in available school descriptions; the refusal to participate by one *Bundesland* with the loss of more than 100 designated schools; and a high refusal rate by individual schools. In the remaining Bundesländer at Population I, 108 schools were designated and testing took place in 36; at Population II, 110 schools were designated and testing took place in 45. It is clear that the data from this country should be examined with some caution.

Finland. In Finland Population II was tested between February 20 and March 10, 1971 (with a notional testing date of March 1). Population IV was tested October 25 through November 13 (with a notional testing date of November 1, 1971). The reason for the discrepancy was that the Population IV pre-university students were preparing for their examinations and ended their regular school work in February. Population II was defined as all Finnish-speaking 14-year-olds attending either a civic school or a secondary school. Population IV was defined as all Finnish-speaking students at the pre-university grade of the secondary school. Less than 10% of the students in Finland speak only Swedish; they were not included in the population definitions. The sampling of schools for Stage 2 was the basis of sampling for the Civic Education testing in Stage 3. Schools were stratified according to type (Civic—Population II only; secondary—state; secondary private or communal; secondary municipal), by locale (urban areas classified as 1st or 2nd class towns or rural) and by size of school. Testing was conducted in 72 schools for Population II and 73 for Population IV.

Iran. In Iran testing was conducted from March 15 to 31, 1971. Population II was defined as all 14-year-old students in grades 7, 8, or 9. In each chosen school every 14-year-old in any of these three consecutive grades was tested. Population IV was defined as those students in the 12th grade, which is the pre-university year (most of the respondents were 18 years old).

52

Sampling was carried out in three stages instead of two in Iran. First, from among the 152 regions (Shahazatan), 20 were drawn. The second stage was a draw of schools stratified by type (public–private) and sex (boys or girls). Five schools were selected in each locality for each age group in proportion to the total number of schools of each type. As indicated above, once a school had been chosen, all 14-year-olds in the three adjacent grades or all students in the pre-university grade level (whichever level the school represented) were tested. If the number of students thereby tested in any given school was greater than thirty, every other child was subsampled.

Testing was conducted in 60 schools for Population II and 58 schools for Population IV. As already indicated, outcome data for Iran are presented only in the general test development section in Chapter 8.

Ireland. The notional testing date in Ireland was October 1, 1971. Population II was defined as all students in post-primary education who were aged 14 and were enrolled in post-primary schools. Population IV was defined as all students in their pre-university year at school on October 1, 1971. Their ages could range from 16 to 20.

The basic design entailed stratification of pupils in post-primary education according to sex, school type (secondary or vocational), religious affiliation of school (Catholic or non-Catholic), region (Dublin; other cities; remainder of Ireland). Slightly more than 20 % of the selected schools refused to participate, and within participating schools 40 % of the teachers declined to answer the teacher questionnaire. Testing was conducted in 43 schools for Population II and 38 schools for Population IV.

Israel. The notional date for Civic Education testing in Israel was May 1, 1971. Population I was defined as all 10 to 11-year-olds who were studying in the state and independent school systems, excluding those in schools for physically and mentally handicapped (about 3 %). Population II was defined as all students aged 14 and 15 currently enrolled in elementary, middle or secondary schools. Some of these students were in grade eight but the majority were in grade nine.

The basic sampling design entailed stratification of students in all populations according to size and type of school. Type of school was especially important in Population II where the following types were used: secondary mixed sex; secondary boys; secondary girls; agricultural; continuation; teacher training; vocational mixed sex; vocational boys; vocational girls; multi-type and elementary. At Population I testing was conducted in 16 schools; at Population II testing was conducted in 47 schools. In Population I the schools chosen were those judged by the National Center to be representative; they were not systematically sampled.

Italy. Testing was conducted during the first week in December, 1971. The notional date was March 31, 1971. Population I was defined as students who were 10-year-olds and who were studying in the fifth grade. Population II was defined as students who were 14 years old, who were in the eighth or ninth grade and who were taking English (the other subject area in which Italy was testing). Population I schools were stratified according to geographic region (Northern, Central and Southern including islands), and by size of schools (4 categories). Population II schools were stratified according to geographic region, size, and type of school (secondary middle, classical and scientific lyceums, teacher training colleges, technical institutes, vocational institutes). At Population I testing was conducted in 127 schools; at Population II testing took place in 67 schools.

Netherlands. Testing took place between October 15 and December 1, 1971. The definition of target populations was as follows: Population I, 10-year-old students enrolled in primary education excluding those in schools for mentally or physically handicapped. Population II, 14-year-old students enrolled in four major school types comprising 85 % of the total school enrollment (VWO/HAVO—general secondary of an academic type; MAVO—general secondary; LTS—mixed general and vocational education for boys; LHNO—mixed general and vocational elucation for girls). Population IV was defined as all students in examination classes from *gymnasium* and *atheneum* (general secondary education of an academic type), MMS and HAVO (see above) and teacher training academies. This comprised essentially all the students who are in school at this level.

The sampling frame for Population I distinguished schools by type of residence area (areas of more than 50 000; suburban of 20 000 to 50 000; rural of less than 20 000) and denomination (Protestant-Christian, Roman Catholic, public, private). At Population I, 172

54

schools were contacted and 78 tested. For Population II the stratification of schools was done on the basis of school type (VWO/HAVO, MAVO, LTS, and LHNO) and denomination (public, Protestant-Christian; Roman Catholic; and private). Of 178 schools contacted at Population II, 74 were actually tested.

At Population IV an ideal sampling grid was formed on the basis of school type and denomination, as in Population II. Because a large proportion of refusals was expected here, three different samples were drawn, two of them including Civic Education. Of 231 schools contacted, 46 were tested. In view of the large refusal rate, data from this country should be examined with caution also.

New Zealand. The testing period in New Zealand was August 9 to 17, 1971 (notional date July 1, 1971). Population II was defined as all students who were 14 years old. Population IV was defined as all students in Form VII (grade 13). The sample was very similar to that used in Stage 2 of the IEA project—many of the same schools participating again. The schools were stratified by size (3 categories), coeducational status (boys, girls, coeducational), and location (urban center of 20 000 or more, or rural). Thirty students were tested in each school. Testing was completed in 76 schools at Population II and 68 at Population IV.

Sweden. Testing took place from May 15 to June 9, 1971; notional date was May 15, 1971. Population IV was the only group tested in Civic Education and was defined as all students in Grade 3 of *Gymnasium* or grade 2 of *Fackskola* or combination thereof. Every school with Population IV students enrolled was included in one of the three subject areas testing at Stage 3. Therefore every third Population IV school in the country was used for Civic Education. Within each selected school one student was drawn at random and the class or track to which he belonged was tested as a class group. Since classes are not streamed, each class is a reasonable sample of the school as a whole. The result was that 11 schools which could be classified as *Gymnasia*, 69 classified as *Gymnasia/Fackskola* combination, and 8 *Fackskola* were tested in Civic Education.

United States. Testing was conducted from April 1 to May 1, 1971 with a notional testing date of April 15, 1971. The definitions of target population were identical to internationally defined populations (with the exclusion of retarded and handicapped). Three-stage sampling was conducted in the United States with communities being sampled at the first stage. At the second stage schools within selected communities were sampled. At the third stage, students were sampled. Twenty-eight possible combinations of community size, type of school, and socio-economic status formed the stratification categories (with independent private schools forming the twenty-ninth category). For Population II a total of 127 schools participated in testing; for Population IV the figure was 120.

Design Effect

Simple random sample formulae for estimating errors are inappropriate for use in a two- or three-stage sampling design such as that used in this study. For between-student analysis the simple random sample estimate of error based on the N of students in the sample is too small because there is a clustering effect of students within schools. A measure to assess the magnitude of this effect is the design effect (DEFF). DEFF is defined as the square of the ratio of the assessed standard error of the estimate to the expected standard error for a simple random sample of the same size. In testing mean values, correlation coefficients, and regression coefficients for significance it is necessary to multiply the simple random sample standard error by $DEFF^{\frac{1}{2}}$. This multiplier has been estimated to be about 2.0 for the standard error of means and 1.5 for the standard error of correlations. These figures for Civic Education data are taken from an extensive analysis by Peaker, (1975).

ADMINISTRATION OF DATA COLLECTION AND ANALYSIS

The Main Testing Program

The procedures to be followed in the main testing, both at national and at school levels, were set out in detail in three manuals. Just as the National Technical Officer, working at the National Center, was the link between a country and IEA International, so the school coordinator, who was usually but not always the principal or headmaster, was the link between a school and the National Center. The school coordinator was responsible for all the arrangements made within the school. This included producing the school lists from which the samples were drawn, the reception, distribution, collection, and return of tests and questionnaires, the nomination of the teachers asked to respond to the Teacher Questionnaires and the completion of the School Questionnaire.

Once the total sample of students had been drawn, packets of all the materials required by each student together with return envelopes were made up and dispatched to schools by the National Centers. This included appropriate machine-readable cards (MRC) for responses in those countries which were using them. It was then that the school coordinator took over.

In many cases regional meetings of school coordinators were held to familiarize them with the materials and procedures. Two manuals, one for coordinators and one for test administrators, gave full details and clear instructions. Most of the tests were administered by classroom teachers or university students hired by the National Center. They gave the respondents general instructions as to the form of answering the Civic Education Cognitive, Civic Education Affective and Civic Education Background Questionnaires but did not answer specific queries during the testing itself. Teachers did help the students fill in other background information including father's occupation. The average time for completing the battery of Civic Education tests was approximately two hours. Students were not asked to put their names on the tests and there was no indication as to which students had studied with which teachers. All material from each school was packed together and returned to the National Center.

The Initial Processing of the Data

National Centers had the responsibility of ensuring that the identification sections on all the forms were correctly filled in and of performing certain coding operations on items such as age, grade, father's occupation and expected occupation.

The National Centers sent the student materials either on MRC cards to the Measurement Research Center, Iowa City, Iowa scoring service or on punched cards or on magnetic tape (card images) to the IEA Data Processing Center at Teachers College, Columbia University, New York. Several National Centers asked extra questions or gave extra tests to additional populations that were of special interest within their own countries. The results of these special analyses will be reported separately by the respective National Centers.

The Analysis of the Data

MRC cards were scored by the Iowa scoring service and the results transmitted to the New York Data Processing Center on magnetic tape. All data were edited, sorted, and filed by the Center. Total scores and subscores for each student and' for all predictor and criterion variables were then computed and the weighted files were produced, as indicated in the previous section.

For each population, country by country, weighted means, standard deviations, and frequency distributions were produced. Weighting was applied for each stratum employed in the sampling plan to correct for any shortfall of schools or students within the stratum.

For use of those analyzing the data, item analyses and analyses of scale reliability were produced by the New York unit for each test for each country. For each population tested, student, teacher, and school files of edited data were prepared in New York and then sent to a second IEA Data Processing Unit in Stockholm where the main work of the bivariate and multivariate analyses was carried out.

Chapter 3

Characteristics of Participating Schools, Teachers and Students

The purpose of this chapter is to present information about the characteristics of the student and teacher participants as well as the schools in which the Civic Education survey was conducted. Some information about the general character of education in these countries will also be summarized.

DESCRIPTIVE INFORMATION CONCERNING NATIONS AND RESPONDENTS

The material in this chapter comes from a variety of sources—from student background questionnaires, from questionnaires filled out by the school principal or headmaster, from questionnaires filled out by the teachers and from national summary reports.

Table 3.1 presents some of the demographic and political characteristics of the participating nations. With the exception of Iran these are all major industrialized nations where half or more of the population live in urban areas. Two of the countries have federal systems of government (the United States with 50 states and the Federal Republic of Germany with 10 *Länder*); the remainder have unitary systems.

Table 3.2 summarizes major characteristics of the educational systems (considered at the national level). The age of entry into school and the duration of compulsory education vary. The most important information on this table for our purposes is the percentage of an age group which is still in school at the pre-university level (Population IV).

The nations involved in this study have high rates of literacy, lengthy periods of compulsory education, and fairly elitist patterns for secondary school attendance and post-secondary transfer (except in the cases of the United States and Sweden). Educational tracking

Table 3.1. *Demographic and Other Principal Characteristics of the Ten Countries*

Country	Area (1 000 sq mi)	Population (1 000 000's)	Employment in: (%) Agri-culture	Industry	Other	Per capita income (US $)	% of GNP spent on education	Private autos	Telephones	Radios	T.V. Sets	Newspapers	Percent urban population	Type of government
FRG	96[a]	59.5[a]	9[c]	48[c]	43[c]	2 520[c]	3.6[e]	196[d]	209[d]	329	277	331[d]	79	Federal Republic
Finland	130[c]	4.7[c]	19[c]	27[c]	54[c]	1 700[c]	6.4	151[c]	232[c]	374[b]	229[b]	405[c]	50.5	Unitary Republic
Iran	636[a]	30.5[a]	42[c]	17[c]	41[c]	321[c]	N/A	5.5[f]	8.2[d]	56[e]	6.5[e]	17	31	Unitary Monarchy
Ireland	27[b]	3[b]	26[c]	28[c]	46[c]	953[d]	4.4[f]	131[c]	92[c]	58	132	239	49.2	Unitary Republic
Israel	8[a]	3.2[a]	12[d]	25[d]	63[d]	1 663[d]	3.4	35[e]	127[d]	190[d]	23[d]	210	82	Unitary Republic
Italy	116[a]	54.5[a]	21	40	39	1 525[d]	4.8[e]	166[d]	157[d]	206[c]	165[c]	127	48	Unitary Republic
Netherlands	13[c]	13.1[c]	7[c]	39[c]	54[c]	1 797[d]	6.9	192	154	284	234	320	52.7	Unitary Monarchy
New Zealand	103[a]	2.9[a]	14[c]	35[c]	51[c]	1 762[c]	7.4	310	413	237	201	378	77.3	Unitary Commonwlt
Sweden	173[a]	8.2[a]	7	39	54	3 553[d]	4.4	277[c]	501[d]	Combined 295[d]		514	77	Unitary Monarchy
United States	3 617[c]	203.1[c]	6[a]	34[a]	60[a]	4 440[a]	7.7	442[c]	591	1 403	399	305	73.5	Federal Republic

Note: Data are for 1973 unless otherwise noted.

Source: The Official Associated Press Almanac. New York: Almanac Publishing Company, Inc., 1973, 673–783.

Table 3.2. *Selected Structural Features in National Systems of Education*

	FRG	Finland	Israel[e]	Ireland[f]	Iran	Italy	Netherlands	New Zealand	Sweden	United States
Age of entry to compulsory education	6	7	5	6	6	6	7	6[c]	7	6
Age at which compulsory education ends	15[a]	16	14	14	14	14	15	15	16	16
Duration of compulsory education in years	9	8	9	8	6	8	8	9	9	10
Modal age of transfer from primary to secondary education	10–12[a]	11	14	12	10–11	13–14	11	13	14[i]	11–12
Percentage of age group in school:										
Population I	99	99	99	99	75	99	99	99	99	99
Population II	94	99	84	82	25	55	98	99	99	99
Population IV	9[b]	21	39	38[g]	9	16	13	13[d]	45[h]	75

Note: Data in this table are for 1969 unless noted otherwise.

[a] Some schools have an observation or guidance period associated with transfer from primary to secondary education.

[b] This figure is for the *Gymnasia* only; there are many students of Population IV age in other schools such as higher technical schools.

[c] Six is legal age of entry but most children start school at five.

[d] This figure is for the terminal grade of the secondary school system, i.e., the grade which was sampled. It is also possible to proceed to university from the previous grade.

[e] Data for Hebrew speaking schools only.

[f] Data for year 1971.

[g] Data for 17 year olds only.

[h] If vocational and technical education is included, this figure is 75 %.

[i] Primary and secondary schools are not distinguished administratively.

occurs early in about half the nations (Federal Republic of Germany, Iran, Ireland, the Netherlands and New Zealand; Finland at the time of this survey) and later in the other half.

More extensive descriptions of the educational systems in these countries may be found in Passow et al. (1975).

Table 3.3 presents the mean age in years for the student respondents to the IEA Civic Education survey. Population I and II were defined as age groups. These means indicate that in the majority of

Table 3.3. *Mean Student Age in Years (Excluding Omits)*

Population I		Population IV	
FRG	10.4	FRG	18.9
Italy	10.5	Finland	19.0
Netherlands	10.5	Iran	19.0
		Ireland	17.2
Population II		New Zealand	17.5
FRG	14.4	Netherlands	17.8
Finland	14.5	Sweden	19.3
Iran	14.4	United States	17.5
Ireland	14.5		
Israel	14.5		
Italy	14.5		
Netherlands	14.5		
New Zealand	14.4		
United States	14.9		

countries tested students were on the average 10.5 and 14.5 years old. In the United States, the average student was about five months older. Population IV is defined as a grade group rather than an age group. There is, for that reason, considerably more variability in the age of Population IV students both within and between countries. Students tended to be younger in Ireland, New Zealand, the Netherlands, and the United States (average age below eighteen years), and older in the other countries (average nearly nineteen or older).

Table 3.4 presents the mean grade level of student respondents. This reflects the sampling plan adopted at the national level which sometimes included more than one grade level at Population II and sometimes more than one type of school and grade level at Population IV.

Table 3.4. *Mean Student Grade Level (Excluding Omits)*

Population II		Population IV	
FRG	8.2	FRG	13.0
Finland	7.7	Finland	12.1
Ireland	10.4	Ireland	13.0
Israel	8.8	Netherlands	11.3
Italy	8.5	New Zealand	13.0
Netherlands	8.7	Sweden	11.7
New Zealand	9.8	United States	12.0
United States	9.0		

Table 3.5. *Student Distribution by Sex (Excluding Omits)*

Country	% Male	% Female
Population I		
Israel	43.6	56.4
FRG	50.3	49.7
Italy	55.5	44.5
Netherlands	48.4	51.6
Population II		
FRG	51.9	48.1
Finland	51.0	49.0
Iran	59.1	40.9
Ireland	49.2	50.8
Israel	54.3	45.7
Italy	61.5	38.5
Netherlands	50.5	49.5
New Zealand	49.9	50.1
United States	52.1	47.9
Population IV		
FRG	70.4	29.6
Finland	40.6	59.4
Iran	58.2	41.8
Ireland	47.6	52.4
Netherlands	58.6	41.4
New Zealand	67.2	32.8
Sweden	48.1	51.9
United States	51.5	48.5

Table 3.5 gives the distribution of students by sex. Italy and Iran are the only countries where the male/female ratio departs from an even split by more than 5 % at the Population I or II level. At Population IV the Federal Republic of Germany, Iran, the Netherlands, and New Zealand all have more than 55 % male students. Finland, on the other hand, enrolls more than 55 % female students at Population IV. The majority of schools in which testing was conducted were co-educational except in Iran and Ireland, where the majority of schools were segregated by sex. A number of single-sex schools were reported in Italy, the Netherlands and New Zealand as well.

Table 3.6. *Student Reports of Father's Occupation by Country, Population and Occupational Category (Excluding Omits)*

Country	Unclas-sified	Unskilled and semiskilled	Skilled and clerical	Professional and manager-ial
Population I				
FRG	1.1	3.4	84.6	10.9
Israel	4.5	23.0	50.1	22.3
Italy	4.2	23.0	65.3	7.5
Netherlands	4.3	9.4	58.1	28.1
Population II				
FRG	2.3	8.1	75.6	14.0
Finland	3.1	31.7	59.2	6.0
Ireland	5.8	17.5	55.2	21.6
Israel	8.7	17.0	54.1	20.3
Italy	4.6	30.0	53.5	11.9
Netherlands	4.9	11.1	52.4	31.6
New Zealand	7.6	27.7	51.8	12.9
United States	7.8	15.1	40.5	36.5
Population IV				
FRG	1.8	0.8	52.6	45.0
Finland	3.2	15.5	67.0	14.3
Ireland	3.3	12.1	58.7	26.2
Netherlands	5.2	3.3	41.8	49.6
New Zealand	8.8	9.5	48.8	32.9
Sweden	5.9	22.5	43.6	28.1
United States	6.4	14.0	37.3	42.3

Table 3.6 presents the distribution of fathers' occupations according to student report. Students in each country were asked to write down their father's job title and a short description of his job. Each National Center then developed a classification system for occupations (in most cases utilizing categories from 0–9, zero being for unclassifiable jobs). The Centers were urged to use several categories each for "unskilled," "skilled," and "professional or managerial" type jobs. In Table 3.6 the national codes have been grouped according to these broader categories. The proportion of unclassifiable jobs is also shown.

Schools become more class biased from Population I to Population IV. This is particularly evident when one traces the proportions of

Table 3.7. *Mean Student Report of Father's Education (in Years) by Country and Population (Excluding Omits)*

Population II		Population IV	
FRG	8.9	FRG	11.2
Finland	7.4	Finland	8.7
Iran	6.0	Iran	6.1
Ireland	9.8	Ireland	10.4
Israel	9.0	Netherlands	10.6
Italy	7.2	New Zealand	11.1
Netherlands	9.7	Sweden	[a]
New Zealand	10.0	United States	12.3
United States	12.4		
International Mean	8.9	International Mean	10.0

Note: This information was not asked for in Population I.

[a] No figures are given because of ambiguity in the wording of the question.

students whose fathers are professionals or managers from population to population (in the Federal Republic of Germany 10.9 % at Population I; 45 % at Population IV). Because of differences in scale and classification systems, between-country occupation comparisons are not justified.

In order to include father's occupation as a major component in the block of home background variables for the regression analysis, a procedure similar to that followed in other IEA subject areas was used in Civic Education. Within each country the occupation categories 1–9 plus missing and unclassifiable were criterion scaled using Reading Comprehension achievement (or where that was not available, using Word Knowledge). This resulted in each of the 11 occupational categories being assigned a *score on Father's Occupation* ranging from 0–9. This computation of the scale score for each occupational category by criterion scaling was done at Stage 2 of the IEA surveys (using data from Science, Literature, and Reading Comprehension). The same category scores were used in the Civics regression analysis; National Centers used the same occupational categories in Stage 2 and 3. For further information on this technique see Peaker, (1975).

The means of student reports of father's and mother's education appear in Tables 3.7 and 3.8. The somewhat higher parental education figures reported by the Population IV students are an indication of the selectivity of the school systems in some countries. Students

Table 3.8. *Mean Student Report of Mother's Education (in Years) by Country and Population (Excluding Omits)*

Population II		Population IV	
FRG	8.2	FRG	9.6
Finland	7.7	Finland	8.6
Iran	3.7	Iran	3.6
Ireland	9.8	Ireland	10.3
Israel	8.1	Netherlands	9.1
Italy	5.9	New Zealand	11.0
Netherlands	8.5	Sweden	a
New Zealand	10.2	United States	12.1
United States	12.1		
International Mean	8.2	International Mean	9.1

Note: This information was not asked for in Population I.
a No figures are given because of ambiguity in the wording of the question.

from high socioeconomic status homes with high levels of parental education are more likely than those less privileged to be enrolled in the final year of pre-university education in selective school systems.

SCHOOL, TEACHER, AND STUDENT CHARACTERISTICS USEFUL IN THE PREDICTION OF ACHIEVEMENT IN CIVIC EDUCATION

Only tentative arguments can be made concerning the *causal* links between characteristics of schools or teachers and country performance on either attitudinal or cognitive outcomes of Civic Education. However, by utilizing data from the three available sources of information: school, teacher and student, it is possible to characterize the educational inputs in different countries permitting us to gain a better understanding of the patterns of achievement which we observe.

First there is a need to examine the formal curriculum and the exposure of students to it. Data collected from National Centers and from school administrators were not always consistent with regard to the teaching of Civic Education as a separate subject. These two sets of data indicate that Civic Education as a separate subject is probably taught in one third to one half of the schools sampled in the Federal Republic of Germany at the Population I level, but is not taught in Italy or the Netherlands; other Social Studies or History courses

Table 3.9. *Students' Report on Current Enrollment in Civics, Social Studies, History or Current Events Classes by Country (Percentage excluding omits)*

Country	Report Current Enrollment
Population I	
FRG	No data
Italy	88.9
Netherlands	74.7
Population II	
FRG	93.0
Finland	95.5
Iran	83.1
Ireland	94.9
Israel	77.5
Italy	95.3
Netherlands	89.4
New Zealand	96.4
United States	86.6
Population IV	
FRG	98.8
Finland	95.9
Iran	57.0
Ireland	69.7
Netherlands	89.0
New Zealand	57.7
Sweden	83.8
United States	90.7

seem to be taught instead. At the Population II level Civic Education is reported to be taught in the Federal Republic of Germany, Iran, Ireland, Israel, the Netherlands and in about half of the United States and Finnish schools; reports indicate that it is not taught in Italy or New Zealand.

History is more widely taught and has more time devoted to it in all countries reporting. The subject "social studies" (often integrating aspects of geography, history, and civic education) is taught in Italy, the United States and to some extent in New Zealand. The Population IV curricula are so varied in specialization and content that it is difficult to make an assessment. History and a variety of other social sciences are likely to be included in the curriculum according to the reports of National Centers. A substantial number of schools in every country but New Zealand report some Civic Education courses at the pre-university level.

Students' reports of current enrollment in social studies, history, civics or current events classes indicate that more than 75 % are enrolled at Population II and IV in all countries except Iran, Ireland and New Zealand at Population IV (see Table 3.9).

Various sources of information give slightly different pictures concerning the level of student interest in Civic Education courses (Table 3.10). Evidence from this table, and another question where students were asked about their liking for other classes, indicate that civics and history classes are least popular in Finland and the United States. Student interest in these classes also is relatively low in the Netherlands and to some extent Israel. Students in Ireland and New Zealand report high interest in these courses.

Judging by student report, there is some connection between the stress on learning facts or memorizing dates and low student interest in civic education classes. At Population II the greatest stress on facts is reported by students in Ireland, Israel and the United States. As noted previously, interest in such classes is low in two out of these three countries, but is very high in the other.

The proportion of students enrolled in Civic Education classes may be helpful in providing some explanation of differences in educational outcomes. Information from the teachers can be used to form quantifiable educational indices (e.g., level of teacher training) and can also give information about the kind of materials which are used, topics emphasized, and the climate of the classroom.

The percentage of teachers who report that they are specialists in teaching civics or social studies, the mean number of years of post-secondary education and the percent who report that they have been teaching for 20 years or more are reported in Table 3.11. This is listed separately for the teachers of each population and each country. Several trends may be noted. For teachers in the three countries testing at Populations I and II, those teaching at the higher level are more likely to be specialists, and have a larger mean number of years of post-secondary education. Italian schools at both Population I and II have the largest proportion of teachers with more than 20 years experience.

The next comparison is between teachers instructing Population II and IV. In some countries there tends to be more specialization and more training for those teaching the higher grade (in the Federal

Table 3.10. *Students' Report on Civics, Social Studies, History or Current Events Classes (General Liking and Stress on Factual Learning) by Country*

Country	General liking of these classes		Stress on factual learning in these classes	
	Mean[a]	S.D.	Mean	S.D.
Population I				
FRG[b]	—	—	—	—
Italy	3.7	0.9	3.0	1.1
Netherlands	3.3	0.8	3.2	1.0
Population II				
FRG	3.4	0.7	3.1	0.8
Finland	3.1	0.7	3.2	0.8
Ireland	3.5	0.8	3.4	0.8
Israel	3.2	0.9	3.4	0.9
Italy	3.4	0.8	2.9	0.8
Netherlands	3.3	0.7	3.1	0.8
New Zealand	3.5	0.7	3.2	0.7
United States	3.0	0.7	3.4	0.8
Population IV				
FRG	3.5	0.7	3.1	0.7
Finland	3.1	0.6	3.2	0.6
Ireland	3.6	0.7	3.2	0.8
Netherlands	3.3	0.7	2.8	0.9
New Zealand	3.5	0.6	3.2	0.8
Sweden	3.4	0.6	3.2	0.8
United States	3.1	0.6	3.4	0.8

[a] These country means represent the average response on a five point scale (excluding omits). Students were asked how often they liked the above courses and how often facts were stressed in them. The responses were coded as follows: 1 Never, 2 Rarely, 3 Sometimes, 4 Often, 5 Always.

[b] These questions were not asked at Population I.

Republic of Germany, Finland, the Netherlands). The specialization and training in Ireland, New Zealand, the United States seems about equivalent for teachers of Population II and Population IV.

At Population I teachers in the Federal Republic of Germany are the least specialized but have the highest number of years of post-secondary education; teachers in Italy are the most likely to be specialized but have the fewest years of post-secondary education

Table 3.11. *General Description of Teachers Answering Questionnaire by Country and Population*

	% Specialist teachers	Mean years post secondary education	% More than 20 years experience
Population I			
FRG	12.8	3.3	24.3
Italy	32.9	1.0	49.3
Netherlands	31.3	3.0	19.6
Population II			
FRG	15.4	3.6	21.9
Finland	54.4	4.1	19.9
Ireland	38.5	3.5	20.1
Israel	58.6	3.9	17.1
Italy	66.9	3.6	26.1
Netherlands	54.8	2.9	20.7
New Zealand	41.0	3.5	14.4
United States	57.2	4.6	15.6
Population IV			
FRG	45.4	4.8	14.2
Finland	77.2	4.6	12.5
Ireland	37.4	3.6	25.0
Netherlands	88.4	3.4	16.9
New Zealand	39.3	3.6	14.6
Sweden	72.4	4.4	21.1
United States	56.4	4.8	21.9

Note: The approximate number of teachers responding to each of these questions may be determined by reference to Table 2.1.

(this may be an artifact of the large proportion of them who were trained more than 20 years ago). Also at Population II, the highest degree of specialization of teachers is in Italy and the lowest in West Germany. Teachers report the highest level of post-secondary education in the United States and the lowest in the Netherlands. At Population IV, the largest percentage of teachers are specialists in the Netherlands, the lowest percentage in Ireland. Teachers report the highest level of post-secondary level education in the Federal Republic of Germany and the United States and the lowest level in the Netherlands.

Other relatively standard measures of teacher training and input

Table 3.12. *Teachers' Report of Preparation and Professional Activities*

Country	Mean hours preparation per week	Mean number of semesters pre-service in social sciences	Mean number of weeks in-service training social science	% Participated curriculum reform project	% Member of subject matter association
Population I					
FRG	8.6	No data	No data	No data	No data
Italy	7.2	1.4	1.1	2.1	0.7
Netherlands	6.1	2.9	6.1	22.3	0.8
Population II					
FRG	11.0	4.9	2.1	6.6	1.4
Finland	7.3	4.0	3.9	12.2	35.1
Ireland	6.9	3.2	5.5	3.5	25.0
Israel	8.7	No data	No data	No data	No data
Italy	7.0	3.7	1.3	5.1	0.8
Netherlands	7.3	4.3	9.1	23.1	10.5
New Zealand	8.7	4.8	1.5	15.6	40.1
United States	8.5	9.9	6.4	38.6	14.7
Population IV					
FRG	14.3	6.5	4.0	11.3	6.0
Finland	10.3	5.5	3.2	15.5	67.2
Ireland	6.9	3.1	5.9	5.5	34.7
Netherlands	9.4	6.9	10.1	24.8	15.9
New Zealand	8.9	5.1	1.6	18.4	40.0
Sweden	12.3	5.2	3.8	25.1	63.2
United States	8.8	10.8	7.2	52.6	19.1

are contained in Table 3.12. Teachers in the United States in addition to having the highest general level of post-secondary education also seem to have had a larger number of semesters of study in the social sciences. This is true for those who teach at Population II as well as those teaching at Population IV. At Population II the teachers in the Federal Republic and New Zealand have received the next highest amount of post-secondary social science training.

Given that Population IV teachers in the Netherlands have attended a relatively small number of years at the post-secondary level, they have studied social sciences for an unusually high proportion of their pre-service training. Also it may be noted from Table 3.12 that teachers in the Netherlands at both the Population II and IV levels report more weeks of in-service instruction in the social sciences than do the teachers in any other country.

In pre-service education, general and specialized, teachers in the United States seem the best prepared. On the basis of training specifically in the social sciences, teachers in the Netherlands seem especially well prepared. Teachers in the Federal Republic of Germany, Finland, New Zealand and Sweden also have relatively high levels of pre-service training in social sciences (considerably more than teachers in Ireland or Italy). In-service social science training seems most extensive in Finland, the Federal Republic of Germany, Ireland, and Sweden (in addition to the Netherlands and the United States). Extensive in-service training is not provided to teachers in Italy or New Zealand. History is the most frequent discipline mentioned for both pre-service and in-service studies.

Membership in organizations of teachers of social studies or Civic Education is clearly more popular in some countries than in others. More than 35 % of teachers in Finland, New Zealand, and Sweden report such membership at both Population levels, with a larger percentage among teachers of older students.

Table 3.12 also presents data on the mean number of hours a week during which teachers prepare. At all Population levels this is the highest for teachers in the Federal Republic of Germany and also very high in Sweden.

Considering formal training, professional participation and hours of preparation, teachers in the United States appear to have high levels of general preparation and teachers in the Netherlands to have high levels of social science training (especially in-service). West German and Swedish teachers have moderate levels of training and prepare especially diligently for classes. At some levels this is also true in Finland and New Zealand. In general teachers in Italy and Ireland seem less well trained and less involved in professional matters. Comparable data on teachers in Israel are missing.

Table 3.13 presents teachers' reports concerning the use of various kinds of instructional material. There is remarkable similarity in the reports of Populations II and IV teachers. In general the most frequently used materials and methods are textbooks, questioning of students and discussion. The Netherlands is an exception to this pattern. Whereas every other country ranks textbooks, questioning, and discussions as among the most frequently used, the most popular methods in the Netherlands are individualized materials, indi-

Table 3.13. *Teachers' Report of Use of Instructional Materials and Techniques by Country and Population (% Reporting They Use Technique "Often")*

Country	Text-book	Printed drill	Individual material	Small group	Individual conference	Audio-visual	Field trips	Lectures	Question-ing	Discus-sion	Student reports
Population I											
FRG	65.6	46.1	9.3	17.2	16.0	19.3	9.7	25.3	62.4	82.8	—
Italy	64.7	18.8	29.9	47.1	64.4	21.9	4.6	1.6	81.2	86.1	26.5
Netherlands	0.0	6.9	50.4	9.2	23.8	5.9	43.7	0.0	0.3	2.5	5.3
Population II											
FRG	74.3	45.8	4.3	12.2	9.6	36.1	5.8	26.7	60.7	78.6	23.0
Finland	88.7	35.2	8.2	16.0	13.1	33.6	5.6	26.2	62.0	50.5	7.8
Ireland	77.2	15.2	7.7	9.9	15.1	18.4	8.0	70.6	71.3	95.5	8.4
Israel	71.5	20.3	7.8	4.0	2.2	10.2	3.2	22.6	73.9	78.4	—
Italy	81.3	4.7	7.5	24.1	31.8	14.1	1.7	2.3	86.3	88.6	34.0
Netherlands	4.1	30.3	81.2	29.2	70.9	23.9	42.1	1.0	1.3	2.5	11.6
New Zealand	54.0	10.4	12.6	17.7	9.5	27.0	5.7	7.1	80.0	73.0	19.7
United States	57.0	10.0	10.7	29.1	18.8	46.9	4.8	30.1	76.4	77.3	29.5
Population IV											
FRG	64.6	39.3	10.0	8.4	4.8	14.7	2.0	32.1	76.7	83.5	37.3
Finland	91.3	26.6	7.5	13.4	6.1	42.0	7.1	28.6	70.9	53.0	11.6
Ireland	78.6	13.8	6.5	10.7	11.6	17.1	5.1	70.7	73.5	46.6	10.5
Netherlands	10.5	33.6	86.3	32.8	78.7	45.7	45.9	0.0	0.0	2.7	7.1
New Zealand	56.1	11.9	18.4	19.9	11.7	28.3	8.6	9.0	79.7	73.6	24.5
Sweden	84.7	17.3	4.6	32.9	26.9	53.4	6.2	3.4	55.0	60.4	17.7
United States	55.4	5.5	14.0	27.1	24.3	43.4	6.7	29.7	66.3	80.4	26.7

Note: If fewer than 60% of the teachers surveyed responded to a question this information was omitted from the table.

Table 3.14. *Teachers' Report of Evaluation Methods by Country and Population (Percentage Reporting "Frequent Use")*

	Stand-ardized tests	Teacher-made essays	Teacher-made objective tests	Perform-ance on homework	Perform-ance on term papers
Population I					
FRG	6.9	91.9	19.5	21.1	4.5
Italy	4.6	74.7	27.1	51.6	33.2
Netherlands	10.6	82.6	13.7	26.1	24.8
Population II					
FRG	7.1	85.8	12.5	20.8	12.7
Finland	1.3	29.8	34.9	12.7	5.5
Ireland	19.5	38.5	22.9	73.6	29.5
Israel	7.6	92.2	9.2	72.4	34.5
Italy	1.3	67.7	19.8	67.2	65.9
Netherlands	3.5	82.0	14.9	36.0	21.8
New Zealand	9.5	48.7	45.5	32.7	34.5
United States	11.6	48.0	68.8	43.9	37.2
Population IV					
FRG	4.6	81.9	9.0	34.3	11.9
Finland	2.2	37.6	32.5	11.1	4.9
Ireland	18.9	42.1	23.5	71.9	23.1
Netherlands	0.0	77.2	14.7	31.0	21.2
New Zealand	10.3	50.3	45.4	31.8	38.2
Sweden	1.1	15.2	31.5	58.5	30.7
United States	10.5	55.2	54.1	40.3	42.0

vidual conferences, and field trips with students. This is true at both Population I, II, and Population IV. On the basis of this information the Netherlands appears to have the most individualized Civic Education program.

Other country patterns are relatively similar to that discussed above. Teachers in the Federal Republic of Germany report more frequent use of printed drill than teachers in other countries; teachers in Ireland favor lectures somewhat more than those in other countries; those in the United States at Population II use audio-visual aids more than any other country.

When teacher use of evaluation techniques is examined (Table 3.14), there is no single popular rank order as there is for teaching

Table 3.15. *Teachers' Perceptions of the Importance of Various Topics for the General Education of Students Grades 7–12 by Country and Population (Percentage responding "Essential")*

1. Activities/political figures.   2. Functions/political institutions.   3. Local government and social services.   4. Ideology of democracy.   5. Ideology of political parties.   6. "Non-Western" cultures.   7. Political history of country.   8. National social problems (e.g., racial or crime).   9. International problems (e.g., overpopulation).

	1	2	3	4	5	6	7	8	9
Population II									
FRG	41.7	59.4	61.9	67.9	35.9	37.4	75.4	82.0	82.2
Finland	64.7	37.1	74.9	58.6	44.9	28.7	46.8	72.9	63.3
Ireland	50.4	65.1	73.0	63.4	43.1	31.6	64.6	73.1	61.1
Italy	80.5	86.8	86.6	86.5	60.0	45.6	91.2	89.1	91.5
Netherlands	29.1	42.6	41.5	56.5	23.2	22.2	14.1	60.3	66.6
New Zealand	46.6	65.5	67.1	63.4	36.5	65.4	28.5	79.1	84.9
United States	71.7	73.8	75.0	87.9	52.2	51.6	59.2	87.0	84.1
Population IV									
FRG	46.4	84.5	55.5	79.6	64.3	42.4	79.0	89.0	85.6
Finland	73.1	45.4	78.7	62.2	49.0	36.9	56.9	82.2	79.0
Ireland	50.2	61.8	70.2	66.3	42.2	28.3	64.8	72.9	63.9
Netherlands	28.2	52.4	24.3	73.7	40.1	38.0	11.4	52.5	73.3
New Zealand	45.6	64.7	66.3	62.8	35.9	63.3	28.7	78.7	86.4
Sweden	37.2	83.7	73.0	81.1	66.5	70.8	44.1	77.8	94.5
United States	68.3	83.0	73.6	85.9	54.8	54.3	57.2	91.1	85.4

Note: Population I teachers were not asked these questions.

methods. However, most countries do show very similar patterns at Population II and IV. Teachers in the Federal Republic of Germany and the Netherlands seem to use teacher-made written or essay tests much more frequently than any other method. Teachers in Finland rely on these as well as teacher-made objective tests. Teachers in Italy and Israel use teacher-made essays, performance on homework and term papers (Italy only). Teachers in New Zealand and the United States report extensive use of four evaluation methods at roughly equivalent rates: teacher-made essays, teacher-made objective tests, performance on homework, and term papers. Ireland stands out as the country which at both population levels uses homework performance as the major method of evaluating students (with teacher-made essays second in frequency of use). Sweden also puts some reliance on homework using teacher-made objective tests as well. *Standardized* tests are not frequently used although Irish teachers report them more frequently than others do.

Teacher reports on the topics in the curriculum which they consider most important for the general education of students grades 7 to 12 are given in Table 3.15. The two topics which over all countries have the greatest importance in the minds of teachers are "important national social problems like racial tension and crime" and "important international problems, such as overpopulation." In some countries other topics received frequent emphasis; again the data are very similar for teachers from the Population II and IV levels. Finnish teachers believe that the workings of local government and activities of political figures are as important or nearly as important as national and international social problems. Teachers in the Federal Republic of Germany (and also the Italian Population II teachers) stress "the political history of the country" about as much as national and international problems. Irish teachers report that they consider national problems and the working of local government particularly important. Their lack of emphasis upon international problems may be due to the example of "overpopulation" which was not the most appropriate one to assess international orientation in a Catholic country. Teachers in the Netherlands thought that national and international problems were important, as well as "the ideology of democracy." Teachers in New Zealand reported emphasis on many topics—national problems first, followed by several others previously listed including "non-Western" studies. Teachers in Sweden put more stress on international rather than on national problems and also listed "non-Western" studies more frequently that did the teachers in any other country.

Teachers in the United States were characterized by their stress on national problems and on the ideology of democracy (to a greater extent than the teachers in any other country). International problems were also viewed as important by many of them.

These brief profiles deserve further exploration. There is no evidence that these are the topics which are actually stressed, only that teachers think they are important. Actual time or emphasis in the classroom would also depend, of course, on curriculum plans, available materials, and student interest.

Table 3.16 presents the teachers' assessment of the appropriateness of allowing various political activities or kinds of political discussion in class. Teachers were asked how appropriate each activity was, given that a teacher wanted to engage in it; it was not that the teacher

Table 3.16. *Teachers' Report of Perceived Appropriateness of Various Teacher Behavior in Class by Country and Population (Percentage Reporting "Should Engage in Activity")*

1. Explain reasons for preferring one party over another in a national election.   2. Allow atheists to express views before school classes.   3. Argue against censoring of literature by those who feel it is controversial or immoral.   4. Speak out against fascist and objectionable or unpopular political groups.   5. Speak out in favor of nationalization of large privately owned industry.   6. Speak out in favor of the political and economic union of Europe. 7. Allow the distribution of free enterprise literature put out by the stock exchanges or national chamber of commerce and banking groups.   8. Speak favorably about Marxist communism and circulate appropriate material.   9. Argue that labor unions should be further regulated or controlled by the government.   10. Speak out against the government.   11. Speak out against racial discrimination.

	1	2	3	4	5	6	7	8	9	10	11
Population I											
Italy	31.0	43.8	25.8	20.5	41.3	96.7	49.8	2.3	21.4	15.6	86.9
Netherlands	22.6	35.9	36.2	66.3	16.8	86.2	56.6	22.9	13.1	15.3	87.2
Population II											
FRG	17.6	94.6	60.5	62.5	40.9	96.8	88.2	39.4	9.0	44.3	81.5
Finland	17.5	59.4	23.6	16.6	10.6	65.4	80.7	31.3	5.7	20.6	83.6
Ireland	28.3	39.7	39.4	54.6	29.5	60.3	84.4	12.3	43.9	29.5	90.7
Italy	33.9	64.3	45.7	25.9	36.1	97.3	55.7	6.2	19.0	28.4	91.5
Netherlands	17.8	55.9	39.4	70.1	35.5	92.0	71.1	37.5	13.5	38.6	89.3
New Zealand	37.6	75.0	60.6	58.5	38.2	62.1	86.0	36.0	43.8	46.9	88.7
United States	39.5	66.0	60.2	68.2	29.3	64.0	91.1	21.8	34.7	48.1	87.8
Population IV											
FRG	12.3	96.3	63.4	66.6	31.2	96.2	84.7	45.3	6.2	51.3	89.1
Finland	18.0	65.6	27.4	18.6	11.2	53.2	80.9	34.5	5.7	25.8	85.1
Ireland	29.4	44.0	40.0	55.5	24.9	55.7	84.0	9.3	44.6	31.6	91.4
Netherlands	11.3	67.8	55.1	74.9	29.8	95.8	88.1	49.6	28.1	45.2	93.8
New Zealand	34.5	77.6	54.2	51.1	35.3	57.5	83.2	36.0	43.9	42.5	83.6
Sweden	6.9	86.2	73.6	25.1	4.9	13.7	96.0	2.2	3.1	8.1	82.2
United States	44.6	75.1	66.5	70.8	30.7	59.6	96.5	27.9	46.9	37.2	87.6

Note: If fewer than 60 % of the teachers surveyed responded to a question, this information was omitted from the table. Consequently, the table contains no figures for Israel and FRG (at Population I).

was to be forced to engage in it. Responses to these items were combined in later analysis into a scale measuring readiness to engage in discussion of sensitive issues in the classroom. Teachers in Finland appear to believe that only a few of these issues are appropriate for classroom discussion (the percentage endorsing these activities as appropriate was lower in Finland for six of the 11 issues than it was in any other country at Population II). Teachers in Ireland also seemed to be reticent to discuss many of these issues. The proportion who felt such issue discussion was appropriate was highest in the Federal Republic of Germany, the United States, and New Zealand. These discussion preference patterns are similar at Population IV, with Finnish teachers still regarding them as least appropriate and teachers in the United States, the Federal Republic of Germany, and also the Netherlands tending to be willing to discuss many issues. Teachers in Sweden present a most interesting pattern at this level, showing a considerable degree of variation with respect to discussion. They report very high willingness to allow atheists to express their views, to argue against the censorship of literature and to allow the distribution of stock exchange literature. They are *less* willing than the teachers of any other nation to explain reasons for preferring a particular political party, speak out in favor of an industry's nationalization, speak in favor of the political and economic union of Europe, speak favorably about Marxist communism, argue that labor unions should be regulated, or speak out against the government. It is clear that the input which teachers are likely to provide regarding contemporary issues varies a great deal according to the content of the issue. Summations over such diverse issues may not provide the information which is most useful for understanding the process of attitude formation.

Student reports on the encouragement of the expression of independent opinions in the classroom tend to confirm their teachers' reports. Finnish students report low levels of encouragement of such expression; students in the Federal Republic of Germany, Ireland, New Zealand and the United States report high levels of encouragement (Table 3.17).

Teachers were also questioned about less controversial issues and about student participation in their school affairs (Table 3.18). Nearly all agreed, that students should make decisions about school activities like clubs, and take part in voluntary social work. Over 85 % in all countries agreed that students should be allowed to discuss current political issues in class—this is much higher than the

Table 3.17. *Students' Report of Encouragement of Independent Expression in Classroom by Country and Population*

Country	Mean	S.D.
Population I		
FRG	3.5	0.8
Israel	3.3	0.8
Italy	3.4	0.9
Netherlands	2.8	0.9
Population II		
FRG	4.0	0.8
Finland	3.3	0.8
Ireland	3.9	0.8
Israel	3.5	0.7
Italy	3.4	0.8
Netherlands	3.6	0.7
New Zealand	3.9	0.7
United States	3.8	0.8
Population IV		
FRG	3.9	0.8
Finland	3.4	0.8
Ireland	4.1	0.8
Netherlands	3.8	0.7
New Zealand	4.1	0.6
Sweden	3.8	0.8
United States	3.8	0.8

Note: Mean score on a five point scale; 5 being the highest value.

percentages in the previous table where the appropriateness of teachers discussing issues of some controversy was reported.

This is in harmony with previous research showing that general statements of democratic values are much more likely to be endorsed than specified applications of these values in controversial situations.

Teachers in the United States were most willing to allow students to make decisions in the area of curriculum. According to teachers, decisions about discipline should involve students in the Federal Republic of Germany, Finland, and the Netherlands. Working for a political party in school as part of a school project was acceptable in the United States and Sweden. It was in Italy at Population II that teachers were *least* likely to endorse these various kinds of active involvement for students.

Table 3.18. *Teachers' Reports Concerning Appropriateness of Certain Activities in School by Country and Population (Percentage Reporting Students "Should" be Provided Opportunity for Listed Activity)*

1. Take part in making decisions about school curriculum.   2. Take part in making decisions about discipline.   3. Take part in "mock" election campaign in school.   4. Work for political party in election as part of school project.   5. Discuss current political issues in class.   6. Take one side of political issue in school debate.

Country	1	2	3	4	5	6
Population I						
Italy	73.5	77.2	47.8	5.0	85.0	38.6
Netherlands	34.7	59.8	76.2	17.6	87.5	44.0
Population II						
FRG	48.3	98.4	no data	27.7	99.2	7.4
Finland	53.8	92.6	88.4	11.7	86.2	69.4
Ireland	49.4	70.6	75.7	24.6	90.6	58.9
Italy	63.0	65.3	30.7	3.0	92.9	49.5
Netherlands	40.0	92.2	89.7	16.9	99.6	64.1
New Zealand	54.8	80.3	81.9	27.4	98.1	60.8
United States	86.5	83.5	98.3	71.3	99.8	89.6
Population IV						
FRG	50.0	95.3	no data	46.1	98.8	14.5
Finland	67.6	95.6	90.7	12.5	90.6	81.4
Ireland	45.5	73.7	73.4	24.6	95.8	61.9
Netherlands	49.5	93.2	91.0	19.1	97.4	67.2
New Zealand	51.0	72.9	85.8	24.9	96.6	81.2
Sweden	79.9	73.6	95.9	60.4	99.6	94.6
United States	88.9	85.3	97.9	72.6	100.0	86.4

Note: Two items included in the questionnaire, "should provide opportunity to take part in making decisions about initiating and running school clubs and societies" and "take part in voluntary social work" were not included in this table because an average of more than ninety percent of the teachers endorsed them, and with little variation by country or population.

If fewer than 60 % of the teachers surveyed responded to a question, this information was omitted from the table.

Teachers were given the same list of citizenship characteristics as was given to students, and asked to indicate which were "essential to being a good citizen" (Table 3.19). Non-political qualities such as a good citizen "is polite," "works hard," "has good table manners," and "shows respect for a funeral," were most likely to be endorsed in Italy and in Ireland. This is further evidence of the relatively

Behavior is "Essential to being a good citizen")

1. Obey laws. 2. Always polite. 3. Always votes. 4. Loyal to family. 5. Works hard. 6. Political party member. 7. Knows how taxes spent. 8. Good manners. 9. Studies hard. 10. Pays taxes. 11. Keeps up with events. 12. Tries to change government. 13. Get other to vote. 14. Stands for National Anthem. 15. Respects Funeral. 16. Belongs to Labor Union.

	1	2	3	4	5	6	7	8	9	10	11	12	13	14	15	16
Population I																
Italy	98.5	73.2	98.3	95.2	72.9	19.7	66.7	57.3	56.3	97.9	66.0	52.9	77.9	64.5	83.2	35.2
Netherlands	78.0	42.4	87.3	93.7	70.5	16.5	59.1	24.0	46.9	86.5	83.6	60.8	28.0	60.1	39.3	—
Population II																
FRG	93.4	29.0	95.6	66.3	12.9	14.6	92.3	18.5	43.0	87.3	98.9	58.6	87.9	18.1	28.7	19.9
Finland	98.4	45.4	80.5	99.1	65.0	14.8	85.3	47.4	72.1	92.5	86.9	25.3	45.9	62.3	69.4	66.7
Ireland	95.2	53.7	94.7	90.2	92.8	14.2	65.6	35.2	59.6	93.4	77.4	47.6	55.3	68.0	77.1	32.6
Italy	98.4	66.8	92.5	93.7	61.7	10.3	61.5	45.6	43.6	95.7	84.9	60.4	69.0	47.2	75.2	27.8
Netherlands	69.5	30.2	78.7	92.8	51.8	14.6	71.7	16.8	42.2	81.6	85.6	58.4	24.6	52.1	32.8	—
New Zealand	92.7	43.2	86.1	79.4	76.6	5.8	59.0	28.1	39.1	89.2	85.4	36.5	29.6	23.8	61.0	7.8
United States	89.9	46.6	91.6	73.0	80.6	26.2	82.3	22.8	45.1	91.7	94.2	54.2	61.6	58.4	49.1	1.7
Population IV																
FRG	94.4	29.1	90.2	53.6	15.8	29.5	94.9	15.7	32.0	78.7	96.6	61.8	82.4	16.6	30.4	11.6
Finland	93.7	46.8	75.1	97.1	52.6	7.9	80.6	37.8	60.6	89.7	81.1	30.5	37.8	52.0	59.7	39.6
Ireland	95.6	60.2	95.1	92.3	90.8	12.2	61.6	42.1	59.5	92.7	79.8	43.5	51.0	74.6	79.7	28.9
Netherlands	74.0	30.2	81.2	90.0	36.5	25.0	63.0	27.6	44.9	78.0	91.8	62.3	18.2	44.8	30.3	—
New Zealand	92.4	47.8	84.8	81.0	77.3	8.3	56.5	24.5	38.1	88.5	85.7	35.7	26.8	29.2	59.5	8.7
Sweden	99.4	68.4	96.8	83.7	72.4	20.9	87.5	39.9	75.6	96.5	98.9	93.5	67.4	34.8	89.3	66.7
United States	94.6	40.8	91.2	70.0	72.2	23.0	76.7	25.9	41.1	93.5	87.3	51.6	58.3	60.6	55.0	2.9

Note: If fewer than 60% of the teachers surveyed responded to a question, this information was omitted from the table.

Table 3.20. *Ranking of Countries According to Teacher Participation in Policy and Decision Making*

	School Head's Report on Teacher Role in Policy and Rule Making— Population II Schools[a]	School Head's Report on Teacher Role in Policy and Rule Making— Population IV Schools[a]
FRG	2	1
Finland	1	2
Ireland	7	4
Israel	4	–
Italy	6	–
Netherlands	3	3
New Zealand	5	5
Sweden	–	7
United States	8	6
	8 countries	7 countries

[a] School questionnaires included a question about teachers' role in policy and rule making. National mean responses have been ranked to produce this column.

traditional orientation of the Civic Education programs in these Catholic nations. As one might expect, obedience to law and payment of taxes were almost universally perceived as important citizen qualities. Overall it is interesting that teachers did not endorse political party membership as an important quality of citizenship.

There seems to be considerable variation in the extent to which teachers are involved in the educational policy making process. The reports concerning teacher power in each school were available as part of the School Questionnaire (Table 3.20). Teachers in the Federal Republic of Germany, Finland, and the Netherlands tend to have relatively substantial power (and in several areas); teachers in Israel, Ireland, Italy, New Zealand have moderate amounts of power. Teachers in Sweden and the United States tend to be the least powerful in educational decisions made outside their classrooms.

STUDENT ASSESSMENT OF THE IMPORTANCE
OF DIFFERENT SOCIALIZATION AGENTS

When students were asked (in the Background Questionnaire) which source or event had had the *greatest* influence on the formation of their political ideas, at all ages they selected radio or television—especially the broadcast of specific political events (but also programs describing political issues). Teachers were frequently cited only by the 10-year-olds; the importance of parents was fairly well restricted to 10-year-olds and 14-year-olds. Reading which they had done was credited by a number of pre-university students with forming their ideas. In general students did not report that personal

Table 3.21. *Students' Report of Agreement with Father's Political Opinions*

Country	Omit	Don't know his opinions	Agree a lot	Agree a little	Mostly disagree	Student has no opinion
Population I						
FRG	13.6	35.0	23.0	17.1	11.3	0.0
Israel	12.7	21.5	51.0	6.9	0.9	6.9
Italy	8.1	40.6	30.3	5.9	1.6	13.4
Netherlands	4.0	42.4	26.6	8.7	4.5	13.9
Population II						
FRG	3.4	23.7	17.1	31.6	15.8	8.4
Finland	3.3	31.5	20.3	21.6	9.9	13.4
Ireland	3.9	25.3	34.5	23.1	6.5	6.7
Israel	10.9	16.0	46.1	17.6	4.5	4.9
Italy	2.3	40.1	34.3	12.2	5.5	5.7
Netherlands	3.3	39.7	25.6	12.5	5.5	13.5
New Zealand	2.0	28.2	28.3	23.5	7.0	10.9
United States	2.5	26.0	—[a]	—[a]	—[a]	13.9
Population IV						
FRG	3.9	5.1	15.9	43.0	30.0	2.1
Finland	5.6	11.9	25.4	33.7	15.6	7.8
Ireland	3.1	14.1	29.1	31.7	12.8	9.3
Netherlands	9.9	16.1	23.1	24.6	13.9	12.3
New Zealand	3.2	16.2	35.5	28.4	7.7	9.0
Sweden	18.3	9.8	32.1	18.9	10.2	10.8
United States	5.0	19.8	—[a]	—[a]	—[a]	9.6

[a] Printing error in United States' questionnaire.

83

Table 3.22. *Students' Report of Agreement with Mother's Political Opinions*

Country	Omit	Don't know her opinions	Agree a lot	Agree a little	Mostly disagree	Student has no opinion
Population I						
FRG	13.6	25.3	29.3	21.0	10.8	0.0
Israel	12.2	15.9	51.7	11.5	2.5	6.0
Italy	9.0	30.0	33.6	10.3	3.6	13.5
Netherlands	4.0	39.5	28.6	9.9	5.0	12.9
Population II						
FRG	2.7	20.9	22.4	32.7	12.4	8.8
Finland	2.2	30.6	24.8	23.2	8.2	11.1
Ireland	3.2	22.1	33.5	27.2	8.5	5.5
Israel	11.2	16.6	39.4	21.3	7.6	4.0
Italy	1.9	38.0	28.7	16.8	6.9	7.7
Netherlands	2.6	41.9	26.0	13.4	5.5	10.6
New Zealand	1.8	28.3	29.3	25.8	6.1	8.8
United States	2.3	27.9	24.7	22.9	11.5	10.7
Population IV						
FRG	2.2	7.4	14.9	42.2	30.7	2.5
Finland	3.8	12.8	26.8	34.9	14.8	7.0
Ireland	2.5	18.7	25.1	31.2	14.8	7.6
Netherlands	8.4	28.9	19.2	20.0	13.4	10.1
New Zealand	2.3	21.1	29.7	30.2	8.3	8.3
Sweden	17.7	14.1	31.7	17.7	8.6	10.3
United States	4.1	24.5	23.3	29.1	11.6	7.5

experience with school elections or debates had been important, nor personal exposure to a famous person. Friends were more important in some countries than others in forming political ideas.

Students were also asked how much their political ideas agreed with the ideas of their mothers, fathers, civics teachers, and friends (Tables 3.21–3.24). Substantial numbers of students, particularly at Population II, reported that they were unaware of the opinions of these individuals. In particular, the political attitudes of teachers were less well known to students than the opinions of the others listed. In Israel, students are more aware of the political opinions of parents, friends and teachers than students are in any other country.

Looking first at parents, in most countries those Population II

Table 3.23. *Students' Report of Agreement with Civics Teacher's Political Opinions*

Country	Omit	Don't know his/her opinions	Agree a lot	Agree a little	Mostly disagree	Student has no opinion
Population I						
FRG	23.3	30.9	15.4	14.4	16.1	0.0
Israel	16.2	29.6	27.9	6.9	4.2	15.2
Italy	10.0	31.1	26.6	8.3	5.6	18.4
Netherlands	4.8	38.9	20.1	11.2	7.9	17.2
Population II						
FRG	5.1	24.5	9.7	26.4	16.7	17.7
Finland	2.3	53.0	6.2	13.3	11.4	13.9
Ireland	4.3	32.3	25.4	22.9	9.4	5.6
Israel	10.7	26.9	28.5	19.1	9.1	5.7
Italy	2.8	50.3	17.0	11.3	6.6	12.1
Netherlands	12.8	48.1	10.7	11.0	4.9	12.5
New Zealand	2.4	31.4	23.7	24.5	9.6	8.5
United States	2.7	37.9	15.9	22.5	10.2	10.8
Population IV						
FRG	2.2	12.5	12.4	44.8	23.2	4.9
Finland	3.9	39.1	10.0	21.5	18.1	7.4
Ireland	5.8	35.8	11.1	22.5	15.5	9.4
Netherlands	12.6	34.4	12.2	19.8	10.8	10.3
New Zealand	8.3	51.9	9.6	14.5	6.9	8.8
Sweden	17.1	39.7	9.3	14.1	10.6	9.2
United States	4.2	25.7	23.7	28.0	11.1	7.4

students who know their parents' opinions are much more likely to agree with them than they are to disagree. At Population IV there is a great deal more disagreement, especially in the Federal Republic of Germany (where more than 30 % of the students reported disagreement with parents' opinions). Although teachers' opinions are often not well known in both Finland and the Federal Republic of Germany, students are particularly likely to disagree with teachers' opinions (e.g., of those students in Finland who know their teachers' opinions and have an opinion themselves, more than a third disagree with their teachers). Students at Population II are rather unlikely to know their friends' political opinions but if they know them, they generally agree with them.

Table 3.24 *Students' Report of Agreement with Friends' Political Opinions*

Country	Omit	Don't know their opinions	Agree a lot	Agree a little	Mostly disagree	Student has no opinion
Population I						
FRG	14.6	23.6	22.4	21.1	18.3	0.0
Israel	12.2	22.2	26.3	27.0	5.8	6.5
Italy	9.7	28.7	17.5	20.5	7.2	16.4
Netherlands	4.3	36.8	15.1	15.0	10.4	18.4
Population II						
FRG	3.2	22.2	24.8	24.2	14.7	11.0
Finland	2.1	25.4	29.1	24.1	9.6	9.9
Ireland	4.2	27.8	19.6	27.2	14.5	6.7
Israel	10.4	17.3	26.4	31.1	10.3	4.5
Italy	2.7	30.1	27.5	20.7	10.6	8.4
Netherlands	3.2	49.7	16.6	13.4	5.3	11.8
New Zealand	2.0	34.5	16.0	25.4	10.3	11.8
United States	2.1	39.0	18.3	22.4	8.3	9.9
Population IV						
FRG	2.0	3.1	44.0	40.8	8.1	2.1
Finland	3.6	8.8	35.1	35.1	11.6	5.9
Ireland	2.6	19.9	25.5	27.2	16.8	8.1
Netherlands	8.7	25.1	34.7	15.3	5.4	10.7
New Zealand	2.4	22.2	27.3	31.1	9.2	7.8
Sweden	17.2	14.3	33.2	17.5	8.3	9.6
United States	4.1	25.5	28.6	26.0	8.9	6.9

In conclusion, the purpose of this chapter has been to describe the characteristics of the schools, teachers, and students participating in the IEA Civic Education survey. In the chapters which follow, a number of these characteristics which differ between countries will be considered as possible explanations of between-country differences in outcome variables.

Chapter 4

The Civic Education Cognitive Achievement Test: Content Analysis and Test Development

The preliminary work in the development of a common understanding or definition of the subject matter of Civic Education has been described in Chapter 1. In this chapter, the efforts to develop measures of cognitive Civic Education outcomes are described in more detail. Chapter 7 describes parallel efforts to develop measures of attitudinal outcomes.

The principal techniques utilized in this process were: content analysis; development of an international grid of test specifications; pretest of the preliminary instruments; modifications of the international grid, and use of external reviews. The test was constructed so that it included six subtests, a set of equating or "anchor" items and three different difficulty levels. Here a condensed version of the test construction phase is presented.

NATIONAL LEVEL CONTENT ANALYSIS

The International Civic Education Committee's first major task was to analyze the set of documents which each country was asked to provide describing national goals and content of Civic Education at the three population levels. As the discussion in Chapter 1 indicated, this analysis revealed that there was indeed a common "core" of Civic Education topics emphasized in the schools of each country. This core included such topics as the national constitution, law-making processes, basic political rights and duties, governmental structures, voting procedures, international relations, the United Nations Organization and economic processes. A list of 20 basic content topics was eventually compiled, each topic receiving a preliminary weight according to the number of times it was mentioned in national reports (see Table 4.1). A similar list of topics was compiled for the

Table 4.1. *Summary of Content Analysis of National Center Documents*

Rank order	Content title	Number of times mentioned
1	Constitutions—Political Processes and Institutions	232
2	Concepts of Loyalty, Patriotism, Nationalism, Legitimacy—Citizenship Concepts	170
3	Individualism, Democracy, Rule of Law, Freedom Co-operation, Leadership, Participation, Amity, Trust, Equality of Opportunity—Citizenship Concepts	146
4	Power, Authority, Rights, Duties, Obligations and Responsibilities (e.g., minority rights and majority rule)—Citizenship Concepts	139
5	Political–Economic–Historical Development and Socio-Political Dynamics—Change–Political Processes and Institutions	134
6	Concepts of Federalism, Unitary Government, Parliamentary Government, Presidential Government, Coalition Government, Republic—Citizenship Concepts	120
7	Local, Departmental, State (Intermediary Level) Government—Political Processes and Institutions	116
8	Public Opinion, Political Parties, Pressure Groups, Elections, Decision Making—Political Processes and Institutions	103
9	The National Legislative Branch, Law Making—Political Processes and Institutions	86
10	The National Executive Branch, Cabinet Officers, Ministers—Political Processes and Institutions	83
11	Bureaucracy, Civil Service, Administration—Political Processes and Institutions	76
12	Judiciary and Court Systems—Political Processes and Institutions	70
13	Foreign Policy, National Defense, and Foreign Affairs—Political Processes and Institutions	54
14	International Organizations and Relations, Comparative Politics, Cross Cultural and Non-Western Politics—Political Processes and Institutions	50
15	Government and Economic Regulation, Taxation, the Economy and the Government—Economic Processes and Institutions	38
16	Government and Social Services, e.g. Insurance, Working Conditions and Unemployment, Social Security, Welfare, Education, etc.—Economic Processes and Institutions	37
17	The Political Socialization Process (Family, School, Community, Peer Groups, etc.)—Social Processes and Institutions	36

Rank order	Content title	Number of times mentioned
18	Communications, Mass Media, Transportation, Advertising, "Current Events"—Social Processes and Institutions	34
19	The Social Studies and Interdisciplinary Approaches: History, Sociology, Economics, Political Science, Psychology, Anthropology, Geography—Social Processes and Institutions	32
20	Social Interchange, Social–Political Man, Interdependence, Environment—Social Processes and Institutions	30

affective domain. These attitudinal categories were given consideration in the construction of the attitudinal measures, though other factors were also heavily weighted (see Chapter 7, and Oppenheim and Torney, 1974).

The Content/Age Level Grid

The next step in the cognitive test development was to send back to the National Centers the distilled content specification list (see Table 4.1) in the form of a grid (or check list) to which the National Centers were asked to respond by indicating if each topic was actually *taught* at the three age levels to be tested. The National Centers were also asked to indicate which of the topics received special emphasis at the various age levels. This procedure was helpful in the construction of appropriate test questions as well as in the interpretation of results, since it provided a rough "opportunity to learn" index. All of the countries except the Netherlands returned completed check lists.

The content/age level grids were analyzed in much the same way as the national documents, attention being paid to which topics were actually taught at which age levels in the various countries. This step, a refinement of the content analysis, showed that the following topics were taught at Population I in all participating countries: loyalty and patriotism, information about national holidays, flags, patriotic ritual, authority, rights, and the duties and responsibilities of citizens. An emphasis on democratic freedoms was also indicated, though this topic generally received greater attention in later years. Public opinion, political parties, elections and constitutions were indicated in about half the countries. Most of the other concepts received time in the curriculum in fewer than half of the countries at the 10-year-old level. These included federalism, economics, historical development, foreign policy, international organizations, the judicial system, bureaucracy, executive and legislative branches of government.

The same analysis also showed continued emphasis at the Population II level on many of the topics mentioned at Population I. This included concepts of loyalty and patriotism as well as authority, rights and duties. Topics concerning the legislative and executive branches, almost ignored in most countries before 10, were taught almost everywhere in the 10 to 14-year old period (as were the functions of the judicial system, federalism, foreign policy, international relations, social welfare). In at least six countries by the time students had reached the age of 14 they had been introduced to 17 of the 20 topics on the grid.

Generalizations about the topics taught at Population IV are more difficult to make. School systems vary tremendously from country to country in the types of specializations they offer at this level (if indeed, there is any specialization at all). Students may have had the opportunity to learn about a certain content area during any of their school years even though they are not taught about this area in their preuniversity year. The check lists indicated that 19 of the 20 topics had been taught by the terminal secondary school year in at least six countries and the 20th topic, state and local government, by no fewer than five countries.

Content Areas

From the beginning the International Civic Education Committee recognized a need to categorize the various topics into broader content areas. The first rough categorization, following the curriculum analysis, divided the field into three areas: (1) Political Processes and Institutions (60 % of topics), (2) Citizenship Fundamentals (30 %), and (3) Economic and International Topics (10 %). Other groupings considered but eventually abandoned were Current Events, Analytical Thinking and Methods of Social Science Disciplines. Analysis of the national check lists led to a reorganization of the content areas, putting International Topics with Political Processes and Institutions and then splitting the latter into three sub-areas: (1) National Topics—Processes, (2) National Topics—Institutions, and (3) International Topics. In the later versions of the test grid and in the final test itself, the following content areas are represented:

A. *Fundamental Concepts and Nature of Citizenship:* citizenship concepts and definitions of terms: state, government, patriotism, freedom and responsibility, the rule of law and democracy;
B. *Political Processes and Institutions—National Topics, Institutions:* constitutions, historical development, local and state government, national legislative branch, national executive branch, national judiciary branch;
C. *Political Processes and Institutions—National Topics, Processes:* government decision making, elections, the impact of public opinion, political parties;
D. *Political Processes and Institutions—International Topics:* foreign policy, national defense, comparative politics, the international political system and international organizations;
E. *Economic Processes and Institutions:* social services, welfare, taxation, labor organization and occupations;
F. *Social Processes and Institutions:* the family, the school, the mass media, traffic and crime.

A more detailed description of the content areas can be found by referring to Table 4.2 (Revised Civic Education Content Specifications). Also the distribution of test items by content area is spelled out in Table 4.3. These content areas will be analyzed in the next chapter (Chapter 5) as "sub-scores" of the Civic Education cognitive tests.

TEST DEVELOPMENT

Test Items

At the same time National Centers were asked to respond to the check list of topics, they were also asked to suggest test questions which would be appropriate for evaluating "achievement" in the various content areas. The countries were given a sample format and asked to supply at least 100 questions of their own, translated into English. In all, approximately 1 500 draft items were submitted to the Committee.

On the basis of the check list and the draft items, preliminary forms of pretests were prepared for four groups of students: Populations I, II, and IV and a special group of Population IV students who had taken extra or advanced work in civics, history or social studies. Different countries participated at different levels in the pretests, though nearly all tested at the Population I and II levels. Italy later conducted a separate nationwide pretest on its Population IV students. Of the four countries joining the project late, Israel and Ireland did not pretest at any level and the Netherlands and New Zealand participated in the "Dry Run" only.

In addition to information resulting from pretesting, National Centers also provided the Civic Education Committee with feedback as to whether the content of test questions was appropriate in their countries for the various age levels. Questions were revised in some instances so that the items became more appropriate cross-nationally. Disagreement about the significance of items, their balance, distribution, format and appropriateness for age level were frequent. However, very few times was the query "Is this Civics?" made about a test question.

Approximately 375 test questions for Populations I, II, and IV were translated, reviewed, and reproduced by the participating National Centers. Nine test forms were to be pretested using judgment samples of 80 to 195 students for each population in each of the countries. As a result of National Center reports, the Committee reconsidered the use of its test for the specialist groups in each country. There was considerable difficulty in clearly defining these groups. Moreover, the many difficulties in pretesting so many test forms for the six different IEA subject areas was beginning to overtax the resources of many National Centers. Ultimately the specialist group was reintegrated into the general Population IV sample and the specialist items were integrated into the Population IV test.

The final pretest battery included: three pretest forms of 35 items each for Population I, three forms of 45 items each for Population II, and three forms of 50 items each for Population IV.

"Anchor" Items

Each of the nine different test forms had several items in common, called "anchor" items. They were included in order to provide the basis for comparing the level of civics understanding at one age level with that of another. The common items included in each test could also be used for purposes of cross-validation.

In the final versions of the tests 18 items in the Population I test were also included in the Population II test and six of these were included in the Population IV test. Similarly, 18 items which were included in the Population II test also appear in the Population IV test. In the next chapter special attention will be given to the six anchor items which appeared at all three population levels.

Difficulty Levels

After considerable deliberation the Committee divided its conception of the cognitive map of Civic Education into three difficulty levels (also called ability levels by the Committee): simple, complex, and abstract. Test questions which were elementary in formulation and required definition of a fundamental political term or the recall of basic information were labelled "simple." Those which were more involved, more lengthy and required greater knowledge of facts, terminology or a higher level of reasoning were labelled "complex;" those at the highest level of difficulty, requiring much more sophistication, more involved logic or greater skill, were labelled "abstract." Some consideration was also given to the age level of the respondent in labelling these questions. Pretest results also helped the Committee in reaching decisions about categorizing questions. Generally speaking, items which were correctly answered by more than 70 % of the pretest respondents were categorized as simple; those by 40–70 %, complex; those by fewer than 40 %, abstract.

Categorization, as above, according to the numbers responding correctly to an item was fraught with dangers. Simple recall of an obscure fact may be very difficult for even the brightest students and could lead to the classification of an intrinsically "simple" item as "abstract." The vocabular level of the question is also a consideration in classification, since the most basic information ("simple") can be made more complex by the use of unfamiliar or difficult words. As much care as possible was taken, therefore, to consider both the average difficulty of an item and the kinds of mental skills needed in order for a student to answer it correctly.

The final grid sent out for consideration by the National Centers and country experts in Civic Education was a content/ability grid, with various civics topics on one axis and the difficulty or ability level on the other. This grid, which also shows the topics grouped by content area, is reproduced in Table 4.2.

Analysis of Pretest Results

All pretests were designed to be completed within a class period of 45–50 minutes duration. The time taken to complete the test, as well

Table 4.2. *Revised Civic Education Content Specifications*

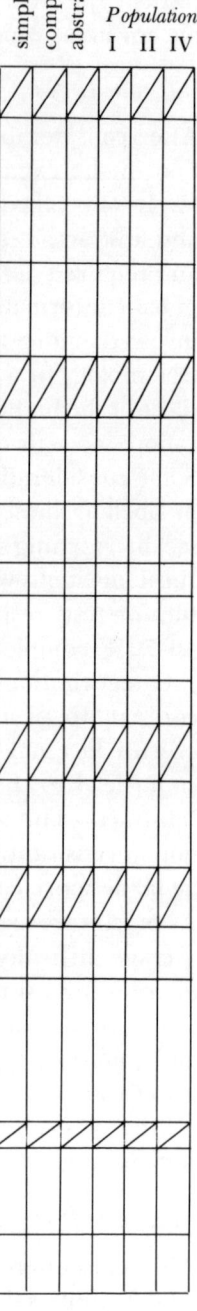

	simple	complex	abstract	Population I	II	IV

A. Fundamentals and Nature of Citizenship–Citizenship Concepts (definitions).
   1. Sovereignty, polity, state, government, political communities, nation, loyalty, patriotism, nationalism, legitimacy, authoritarianism, etc.
   2. Rights, duties, obligations, responsibilities, and power (e.g., minority rights and majority rule), etc.
   3. Individualism, freedom, authority, rule of law, cooperation, leadership, participation, democracy, amity, trust, equality of opportunity, etc.

B. Political Processes and Institutions—National Topics —Political institutions
   1. Constitutions
   2. Historical (social-political-economic) development, including political theory, separation of powers, etc.
   3. Local, departmental, state, province (or intermediary levels) as compared with central government, etc.
   4. The national legislative branch, law making, etc.
   5. The national executive branch (including the bureaucracy, civil service, the administrative branch, and the cabinet, etc.)
   6. The national judicial branch and courts.

C. Political Processes and Institutions—National Topics— Political processes.
   1. Public opinion, political parties, pressure groups, elections, political coalitions, and decision making, etc.

D. Political Processes and Institutions—International Topics.
   1. Foreign policy, national defense, and foreign affairs, etc.
   2. International relations and organizations, cross-cultural, nonwestern, comparative politics and governments (e.g., unitary and federal systems, parliamentary and presidential systems, etc.).

E. Economic Processes and Institutions.
   1. Government and the economy, economic trends, standard of living, foreign aid and trade, technology, etc.
   2. Industrial organizations, labor unions, and agriculture.

Table 4.2. (continued.)

	simple	complex	abstract	Population I	II	IV
3. Money and banking, the market, insurance, inflation, and public finance (taxation).						
4. Demography, natural resources, the world of work, and occupations.						
5. Governments and social services, e.g. insurance, working conditions and unemployment, social security, welfare, education, medical care, health, roads, housing, personal security, etc.						
F. Social Processes and Institutions.	//	//	//	//	//	//
1. Group interactions between the individual, peer group, family, social interchange, school and community, interdependence, and "socio-political" man.						
2. Communications, mass media, transportation, advertising, etc.						
3. Recreation and leisure time, group action, traffic, crime, and service institutions.						

Note: A–F included factors such as current events, the problem solving method, critical thinking, methodology of the social sciences and interdisciplinary approaches.

as the average difficulty scores, gave some indication of the relative difficulty of the various test forms. The pretest results indicated that the judgment samples differed appreciably across, but *not* within, countries, and that the pretests were not speeded, i.e., nearly everyone could complete the test in the time allotted.

Using the pretest scores as a guide, the following general criteria were used in selecting items for the field trial and final drafts of the cognitive test:

1. Is this item measuring what it is supposed to be measuring; is it face valid?
2. Is it important to know this particular piece of information, on the basis of Committee comments, National Center documents, reviewers' comments, etc.?
3. Is the item working well cross-nationally; do the item statistics indicate that the item is discriminating well between high and low scoring students; is the item within an acceptable range of difficulty in each nation; are the distractors working, etc.

Standards for item discrimination and difficulty were set as follows: average discrimination score (point biserial correlation) of an item should be above 0.30, and the difficulty level of the item should range between 40 % and 60 %. Care was also taken to include sufficient numbers of items from each content area and an adequate number (at least six) anchor items.

At this point, as at each point along the way, the National Centers were consulted. They were especially asked to comment upon the national appropriateness of the items and were asked to make any changes in terminology that they considered necessary, i.e., substitution of Prime Minister for President, Riksdag for Parliament, and so forth. In each case, when the National Center changed the wording of an item it was recorded and sent to the International Committee. The balance between national appropriateness (validity) and cross-national comparability was a delicate one and was maintained (though perhaps not perfectly) by constant dialogue between the National Centers and the International Committee.

"Dry Run" and Final Test Development

In May of 1970 a "Dry Run" was conducted involving 1 300 children at the Population II level from England, Finland, Italy, the Netherlands, New Zealand, Sweden, and the United States. It provided an opportunity for the cognitive and affective measures to be used together, along with a new measure called "How Society Works". (See Chapter 7 for a description of the development of the attitudinal measures and "How Society Works".)

Though the main purpose of the Dry Run was to assess how all the tests and questionnaires worked together, it also stimulated additional "cleaning" and comparing of cognitive test items. Care was also taken not to prejudice the outcome in any country because the test format was unfamiliar. All in all, the various tests and questionnaires were "manageable" by the students and the items were deemed acceptable by the National Centers.

External Reviews

Before the finalization of the cognitive tests, comments were solicited from a small panel of reviewers familiar with the educational systems in England, the Federal Republic of Germany, and the United States. These reviews indicated a cautiously positive response to the draft pretests. A number of suggested changes in the pretests were effected by the Committee. A second set of critiques by the IEA professional staff pointed out the test's orientation toward Western style democracy and requested the inclusion of items to expand the universality of the questions. A second criticism was that some questions had more than one correct answer depending upon the perspective of the respondent. Some items were thought to be nationalistic, trivial, inaccurate, or tautological by these reviewers. In response to these criticisms, the International Civic Education Committee met with these staff members in the Fall of 1970 to review all of the cognitive items after Dry Run results were available and before the printing of the final cognitive civics instruments. The tests were again revised, incorporating many of the staff's suggestions.

The Final Civics Cognitive Tests

In their final forms the cognitive tests consisted of 41, 47, and 48 items for the respective populations. The Committee had determined that this would provide an adequate sampling of the content domain and sufficient length to ensure internal test reliability, while at the same time not overtaxing the student who was also required to complete attitudinal and background questionnaires. Table 4.3 shows the total number of items in each test and how they were distributed across the content areas.

As Table 4.3 shows, Fundamentals and Nature of Citizenship contains from 17 to 21 % of the items across the three populations, fairly representing the weight assigned to the subcategory in the original content analysis. The Population IV level has the largest percentage of items in this area, because of the number of questions in this category which test higher order concepts such as constitutional rights, free press and tyranny, individual freedoms, citizenship, nationalism, and anarchism—concepts found to be more difficult or inappropriate for younger age groups.

Also according to Table 4.3 the Political Processes and Institutions categories (B, C, and D) are fairly represented in terms of the original analyses and content specifications with 43 to 54 % of the test questions falling in these three categories.

Because of the international character of the tests and the common pool of information in the international area, Political Processes and Institutions was more heavily weighted toward the international area than towards historical topics, which tended to have primarily national relevance.

The Economic Processes and Institutions and the Social Processes and Institutions categories retained essentially their original weights

Table 4.3. *Final Cognitive Test—Distribution of Civic Education Items by Content Areas for each Population*

Category	Population I		Population II		Population IV	
	Number of Items	% of Total	Number of Items	% of Total	Number of Items	% of Total
A. Fundamentals and Nature of Citizenship	7	17.07	8	17.02	10	20.83
B. Political Processes and Institutions—National Topics—Political Institutions	8	19.52	8	17.02	5	10.42
C. Political Processes and Institutions—National Topics—Political Processes	5	12.20	7	14.89	6	12.50
D. Political Processes and Institutions—International Topics	9	21.95	10	21.28	10	20.83
E. Economic Processes and Institutions	6	14.63	9	19.15	11	22.92
F. Social Processes and Institutions	6	14.63	5	10.64	6	12.50
Total	41	100.0	47	100.0	48	100.0

in the content grid, with more weight given to the former at the Population IV level and more to the latter at the Population I level, because of curriculum emphasis and examination of pretest results at these levels.

An attempt was made to include items from each difficulty level in each content area. This was actually accomplished with the first two difficulty levels, but items of the abstract type could not be included in all content areas at Populations I and II. All content areas were sampled at all three levels of difficulty at Population IV.

Item translations were once again carefully reviewed. National Centers were advised to check the accuracy of certain items where alternative phrasing was utilized and were asked to ensure that a common key was used, i.e., that the correct answer appeared in the same position despite a difference in the terminology used (words such as President, Prime Minister, Parliament, Congress and Riksdag). For each of these tests a full page of directions was provided for the student including sample questions to ensure that students knew the basic test format. The full text of the tests is obtainable from ERIC Document Reproduction Service, P.O. Box 190, Arlington, Virginia 22210, USA. The document number is ED 102 187.

SUMMARY AND CONCLUSIONS

The cognitive Civic Education test, which exists in three forms specialized for Population I, II and IV, was constructed over a four year period with an extensive dialogue between members of the International Civic Education Committee and educational experts in each of the IEA countries participating in the Civic Education survey. A variety of existing national documents describing the objectives of Civic Education were analyzed; in addition, National Technical Officers or Civic Education specialists in each country indicated (in an extensive questionnaire) which topics of Civic Education their countries emphasized at which age levels. A content grid was constructed and repeatedly revised to ensure that the test would adequately reflect the emphases in the curriculum in participating nations. Item analysis based on pretest and Dry Run results as well as the comments of specialists about the items were used in the final revision of the test.

The cognitive test which will be analyzed in the next chapter includes 41 items for Population I, 47 for Population II, and 48 for Population IV. In addition to a total score based on these items, which is corrected for guessing, there are six subscores representing the different content areas and a series of anchor item scores comprising those items used at more than one Population. The psychometric properties of the test and an analysis of between-country differences in performance on the Total Cognitive Civics scores may be found in Chapter 5; the results of attempts to predict between-student variations in cognitive Civic Education achievement within country may be found in Chapter 6.

Chapter 5

Psychometric Properties of the Cognitive Civic Education Test and Between-Country Differences in Achievement

Even a careful process of constructing and pretesting, such as that described in the previous chapter, does not insure the reliability or internal consistency of the items when the test is used on a large scale. This chapter therefore demonstrates the reliability of the Civic Education Cognitive test scores (with some special attention to the reliability of the anchor items). Test length, item difficulty and discrimination indices will be discussed along with the intercorrelations of the content subscores, and the relationship of cognitive achievement in Civic Education to a measure of Word Knowledge.

After presenting the psychometric properties of the cognitive Civic Education tests, the achievement of students in different countries will be indicated. This will include a comparison of total scores, content subscores, and between-population increases in scores on the anchor items. The relationship of cognitive achievement in Civic Education to the selectivity of school systems at Population IV will also be explored. In addition to describing particular strengths and weaknesses revealed by the cognitive subscore analysis for students in different countries, some item analysis will be presented. Data previously presented in Chapter 3 describing student background, teacher and school characteristics will then be related to these achievement patterns.

PSYCHOMETRIC PROPERTIES

Reliability of Scores

The reliability of the Civic Education cognitive total scores (which consisted of 41 items at Population I, 47 items at Population II, and 48 items at Population IV) range from 0.716 to 0.926 (Table 5.1).

Table 5.1. *Reliabilities of Civic Education Cognitive Achievement Total Test Scores and Anchor Subscores (Corrected for Guessing) by Population and Country*

Country	Total cognitive (corrected)	Anchor I–II–IV	Anchor I–II	Anchor II–IV
Population I				
FRG	.870	.410	.727	—
Italy	.926	.667	.871	—
Netherlands	.789	.216	.602	—
Median	.870	.410	.727	—
Number of Items	41	6	18	—
Population II				
FRG	.861	.539	.716	.775
Finland	.873	.543	.788	.742
Ireland	.886	.571	.804	.717
Italy	.889	.595	.776	.814
Israel	.886	.675	.798	.821
Netherlands	.830	.449	.673	.708
New Zealand	.871	.545	.771	.729
United States	.877	.593	.781	.769
Median	.873	.545	.776	.742
Number of Items	47	6	18	18
Population IV				
FRG	.716	.359	—	.517
Finland	.768	.343	—	.525
Ireland	.825	.469	—	.679
Netherlands	.718	.317	—	.475
New Zealand	.779	.321	—	.556
Sweden	.840	.401	—	.654
United States	.866	.590	—	.761
Median	.779	.469	—	.556
Number of Items	48	6	—	18

The figures are high for both the Population I and II tests. The reliabilities are somewhat lower for the Population IV test, but are still within an acceptable range for the planned analysis. The anchor scores are substantially less reliable, as would be expected for scores with a smaller number of items. Performance on the identical anchor items is less consistent at Population IV than at Population II in every country testing. This may indicate that the anchor items for Population IV are too easy and also perhaps that on some items these more sophisticated students go through a more complex reasoning process than is required to choose a correct simple answer. In summary, the reliabilities are of reasonable magnitude for an international test constructed by the process described.

Correction for Guessing

The cognitive test scores were corrected for guessing for each student using the formula: $c=r-w/k-1$ where c is the corrected test score, r the raw test score, w the number of wrong items, and k the number of alternative answers (5 in this test).

Average Difficulty, Median Discrimination Values and Speededness

Despite the varying length of the three tests for the three populations, students were all given 35 minutes to complete the exercise. Data on response levels indicate that the tests were somewhat speeded in some countries and not in others. At the Population I level, using 5 % or more not responding to late appearing items as the criterion, the test proved to be more speeded in the Federal Republic of Germany, less so in Italy and not at all speeded in the Netherlands. For Population II, the test proved once again to be more difficult for Italians and West Germans to finish than for all the other students, except those in Israel. Using the same criterion of 5 % or more, the Italian students began not responding at Item 28, whereas this happened with West German students after Item 36 and with students from Israel after Item 39. For Item 44 all of the countries displayed no-response levels ranging from 6 % to 10 %. At least 13 % in every country failed to respond to the last item. At the Population IV level, using the same criterion of 5 % not responding, students from the United States began to have trouble with Item 39, with 32 % not reaching the last item. For the other nations, the 5 %-no-response level was reached as follows: Ireland with Item 41; Finland and the Federal Republic of Germany with Item 43; and the Netherlands, New Zealand, and Sweden with Item 44.

In summary, then, these three tests appeared to be somewhat speeded for Italian and West German students at more than one population level and students from Finland, Ireland and United States at the Population IV level. Since more than one-third of Italian and West German students at the Population I level and from one-third to one-half of students in these same countries at the Population II level did not complete the tests, this imposes some constraints upon the mean scores for these countries; however, the students who omit or do not respond to a group of questions tend to be the lowest scoring students on the test as a whole.

Statistics on the discriminatory power of each item in each country were also calculated for each population. The median point-biserial correlation is a measure of the extent to which a given item discriminates between the higher and lower scoring students on the test as a whole. The international median *discrimination value* for Population I is 0.355, Population II, 0.332, and Population IV, 0.241. The difficulty levels for the items on the three tests are respectively 49%, 60%, and 60% correct. The standard for an acceptable average item discrimination value is 0.30, which was achieved at two of three population levels. All three tests are of average or middle difficulty (50% to 60%) with the Population I tests being of highest difficulty cross-nationally. All three tests have high enough difficulty values to indicate they were a challenge to most students and all three tests contained a majority of items with positive point biserial correlations.

The cognitive Civic Education items were also scored to form six subscores based on different content areas. These subscores (which correspond to the major categories in the master test grid) are correlated with each other at a moderately high positive level in every country. The correlations between subscores at Population II range from about 0.40 to about 0.60; these subscore intercorrelations are slightly smaller at Population IV. It may be concluded that there is a substantial common cognitive civics ability factor which is represented in all the test items especially at Population II. Analysis of any subscore as tapping a unique content area must be made with some caution. However, the advantage of subscore correlations of this magnitude is that if predictors of the total Civic Education cognitive score can be identified, it is likely that these same variables will also be predictors of the subscore components.

A concern for the general as opposed to the more specific achievements measured by the Civic Education cognitive total score leads to an examination of the correlations between this score and a measure of Word Knowledge, used as a measure of general verbal ability in all the IEA Six Subject surveys.

Table 5.2 presents the zero-order correlations between the Word Knowledge test and the Civic Education achievement measures for two populations. (For a complete description of the Word

Table 5.2. *Correlations of Word Knowledge with Civics Cognitive Total Scores and with Reading Comprehension Scores*

Country	Word knowledge and civic education achievement scores	Word knowledge and reading comprehension scores
Population II		
FRG	.63	—[a]
Finland	.64	.65
Ireland	.63	—[a]
Israel	.63	.67
Italy	.61	.62
Netherlands	.57	.59
New Zealand	.68	.68
United States	.71	.69
Population IV		
FRG	.38	—[a]
Finland	.42	.39
Ireland	.57	—[a]
Netherlands	.33	.31
New Zealand	.43	.54
Sweden	.51	.58
United States	.66	.68

[a] No data available.

Knowledge test, see Thorndike, 1973). About one-third of the variance at the Population II level and one-fifth at the Population IV level in the Civic Education achievement measures can be attributed to the students' general word knowledge or verbal ability. The Word Knowledge tests (consisting of 40 items for Populations I, II and IV) were 10 minute tests in which items opposite or similar in meaning were presented to students for appropriate differentiation. As could be expected, students who are able to understand words such as *absolute and relative, wealthy and impoverished, benevolent and intolerant, hostile and bellicose, misanthropic and sociable,* are more able to answer questions phrased in an abstract vocabulary. The correlations do not indicate that Word Knowledge is a simple surrogate for Civic Education cognitive achievement, but they are high enough to indicate a general verbal factor which seems to be of considerable importance in demonstrating knowledge of civic and political processes and institutions. This relationship will be further explored in Chapter 6.

104

Table 5.3. *Total Cognitive Civics Score (Corrected for Guessing) for Population I, II and IV Tests by Country*

Country	Mean	Rank of mean	SD
Population I (41 Items)			
FRG	13.9	3	8.5
Italy	18.6	1	11.1
Netherlands	15.6	2	7.6
Average	16.0		9.1
Population II (47 Items)			
FRG	26.0	2	8.7
Finland	24.5	5	9.8
Ireland	20.8	8	10.4
Israel	25.6	3	9.6
Italy	22.9	7	9.4
Netherlands	27.3	1	7.9
New Zealand	24.3	6	9.6
United States	24.7	4	9.9
Average	24.5		9.4
Population IV (48 Items)			
FRG	28.2	2	5.8
Finland	26.1	4	6.6
Ireland	16.9	7	8.4
Netherlands	25.5	5	6.5
New Zealand	28.4	1	7.1
Sweden	27.0	3	7.8
United States	21.4	6	9.7
Average	24.7		7.4

Note: Comparison cannot be made between populations as the tests are made up of different items.

BETWEEN-COUNTRY DIFFERENCES IN PERFORMANCE

The scores achieved by each population on the tests designed to measure cognitive outcomes in Civic Education are presented for each country in Table 5.3. Also presented here are the rank order of the means within population, the standard deviations of the score distributions.

For the Population I test out of a total of 41 items the range of country mean scores is from 13.9 in the Federal Republic of Germany to 18.6 in Italy. Italy has the largest standard deviation of the student score distributions. At Population II, out of a total of 47 items the range of country mean scores is from 20.8 in Ireland to 27.3 in the Netherlands. Finland, New Zealand and the United States score very close to the mean for all countries at Population II. Ireland and Italy are both substantially below this international mean, while the Federal Republic of Germany, Israel and the Netherlands are above it. The Netherlands has the lowest standard deviation, Ireland the highest. These between-country differences in achievement in cognitive Civic Education will be related to student, teacher and school characteristics later in this chapter.

On the Population IV test the range of country mean (out of 48 items) is from 16.9 in Ireland to 28.4 in New Zealand. Scores above the mean for all countries were achieved by the Federal Republic of Germany, Sweden, and Finland (as well as New Zealand); a mean close to the overall international mean was achieved in the Netherlands. Students at Population IV in the United States and Ireland scored below the mean for all countries. The standard deviations were especially high in the two countries with the lowest mean scores. Scores on the anchor items, comparing Population I and II indicate gains of considerable magnitude in the scores of the Federal Republic of Germany and the Netherlands on both the 6-item anchor scale and the 18-item anchor scale (see Table 5.4). There is a smaller gain for Italy between Population I and Population II on both sets of anchor items. Italian students in general scored very well at Population I (ranked first of three countries) and less well at Population II (ranked seventh of eight countries). This is difficult to explain.

The difference between the Population II and IV scores on both the 6-item anchor scale and the 18-item anchor scale is large in New Zealand, the Federal Republic of Germany and Finland. No figures are available for Sweden which did not test Population II students. The high position of New Zealand, the Federal Republic of Germany and Finland at Population IV is associated with a considerable increase in scores as one moves from the 14-year old to the pre-university level. In contrast, the relatively small difference between Population II and Population IV in the Netherlands reflected that country's decline from a rank of first out of eight countries at Population II to fifth out of seven at Population IV.

Table 5.4. *Civic Education Cognitive Anchor Item Scores (Corrected) and Differences between Populations by Country*

	Popula-tion I		Popula-tion II		Popula-tion IV		Difference between Populations I and II (Means)	Difference between Populations II and IV (Means)
	Mean	SD	Mean	SD	Mean	SD		
Anchor Items I/II (18 items)								
FRG	4.4	3.9	11.9	3.8			+7.5	
Italy	7.1	5.7	10.6	4.4			+3.5	
Netherlands	5.4	3.7	12.3	3.6			+6.9	
Anchor Items II/IV (18 items)								
FRG			7.7	4.2	14.4	2.4		+6.7
Finland			6.7	4.3	13.5	2.5		+6.8
Ireland			5.1	4.2	9.1	3.9		+4.0
Netherlands			7.6	4.1	13.1	2.7		+5.5
New Zealand			6.2	4.3	13.8	2.8		+7.6
United States			7.1	4.6	10.7	4.4		+3.6
Anchor Items I/II/IV (6 items)								
FRG	0.8	1.5	3.0	1.9	5.4	1.0	+2.2	+2.4
Finland	–	–	3.1	1.9	5.3	1.0	–	+2.2
Ireland	–	–	2.2	2.0	3.3	1.8	–	+1.1
Italy	1.9	2.0	2.6	1.9	–	–	+0.7	–
Netherlands	1.3	1.6	3.4	1.8	4.8	1.2	+2.1	+1.4
New Zealand	–	–	2.9	2.0	4.9	1.2	–	+2.0
United States	–	–	3.1	2.0	4.2	1.8	–	+1.1

It is, of course, not entirely fair to compare the cognitive Civic Education scores from different countries at the Population IV level without taking into account the selectivity of the school system at the pre-university level. New Zealand and the Federal Republic of Germany, which rank first and second in their Civic Education cognitive scores are also the most selective of the school systems, retaining presumably the most able students. In the Federal Republic of Germany, only nine percent of the age cohort is still in school at the Population IV level. In New Zealand this figure is 13 %. However, it should be recalled that the Federal Republic of Germany only included students from the *Gymnasia* in Population IV and New Zealand excluded those students in Grade 12 who proceeded directly to University without completing a Grade 13 year. Finland retains

21 % in school at this level, and its cognitive score is fourth in rank. Among those countries which score above the international mean at Population IV Sweden is an exception to this argument of associating high scores with selective systems. The Swedish cognitive total mean ranks third out of seven countries; yet 45 % of the students are still in school at the Population IV level. Swedish students, even those who are less able (if we use retention in school to the pre-university year as an indicator) have relatively high Civic Education cognitive scores. Also an exception to the selectivity relationship, but of the opposite kind, is the Netherlands. Although one of the most selective systems at Population IV (with only 13 % still in school) Dutch students rank fifth out of seven countries in the mean score at this level. The United States, which retains 75 % of the age cohort, ranks sixth out of seven. Ireland, retaining 38 %, is more selective than the United States or Sweden but has the lowest cognitive score.

If one is willing to make the assumption that each school system retains only the best of its students at the pre-university level and that Population IV as tested is a true sample of that group, it is possible to make some adjustments in the mean scores to equalize the impact of selectivity upon the cognitive scores. The procedure involves taking the country with the smallest proportion of the age group in school at Population IV (in this case the Federal Republic of Germany) and using its mean without correction as representing the score of the top nine percent of all youth of that age in that country. The mean score of the top nine percent of this age group in each of the other countries is then computed making an adjustment for the proportion of students still in school: a country which retains one hundred percent of its students would have only the scores of the top nine percent of their tested students averaged. In fact no country retains one hundred percent of the pre-university level, but a country which retains 75 % of its students will have only the top 12 % of the scores considered in computing this adjusted mean. This procedure probably penalizes some countries unduly. For example, in the base country, where 100 % of the scores are averaged, any extremely low student scores may artificially lower the mean since the distributions in countries where the adjustment is being applied are truncated excluding the lowest scores. The use of a median helps this problem slightly, but that would differ from previous IEA computations comparing the top nine percent.

The data in Table 5.5, which correspond to the tables in other IEA

Table 5.5. *Means for Civic Education Test Scores for Total Sample and for Top 9 % of the Age Group in Each Country—Population IV*

Country by full sample mean ranking order	% of age group Population IV	N	Corrected score[a] means for full sample	Corrected score means for top 9 % of age group
New Zealand	13	1 665	28.4	31.28
FRG	9	1 163	28.2	28.20
Sweden	45	1 252	27.0	35.48
Finland	21	2 315	26.1	31.38
Netherlands	13	1 296	25.5	28.96
United States	75	3 016	21.4	35.23
Ireland	38	786	16.9	28.50

[a] The maximum corrected test score was 48.

volumes, estimate the mean scores which would exist if all schools were equally selective, retaining only the best nine percent of the age cohort with regard to their Civic Education knowledge. As a result of this adjustment, Sweden becomes the highest scoring country at Population IV. Sweden, in spite of relatively high retentivity, has a high achievement score. When scores are adjusted for selectivity, the United States ranks second, primarily due to the very large proportion of students retained there. Finland and New Zealand score at a moderate level resulting from quite high scores and relatively high selectivity. The adjustment for selectivity further reduces the Population IV rank for the Netherlands; these students do not do as well at Population IV as they would have been expected to on the basis of the school's selectivity. This is in contrast to the performance of the Netherlands at Population II; at the 14-year old level the highest mean was achieved in the Netherlands, and nearly 100 % of the age group is still in school at that level. Ireland's position is not improved appreciably by the adjustment for selectivity, since this country has a low mean score and only a moderate level of retentivity. The score for the Federal Republic of Germany now ranks seventh of seven, but this must be cautiously interpreted due to the tentative nature of the required assumptions of this adjustment procedure.

To use the phraseology of the other IEA subject areas, "more" (in the sense of a retentive school system) does not necessarily mean "worse" (in the sense of lower scores) in Civic Education. When adjustments for selectivity are made, the scores in Sweden and the United States, the most comprehensive systems, rise appreciably.

Analysis of Subscores

Analysis of the items categorized as "simple"—requiring a factual or definitional answer—shows that the rank order of country performance on these items at Population II is identical to the rank ordering based on cognitive total score. Further analysis of the simple-complex-abstract subscores is therefore omitted.

The mean scores reflecting performance on the content-defined subscores of the cognitive civics instrument are presented in Table 5.6. Originally an elaborate z-score analysis was undertaken in order to determine whether students in a given country performed better or worse in a given content area than would be expected from their total performance. Given the high correlations between subscores on this instrument and the unreliability of relatively short scales, it seems more appropriate to consider general patterns rather than the z scores. This can be most easily accomplished by ranking each country's performance on a given subscore within population. Subscore patterns must be understood, however, in the context of a country's performance on the cognitive test as a whole. There is considerable consistency in the patterns of subscores within a country. A country which has a low score on the cognitive total tends to have low scores on almost all of its components (e.g., Ireland, which ranks eighth out of eight in total cognitive score also ranks eighth on four of the six cognitive subscales at Population II and seventh out of seven on all six cognitive subscales at Population IV). Countries with higher performance levels are a little more variable in subscore performance; for example, no country ranks first or second on all subscores at a given population level.

Summary of Cognitive Civic Education Results by Country

The conclusions with regard to the performance on the total test and the subtests in cognitive civics by country may be summarized as follows:

Federal Republic of Germany. Students in the Federal Republic of Germany rank relatively low in the cognitive Civic Education score at Population I. They show a considerable increase, indicated by anchor items, between the 10 and 14-year-old level placing them

Subscore …	1 Fundamentals of citizenship		2 Political institutions		3 Political processes		4 International topics		5 Economic processes/institutions		6 Social processes/institutions	
Country	Mean	Rank	Mean	Rank	Mean	Rank	Mean	Rank	Mean	Rank	Mean	Rank
Population I												
FRG	2.1	–	2.7	–	1.6	–	2.6	–	2.9	–	2.2	–
Italy	3.1	–	4.2	–	2.2	–	4.4	–	3.0	–	1.8	–
Netherlands	3.1	–	3.0	–	1.4	–	3.6	–	3.0	–	1.6	–
Population II												
FRG	5.0	4	4.2	7.5	3.9	3.5	5.1	2	4.7	2	3.3	2
Finland	4.9	5	4.8	1.5	3.6	6	4.9	3	3.8	6	2.7	5.5
Ireland	4.1	8	4.6	5.5	3.1	7	3.7	8	3.3	8	2.2	8
Israel	5.4	1	4.7	3.5	4.1	1	4.3	5.5	4.6	3	2.7	5.5
Italy	5.0	3	4.6	5.5	3.0	8	4.4	4	3.7	7	2.3	7
Netherlands	5.3	2	4.2	7.5	3.9	3.5	5.3	1	5.3	1	3.4	1
New Zealand	4.2	7	4.8	1.5	3.8	5	4.3	5.5	4.4	5	2.9	3.5
United States	4.9	6	4.7	3.5	4.0	2	3.8	7	4.5	4	2.9	3.5
Population IV												
FRG	6.5	1	2.8	3	3.7	1.5	5.2	5	5.5	2	4.7	1
Finland	6.1	2	3.0	1	3.1	5.5	5.8	3	4.2	5	4.1	3
Ireland	3.8	7	1.8	7	2.4	7	3.2	7	3.1	7	2.7	7
Netherlands	5.7	5	2.4	5	3.3	3	5.3	4	4.9	3	4.0	4.5
New Zealand	6.0	3	2.7	4	3.7	1.5	5.9	1.5	5.8	1	4.3	2
Sweden	5.9	4	2.9	2	3.1	5.5	5.9	1.5	5.2	4	4.0	4.5
United States	5.4	6	2.0	6	3.2	4	3.6	6	3.9	6	3.4	6

above the mean for all countries and second in rank out of eight countries at Population II and also at Population IV. When the mean scores are adjusted for selectivity in Population IV, their rank falls considerably. West German students, relative to those in other countries and to their own general level of performance, do slightly worse than would be expected on Political Institutions at Population II and on International Topics at Population IV.

Finland. Students in Finland score at the mean for all countries at Population II and slightly above the mean for all countries at Population IV. They rank fifth of eight countries at Population II, and fourth of seven at Population IV. There is a considerable difference between the performance of their Population II and IV students as measured by the anchor items, with the older students having a substantially higher mean on both the six and 18 item scales. Their performance at Population IV is not modified very much by adjustment for the selectivity of their system. On the subscores, Finnish students, relative to those in other countries and to their own performance overall, do especially well on the items on Political Institutions at both the Population II and IV levels.

Ireland. Students in Ireland perform less well on the total cognitive test than those in any other country at both the Population II and IV levels. The difference between 14-year-old and pre-university student in the average number of anchor items answered correctly is also small. The adjustment for selectivity at Population IV does not improve the standing of Ireland very much. Poor performance is reflected in all of the content subscores with the possible exception of Political Institutions, where they are tied for fifth rank out of eight Population II countries. Otherwise Irish students have the lowest or next to lowest mean on every subscale.

Israel. Students in Israel were administered the cognitive test only at Population II. Their performance ranks them above the international mean and third out of eight countries. Their subscore pattern is relatively consistent, with slightly lower performance on International Topics and Social Processes than might be expected on the basis of total performance.

Italy. Students in Italy have the highest score of the three countries testing at Population I. The difference in performance on the anchor items repeated at Population I and II is very small. The mean for Italian students at Population II is below the mean for all countries and ranks them seventh out of eight countries at Population II. Italian students perform somewhat better on Fundamentals of Citizenship and on International Topics than might have been expected on the basis of their overall scores.

Netherlands. Students in the Netherlands achieve a moderate mean score at Population I, the highest mean of all countries testing at Population II, and a mean score very near the average level for all countries at Population IV (ranking them fifth out of seven countries). This decline in performance at Population IV is also reflected in a relatively small difference score between Population II and Population IV on the anchor items. Adjustment for selectivity reduces the ranking of the Netherlands even further at Population IV since their system is a relatively selective one. The subscore performance at Population II shows one low point—Political Institutions. At Population IV their performance is consistent across subscales though, as mentioned, at only a moderate level of achievement. One of the phenomena for which an explanation must be sought is the difference in the performance of the Dutch students at the Population II and IV levels.

New Zealand. The students in New Zealand score very near the mean for all countries at Population II (ranked six out of eight countries). These students achieve the highest mean score on the Population IV test. Their gain between Populations II and IV, as one might expect, is moderately high. Since New Zealand has a quite selective school system, its adjusted rank order is lowered. The subscore performance is better than expected on Political Institutions at Population II. Performance on subscores is very consistent at Population IV.

Sweden. The students in Sweden, who were tested only at Population IV, achieve a score which is considerably above the mean and ranks third out of seven countries. Since Sweden has a moderately unselective school system, the adjustment for selectivity gives them the highest cognitive mean at Population IV. Their subscore performance is relatively consistent with the exception of a lower than expected score on Political Processes.

United States. At Population II the students in the United States achieve a mean score which is near the mean for all countries and ranks them fourth out of eight countries. At Population IV their performance is below the mean for all countries and their rank is sixth out of seven. The school system in the United States at the pre-university level is the least selective of all those tested. When the mean is adjusted for selectivity, the United States ranks second only to Sweden in Population IV performance. Subscore performance in the United States is relatively consistent with that on the total test, with the exception of a relatively poor performance on the International Topics items at Population II.

Although these national profiles of performance on the total cognitive test, the subscores and the anchor items, are revealing with respect to the outcomes of Civic Education, much of the flavor of the students' understanding and misunderstanding in the area of civics and politics can only be shown by an examination of the results at the item level.

Analysis of Anchor Item Responses

There were six items which were included in identical form in the tests at each population level. In Tables 5.7 to 5.11 the responses to five of these items (identified as Anchor Items 1–5) are presented in some detail in order to show the changes in response patterns from population to population and differences from country to country. Particular attention will be paid to the most commonly chosen distractors at each age level. The tables give the anchor question text, the percent choosing the correct response and the percent choosing the various distractors or omitting the question altogether. It should be noted that a percentage has been included in these tables *only* if it is equal to or greater than 10 %.

Overall, Tables 5.7 to 5.11 confirm what has already been pointed out: in all countries the percentages of correct responses increased from Population I to Population IV. In some cases the increase was dramatic, as in the Federal Republic of Germany where the percent correct on Item 1 increased 41 percentage points between Population I and Population II or in Finland where the percent correct doubled (from 41.1 % to 84.8 %) on Item 4 between Population II and Population IV. In other cases the increase was quite modest, for example, in Italy, Item 3 where the increase between Population I and Population II was only 2.3 percentage points.

Taking the items one at a time the most commonly chosen dis-

114

Table 5.7. *Analysis of Anchor Item 1 by Country and Population*

Question: Which of the following nations have largely socialized economies and governmental systems in which political debate and competition are carried on inside the single national political party?

A. Canada and Switzerland
B. Austria and Australia
C. Japan and Israel
D. Norway and Greece
E. The Soviet Union and Yugoslavia

Country	Per-centage correct	Percent choosing[a]					
		A	B	C	D	E	NR[b]
Population I							
FRG	32.4	10.2		22.9		×[c]	22.3
Italy	49.4			11.8		×	20.4
Netherlands	47.7			12.9	11.1	×	10.1
Median	47.7						
Population II							
FRG	73.0					×	10.7
Finland	61.7			10.4		×	11.4
Ireland	59.2					×	14.0
Israel	66.1	10.9				×	
Italy	56.9					×	16.5
Netherlands	71.4			11.8		×	
New Zealand	57.9	10.1				×	13.8
United States	56.7	12.0				×	14.0
Median	60.4						
Population IV							
FRG	96.1					×	
Finland	96.4					×	
Ireland	70.2					×	15.1
Netherlands	86.6					×	
New Zealand	82.8					×	
Sweden	86.4					×	
United States	67.1					×	13.3
Median	86.4						

[a] The percent choosing a particular distractor is included only if it is equal to or greater than 10 %. Therefore the row percentages do not sum to 100.
[b] NR includes those cases where a question has been omitted, not the cases where the question has not been attempted because of lack of time.
[c] × indicates the correct response.

115

Table 5.8. *Analysis of Anchor Item 2 by Country and Population*

Question: In a democratic political system which of the following ought to govern the nation?
A. One strong leader
B. A small group of well-educated people
C. Popularly elected representatives
D. Large land owners and important businessmen
E. Experts on government and political affairs

Country	Per-centage correct	Percent choosing[a] A	B	C	D	E	NR[b]
Population I							
FRG	21.3	17.0		×[c]		40.4	15.4
Italy	62.3			×		13.9	
Netherlands	28.2	13.9		×		37.5	
Median	28.2						
Population II							
FRG	63.8			×		26.4	
Finland	76.0			×		10.0	
Ireland	38.7			×		38.2	
Israel	82.8			×			
Italy	82.4			×		14.0	
Netherlands	60.5			×		28.5	
New Zealand	46.6			×		39.2	
United States	44.7			×		37.4	
Median	62.1						
Population IV							
FRG	90.4			×			
Finland	94.9			×			
Ireland	59.2			×		24.8	
Netherlands	85.6			×		11.3	
New Zealand	80.9			×		15.8	
Sweden	96.5			×			
United States	67.8			×		20.0	
Median	85.6						

[a] The percent choosing a particular distractor is included only if it is equal to or greater than 10 %. Therefore the row percentages do not sum to 100.

[b] NR includes those cases where a question has been omitted, not the cases where the question has not been attempted because of lack of time.

[c] × indicates the correct response.

116

Table 5.9. *Analysis of Anchor Item 3 by Country and Population*

Question: Which of the following is an important activity carried on by both your national and local governments?
A. Issuing postage stamps
B. Issuing passports
C. Issuing currency
D. Building roads
E. Sending ambassadors to foreign countries

Country	Percentage correct	Percent choosing[a]					
		A	B	C	D	E	NR[b]
Population I							
FRG	23.0		11.3	20.2	×[c]	28.4	
Italy	52.5			10.1	×		
Netherlands	42.4			28.6	×	15.1	
Median	42.4						
Population II							
FRG	40.5			18.6	×	25.8	
Finland	79.6				×		
Ireland	41.8			23.2	×	17.1	
Israel	38.5			18.0	×	24.8	
Italy	54.8		14.1	11.0	×		
Netherlands	55.8		14.2	22.4	×		
New Zealand	45.1			23.8	×	19.1	
United States	49.1			21.2	×		
Median	46.7						
Population IV							
FRG	78.9				×		
Finland	94.6				×		
Ireland	54.1			15.4	×	16.8	
Netherlands	76.7		11.9		×		
New Zealand	73.1				×		
Sweden	77.1				×		
United States	74.3			10.2	×		
Median	76.7						

[a] The percent choosing a particular distractor is included only if it is equal to or greater than 10 %. Therefore the row percentages do not sum to 100.
[b] NR includes those cases where a question has been omitted, not the cases where the question has not been attempted because of lack of time.
[c] × indicates the correct response.

Table 5.10. *Analysis of Anchor Item 4 by Country and Population*

Question: Which of these services is *not* correctly matched with the level of government (local or national) which usually finances it in your nation?

A. Military defense—national
B. Postal service—national
C. Garbage collection—local
D. Social security program—national
E. Street lighting—national

Country	Percentage correct	Percent choosing[a]					
		A	B	C	D	E	NR[b]
Population I							
FRG	23.3		11.9	24.0		×[c]	10.4
Italy	28.0	17.6		15.0	10.7	×	13.3
Netherlands	30.2	11.1	12.1	30.1	10.3	×	
Median	28.0						
Population II							
FRG	52.5		17.3	11.5		×	
Finland	41.1			26.5		×	10.5
Ireland	37.0	10.2		23.8	10.5	×	
Israel	78.3					×	
Italy	35.0	16.7				×	
Netherlands	72.0		10.0	10.3			
New Zealand	59.7			17.7		×	
United States	77.6			10.1		×	
Median	56.1						
Population IV							
FRG	91.9					×	
Finland	84.8					×	
Ireland	51.5			15.0	13.3	×	
Netherlands	89.7					×	
New Zealand	90.3					×	
Sweden	85.7					×	
United States	87.4					×	
Median	87.4						

[a] The percent choosing a particular distractor is included only if it is equal to or greater than 10 %. Therefore the row percentages do not sum to 100.

[b] NR includes those cases where a question has been omitted, not the cases where the question has not been attempted because of lack of time.

[c] × indicates the correct response.

Table 5.11. *Analysis of Anchor Item 5 by Country and Population*

Question: Which of the following is the best way to judge the accuracy of sources of information about public problems?

A. Believe widely expressed points of view which can be easily understood
B. Check the information against other available sources
C. Rely upon the opinions of important people
D. Be automatically negative to new ideas and new sources of information
E. Verify if the sources are in accord with established national traditions

Country	Percentage correct	Percent choosing[a]					
		A	B	C	D	E	NR[b]
Population I							
FRG	28.4		×[c]			23.2	11.6
Italy	29.3	10.4	×			19.3	16.3
Netherlands	37.5		×	12.5		29.5	
Median	29.3						
Population II							
FRG	64.2		×			14.5	
Finland	50.8		×				
Ireland	60.0		×				
Israel	49.7		×			28.3	
Italy	44.0		×			13.8	
Netherlands	70.5		×			18.0	
New Zealand	67.4		×				
United States	67.0		×				
Median	62.1						
Population IV							
FRG	98.7		×				
Finland	86.2		×				
Ireland	76.4		×				
Netherlands	89.9		×				
New Zealand	92.4		×				
Sweden	81.1		×		12.3		
United States	76.4		×				
Median	86.2						

[a] The percent choosing a particular distractor is included only if it is equal to or greater than 10 %. Therefore the row percentages do not sum to 100.

[b] NR includes those cases where a question has been omitted, not the cases where the question has not been attempted because of lack of time.

[c] × indicates the correct response.

tractors can be pinpointed. Anchor Item 1 asked students to identify which of five pairs of nations have largely socialized economies and a single national political party. At Population I roughly 12 to 23 % of the students chose "Japan and Israel" as the answer. At Population II "Canada and Switzerland" was the distractor chosen in most countries (more than 10 % choosing this category in three of eight countries). The median percentage level of non-response was 13.9 %. At Population IV no distractor was chosen by more than 10 % of the students in any country, though in Ireland and the United States the non-response rates were 15 % and 13 % respectively.

Anchor Item 2 asked which person or group ought to govern in a democratic political system, the correct answer being "popularly elected representatives." At Population I, roughly 14 % of Italians, 37 % of the Dutch, and 40 % of the West German youth chose "experts on government and political affairs." At Population II "experts" was again the most common distractor in the Federal Republic of Germany (26.4 %), Finland (10 %), Ireland (38.2 %), Italy (14 %), the Netherlands (28.5 %), New Zealand (39.2 %), and the United States (37.4 %). At Population IV the frequency of incorrect responses decreased but "experts" was still a common choice in Ireland (24.8 %), the Netherlands (11.3 %), New Zealand (15.8 %), and the United States (20 %). Only in the Federal Republic of Germany, Population I, was the number of non-responses above 10 %

Anchor Item 3 asked about the kind of activity carried on by both national and local governments. This is the item for which there were the most incorrect responses. At Population I, "issuing currency" was chosen by a large percent of students in all three countries (median percentage=20.2). "Sending ambassadors to foreign countries" was chosen by West German (28.4 %) and Dutch students (15.1 %). At Population II "issuing currency" was once again the most "popular" distractor, appearing in seven out of eight countries at a median frequency of 21.2 %. "Sending ambassadors" once again appeared at a high frequency in the Federal Republic of Germany, Ireland, Israel, and New Zealand (median frequency 22 %) and "issuing passports" appeared as a relatively popular response in Italy and the Netherlands. At Population IV, the Irish students once again chose "issuing currency" and "sending ambassadors" at a relatively high frequency; roughly 10 % of the American students chose "currency" and about 12 % of the Dutch opted for "passports" again.

The fourth Anchor Item tested whether students could identify the case where a public service was matched with the *inappropriate* level of government for funding it (see Table 5.10).

The fifth Anchor Item asked about the accuracy of sources of information about public problems, with the correct answer being to "check the information against other available sources." At Population I, the most commonly chosen distractor was the option "verify if the sources are in accord with established national traditions," chosen by approximately 19%–30% in all three countries. Non-responses were also above 10% in two of the three countries. At Population II, the "national traditions" distractor was popular in every nation, except Ireland and New Zealand. At Population IV, the correct response rate was generally very high and there were no popular distractors except in Sweden where "be automatically negative to new ideas and new sources of information" received 12.3% of the responses.

Summary of Analysis of Single Items

A fuller understanding of the outcomes of the Civic Education cognitive testing could be achieved by examining all the test items in the same way the five Anchor items have been examined. Such an exercise is obviously beyond the constraints of space in this report. Yet, the examination of the above five items has been fruitful in revealing at least three phenomena. First, with a few exceptions the particular concept measured by an anchor item has been learned by the time Population IV is reached. This is at least what distractor analysis shows; very few distractors attract more than 10% of the responses at this age level. Second, there are some significant areas where information about government and democratic principles appear to have been inadequately learned by students in many countries. The high proportions of students choosing "experts on government" as those who ought to govern in a democracy is a prime example of this. Third, the response patterns also reveal the difficulty of creating questions which are clear and unambiguous in all countries in cross-national research. In some countries a "distractor" may be just as "correct" as the keyed response. The tendency to over-interpret response patterns which differ among the countries in this survey should be tempered by the appreciation of possible differences in the validity of the several items from country to country.

POSSIBLE TEACHER CAUSES OF VARIATION IN COUNTRY ACHIEVEMENT IN COGNITIVE CIVIC EDUCATION

There are no clear cut explanations for the between-country variations in cognitive Civic Education achievement. For example, the high performance of students in the Netherlands at Population II and some decrement in this performance at Population IV have been observed. The characteristics of teachers in the Netherlands which might be associated with this are great stress on study of social sciences (in spite of relatively limited post-secondary training) and the frequent use of individualized methods of instruction at all population levels. This may help to explain the high level of cognitive performance at Population II, but it does not explain the lower Population IV performance.

The strong showing of New Zealand at Population IV is even more difficult to understand, since that country seems to have the least formal program in Civic Education. The characteristics of education in general and social studies in particular were much like other countries except that students reported that teachers encouraged the expression of opinion. Students liked classes moderately well, teachers were moderately well trained and well prepared, and used basically the same methods and stressed basically the same topics as teachers in other countries.

It is particularly difficult to account for different levels of achievement at Population II and IV by showing teacher differences because within a country the teachers at all population levels were remarkably similar in their responses.

The low performance of students in Ireland at Population II and IV may be associated with several factors. First, there are several indications that Ireland has a relatively traditional orientation to Civic Education. Teachers tend to have taken only small amounts of social science pre-service training; facts and memorization seem to be stressed by teachers in civics and social studies classrooms. Teachers in Ireland make extensive use of homework and standardized tests for evaluation and there is little evidence of individualized instruction. Finally, they (as well as those in Italy) place considerable stress on the non-political aspects of citizenship, concentrating on a set of characteristics of a good boy or good girl, and not particularly on those of a politically active citizen. Students report that civics classes are interesting, but that may be in comparison with other classes which are less interesting; they also report that the independent expression of opinion is strongly encouraged in classrooms. Teachers in Italy resemble those in Ireland with regard to holding non-political concepts of what citizenship entails. This may reflect an underlying similarity between basically Catholic countries in their approach to citizenship training. In Italy there is also a low level of active involvement by students in classrooms. However, the data from teachers present no adequate explanation for the high Population I and relatively lower Population II scores in Italy.

In other countries, where the outcome scores are neither especially high nor especially low, different teaching patterns are also found. Teachers in the Federal Republic of Germany spend many hours in lesson preparation, emphasize political history, and discuss willingly many issues in class. They are also quite well trained in social sciences. West German students also report that expressions of opinion in class are encouraged.

In the United States, where cognitive Civic Education scores are moderate, teachers have high levels of training, and seem to encourage a great deal of active involvement in discussion and activities. Students in Finland seem especially unhappy with their Civic Education classes and report less encouragement of independent expressions of opinion than students in any other country. Finnish teachers report very little discussion of controversial issues. The student level of cognitive performance is relatively high in spite of this. Sweden, for which there are only Population IV data, has relatively well trained teachers who are very discriminating in their issue choice and average in the other aspects of educational practice that were examined.

The attempt has been made to describe aspects of educational programs which may help in understanding between-country differences in the cognitive outcomes of Civic Education. However, there is insufficient evidence to label these as causal factors. Some further clues to individual variation in the acquisition of civic knowledge will be given in Chapter 6.

Chapter 6

Predictors of Between – Student Differences in Civic Education Cognitive Achievement

John R. Schwille
Research Officer, IEA International

A major aim in each IEA subject has been to compare the home and the school as explanations of variation in achievement. With the replication of the IEA surveys across countries, it was hoped that certain characteristics of the school and teachers, and in particular certain methods, would emerge repeatedly as being positively related to achievement and making a contribution independent of home background. In this way the studies were to give policymakers guidance in the evaluation of current practices. This chapter deals with these questions as they relate to cognitive achievement in Civic Education, that is, achievement as measured by the total score (corrected for guessing) attained on the cognitive Civic Education tests described in the preceding chapters. The analysis of these scores is based on step-wise multiple regressions. The following summary of results addresses the purposes stated above by focusing on consistency across countries, the relative importance of school and home factors, and the explanatory power of selected school and teacher variables. Chapter 10 contains a similar analysis of two other measures which are affective outcomes of Civic Education, the one an Anti-Authoritarianism score and the other a Participation in Political Discussion score.

REGRESSION ANALYSIS

The reader unfamiliar with multiple regressions can look to Figure 6.1 for a simple illustration of the more important statistical terms used in this chapter. This figure contains two graphs on which the

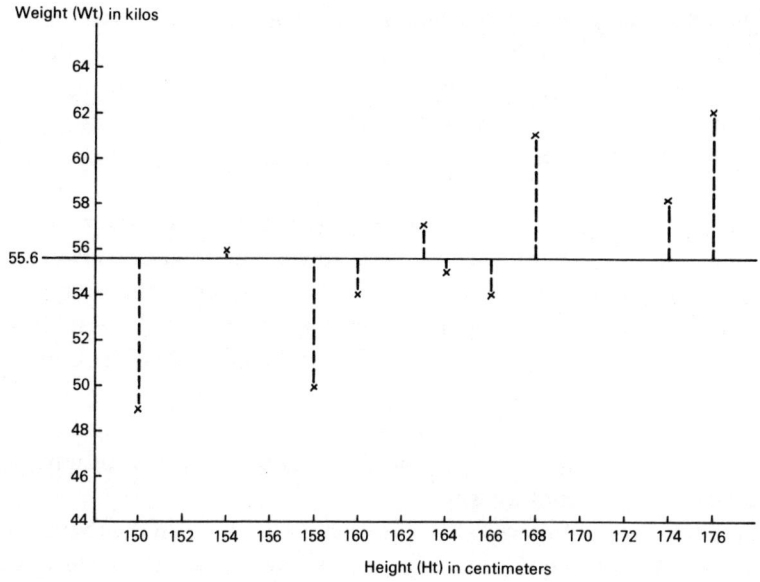

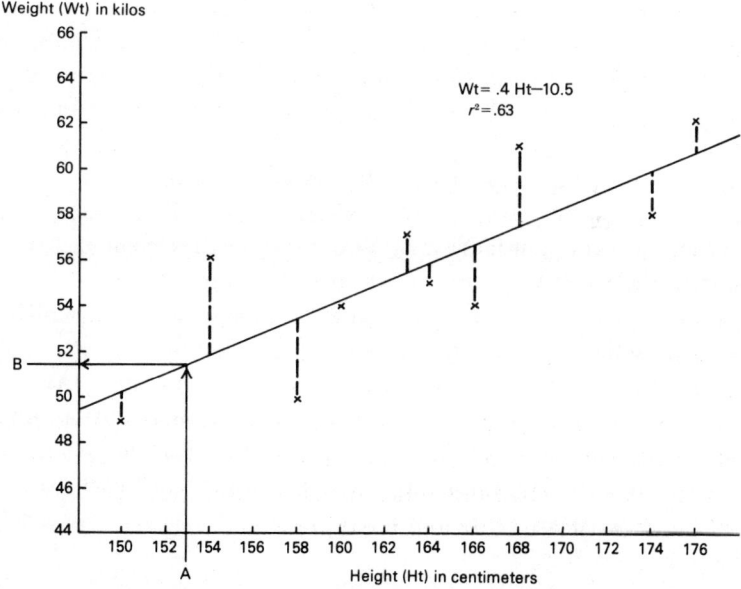

Figure 6.1. Illustration of the Variance Explained by a Regression of Weight on Height.

heights and weights of ten women, the same women in both cases, have been plotted. In the first graph the plots are shown as deviations from a line representing the mean weight, 55.6 kilograms. The magnitude of the deviations (squared deviations, to be more precise) can be summarized by computing the statistic known as a variance.

On the second graph the same plots are shown as deviations from a regression line. This line is, in terms of the mathematical criterion used, the straight line which best allows one to predict the weight of the ten women from their height. In such a case, weight is considered the dependent variable or criterion and height the independent variable or predictor. For example, the weight one would predict for a person of height A is B. It should be noted that, nothing having been said about causation, one could just as well graph another line to predict height from weight.

As a measure of how good this prediction is, one can compare the variance of plots about the regression line to the total variance portrayed in the first graph. In the sense that the regression line has made the deviations smaller, it has explained part of the variance. On each graph one can square and sum the deviations. Then taking the ratio of these two sums, one finds that the original variance is 37 percent unexplained, 63 percent explained by the regression line shown.

If, as in this chapter, many predictors are used at the same time, one can no longer graph the analysis in two dimensions. The purpose, however, is still to explain the variance of some measure, in this case, the Civic Education cognitive test scores. In step-wise regressions the predictors are added one at a time, in an order which is either predetermined by the researcher or left to be settled by statistical tests carried out by the computer. In the latter case the computer picks the best predictor to enter first. It then adds another which, in combination with the first, best accounts for the variance in the criterion variable. In this way one can see how much each adds to those which have been used earlier.[1]

---

[1] Some variables are tried, but do not stay in the regressions. They add so little to the prediction that they fail to pass the F test, a statistical test whose purpose is to exclude variables whose contribution is insignificant. In the IEA regressions the F level for entry ($F=2.0$) was, however, low enough to allow in variables whose contribution in any one country might be considered likely to result from sampling variation. The hope, in permitting such variables to enter, was to see which variables came through consistently across countries even though the magnitude of their contribution in any

BLOCKS OF VARIABLES AND THEIR ORDER

To allow as much comparability as possible across subjects, IEA has tried to follow a standard plan for regression analysis. In particular, variables with certain characteristics in common were grouped together in blocks. These blocks were then used to influence the order in which variables entered the regressions. Blocking, in other words, allowed IEA researchers to determine, in a theoretically defensible way, the order among blocks while the order within blocks was ordinarily, for lack of a better rationale, left to the computer to determine on statistical grounds. Since the principal statistic used in IEA studies to evaluate the importance of a block or variable has been the increase in variance explained over that explained by preceding variables, the order is critical.

The following blocks were created:

1. Student background characteristics (socio-economic status, sex and age within population).
2. Type of school and Type of program in which the student was enrolled.
3. Recent learning conditions (school and teacher attributes).
4. Kindred variables, that is, variables which, though expected to correlate with test scores, did not fit in other blocks, usually because they might be considered either cause or effects of achievement.
5. Two single variable blocks for test scores or affective outcomes which, in this case, were to be used as independent variables.

The justification for the order given by IEA to these blocks is chronological. Characteristics operating over the whole of a student's life were entered first. In this way the variance jointly accounted for by predictors from different blocks could be charged to attributes which had the longest time to take effect. The Home Background,

one country might be small. Variables, once entered, were seldom removed. The F level for removal was set at 0.01, low enough that, when a variable was removed in order to protect the regression matrix, the reduction in variance was negligible. A tolerance check prevented the entry of variables whose own variance was more than 80 percent accounted for by variables already in the regression. In similar fashion, a variable, once in, was removed if more than 99 percent of its own variance was explained by other variables also in the regression.

An extended discussion of the methodological and substantive issues posed by these regressions can be found in Gilbert F. Peaker. *An Empirical Study of Education in Twenty-One Countries: A Technical Report.* Stockholm: Almqvist & Wiksell. 1975.

Sex and Age Block was, therefore, entered first; Type of school or program, next. The first block was judged to be primarily a measure of aptitude for school, early upbringing within the family, and natural maturation, in other words, factors not likely to be greatly changed by the student's most recent school experiences.[2] School type was seen as a surrogate for the student's previous academic success since schools differentiated by curricula—or even other characteristics like region—tend to draw students whose abilities differ at the point of entry. To classify schools by type is, to some extent, to classify them by selectivity. Therefore, the IEA view has been that, when average student achievement differs from one type of school to another, such a gap is more likely to result from differences which predate the selection process than from recent differences in home and school conditions.

In contrast to Blocks 1 and 2, which were treated as measures of earlier learning conditions, the third block dealt explicitly with in-school learning conditions existing at the time of the survey. The analysis was an attempt to show how much measures of current or recent conditions added to a prediction based on earlier conditions. The variables in the third block came from three sources: student questionnaires, teacher questionnaires and school questionnaires. Each student was scored not only in terms of his own responses, but also in terms of the mean of responses made by civics teachers in his school and the response made on the administrator's questionnaire for his school.

The Civic Education data having been collected at one point in time, neither the mathematics nor the results of the regression analysis are sufficient to verify or refute this chronological interpretation. Other interpretations are possible. The importance of recent learning conditions may be underestimated if schools which draw disproportionate numbers of capable and socially privileged students also attract teachers who are especially effective in dealing with students of all backgrounds and capabilities. One way to address this difficulty is to vary the order of the regressions (see below). But in the end regression statistics do not speak unambiguously and must be evaluated in light of what is known from other sources.

After the third block, the chronological rationale for ordering the blocks breaks down: additional variables were entered, without any

[2] Age, intended as a measure of maturation, had too restricted a range in Population I and II to be of much importance.

causal assumptions, to see if they accounted for additional variance. This is not to say that such variables were without influence on achievement but simply that the method used did not permit estimating the degree of influence. The fourth block thus consisted of the Kindred variables, the fifth of a vocabulary score, and the sixth of Anti-Authoritarianism, one of the major affective outcomes sought in Civic Education.

CHOICE OF VARIABLES FOR BLOCKS 3 AND 4

In selecting variables for the third and fourth blocks, the International Civic Education Committee had to narrow down the hundreds of school, teacher and student variables on which data had been gathered to a number that would be computationally manageable. About one hundred sixty predictors, which of the total lot seemed most likely to succeed, were examined, one by one, within each country. In each case a partial regression coefficient was computed to show how well the variable in question predicted the Civic Education cognitive score after one had controlled for a measure of socioeconomic status. Reliabilities, correlations with other predictors and missing data problems were also considered. In short, the committee used both statistical criteria and judgments of *a priori* importance in choosing the variables to be tested for entry into the regressions. The selected variables are listed in Table 6.1.

The variables picked for Block 3, the Learning conditions block, represent various aspects of the school environment. In Population I and II this block included the Grade of the student, which in most countries varied considerably among both 10-year and 14-year-olds. Grade was intended to represent exposure to school and in particular to the curriculum in civic education or related subjects. However, the argument could also be made that 14-year-olds who differed in grade differed in aptitude so that this variable, like Type of school or program, might be charged to differences in ability.

Five of the selected variables characterized the school's policies and climate. Although three of these were from the school questionnaire, only one such item, the Use of entry examinations, was included because it passed the statistical screening described above. Proportion minority group and Grade at which social studies began were put in because they were judged too important on substantive grounds to be left out. The other two variables, Patriotic rituals and Equality among students, were both scales based on student re-

Table 6.1. *Variables Tested for Entry into Regressions (Civic Education Cognitive Total Score, Corrected for Guessing, Populations I, II and IV)*

Block 1: Home Background, Sex and Age[a]

Home Background Cluster:	Weights[b]
Father's occupation (Q)[c]	2
Father's education (Q: II–IV)	1
Mother's education (Q: II–IV)	1
Number of books in home (Q)	2

Use of dictionary in home (Q)
Size of family (Q)
Student sex (Q)
Student age (in months) (Q)

Block 2: Type of School and Program

Type of school[d]
Type of program (Q: II–IV)

Block 3: Learning Conditions

Grade (Q: I–II)
Use of entry examination by school (S)
Proportion of school's students belonging to minority group (S)
Grade at which social studies begun (S)
Patriotic rituals practiced in school (Q)
Equality among students in classroom (Q: I)
Teacher sex (T)
Teachers' years of full-time post-secondary education (T)
Amount of teachers' post-secondary education in social sciences (T)
Amount of teachers' in-service training in the social sciences (T)
Membership in social science teachers' association (T)
Teachers' readiness to introduce sensitive issues (T)
Teachers' emphasis on non-political aspects of citizenship (T)
Teachers' emphasis on country's history (T: II–IV)
Teachers' emphasis on non-Western cultures (T: II–IV)
Independence of opinion encouraged in classroom (Q)
Stress on facts in civics class (Q)
Teachers' specialization (T)
Teachers' preparation for lessons, hours per week (T)
Teachers' use of standardized tests (T)
Teachers' use of projects, papers etc. in assessment (T)
Teachers' use of printed drill (T)
Teachers' use of audio-visuals (T)
Teachers' use of lectures (T)
Teachers' use of ability grouping within class (T)

Block 4: Kindreds

Urbanization of community served by school (S)
Parental Intervention to Further Learning
of Language and Arts Cluster:

130

Table 6.1. *(Cont.)*

	Weights
Parents insist on correct speech (Q)	1
Parents check spelling (Q)	1
Parents encourage reading (Q)	1
Parents inquire about school work (Q)	1
Parents encourage visits to museums or concerts (Q: II–IV)	1
Expected education (Q: II–IV)	
Hours of pleasure reading (Q)	
Like school score (Q)	
Participation in political discussion with friends (Q: II)	
Participation in political discussion with friends, parents and teachers (Q: I–IV)[e]	
Interest in public affairs television (Q)	
Participation in civic activities (Q)	
Reports making peer group decisions by voting (Q)	
Asserting independence from parental expectations (Q)	

Block 5: Word Knowledge Test Score (E)

Block 6: Anti-Authoritarianism Score (Q)

Notes: The source for each variable is shown in parentheses (E=test. Q=student questionnaire, T=teacher questionnaire, and S=school questionnaire). When a variable was not available or otherwise could not be used in all three populations, the applicable populations are also shown within the parentheses.

[a] The variables in this block were entered in fixed order.

[b] Weights assigned by G. Peaker and T. N. Postlethwaite based on experience with IEA Stage 2 data.

[c] Generally criterion scaled on Reading Comprehension (Stage 2 sample), except in Ireland and Federal Republic of Germany, where scaled on Word Knowledge score (Civic Education sample).

[d] The source for Type of school was the school's classification in the sampling frame. In deriving this variable, some strata were collapsed. Even so, Type of school refers not only to school programs, but also in some cases to differentiation by region (Italy Pop. I and II, New Zealand Pop. II and IV, FRG Pop. IV), religion (Netherlands Pop. I, US Pop. II and IV), socio-economic status (US Pop. II and IV), sex (New Zealand Pop. II and IV), size of school (Italy Pop. I and II), and size of community (US Pop. II and IV).

[e] Substituted for the preceding variable when, after the Population II regressions had been done, a scoring error was discovered in Discussion with friends.

sponses. The practice of patriotic rituals included singing national songs, displaying pictures of national leaders and participating in flag ceremonies. Equality among students (used in Population I regressions only) was based on the extent to which students reported the absence of cliques and teachers' favorites.

Other variables provided information on teacher background and qualifications. One was the proportion of female teachers in the school. Three dealt with the teachers' level of education and the last with Membership in a professional subject-matter association.

Of a different sort were the variables representing questions which sought the teacher's opinions on professional issues. In one case it was asked whether teachers in general should engage in such activities as explaining to a class why one party should be preferred above another, allowing an atheist to express his views before school classes or arguing in favor of the regulation of trade unions. Another scale asked the teacher whether such nonpolitical qualities as being polite, working hard, and using good table manners were essential to being a good citizen. Finally, the teacher was asked for his opinion of the importance of his country's history, on the one hand, and non-Western cultures, on the other, to a student's general education.

Still another type of variable dealt with specific teaching practices. Here again the reports of students supplemented those of teachers. For example, students responded to four items asking how much freedom of expression was encouraged in their classrooms. They also indicated how much stress they found in civics classes on learning facts, dates or definitions by heart. Teachers, in turn, reported on their teaching experience. Did they teach the subjects in which they specialized during training? How much time did they spend preparing for lessons? How often did they use standardized tests or projects (e.g., term papers) for assessment? How often did they resort to (1) printed drill materials, (2) audiovisual materials, or (3) lectures?

Most Block 4 variables focused on the interest and participation of parents and students in activities related to school or politics. One exception was an item characterizing the community served by the school as urban, suburban, rural, or a combination of these three. The other exception was a seven-item scale concerning the student's reported propensity to engage in activities which might be seen as asserting independence from parents, such as staying out late, drinking beer or spirits, gambling, smoking or getting into trouble with the police.

THE CONTRIBUTION OF THE VARIOUS BLOCKS

Table 6.2 reports, for each population, the total percentage of variance (R^2) explained by Block 1 alone, by Blocks 1–3 together and finally by all six blocks. The total for Blocks 1–6 does not differ

Table 6.2. *Cumulative Percentage of Variance Accounted for by Blocks (Civic Education Cognitive Total Score, Corrected for Guessing, Populations I, II and IV)*

Population ...	Block 1			Blocks 1–3			Blocks 1–6		
	I	II	IV	I	II	IV	I	II	IV
Ireland	–	18.6	9.0	–	40.3	18.8	–	62.2	43.5
United States	–	20.4	18.3	–	30.2	31.4	–	61.8	56.7
Sweden	–	–	7.5	–	–	28.5	–	–	43.2
Finland	–	19.0	13.8	–	39.3	17.6	–	60.6	37.2
New Zealand	–	14.4	8.1	–	41.2	11.6	–	60.0	33.7
FRG	9.2	17.6	4.7	22.7	41.9	12.1	51.2	57.2	27.8
Italy	2.0	8.5	–	29.0	31.3	–	47.2	56.3	–
Israel[a]	–	25.3	–	–	29.0	–	–	56.1	–
Netherlands	12.5	15.3	8.2	22.2	43.0	21.3	46.4	55.2	31.3

Note: For key to blocks, see Table 6.1.

[a] Numerous Block 3 variables not available.

greatly among the countries in Population II, ranging from 55.2 % to 62.2 %. The total for the three Population I countries is in each case somewhat lower than in Population II.[3] It ranges from 46.4 % to 51.2 %. In Population IV the total is generally much lower than in Population II and differs more among countries. Here the range is from 27.8 % to 56.7 %. Throughout the table, the values for percentage of variance explained in Population IV are almost all below, sometimes far below the values for Population II. One reason for these differences is that Population IV was a select population. Variables lose predictive power when their range has been reduced by selection.

In the IEA studies of science and foreign languages, this effect of selectivity was partly overcome by variation in effort expended on a subject; students in the last year of secondary school varied from taking no science to specializing heavily in science. Those who did not take science had little opportunity to learn this subject outside school. Therefore, variation in time spent on science was a good predictor of achievement scores in science. In contrast, within any given country, school exposure to civics, as compared to science, tends to be relatively constant. Moreover, students have considerable opportunity to learn about civics outside school. Since, for these reasons, variation in time spent on civics was not expected to be a

[3] Israel is not included because it did not administer the cognitive test in Population I.

Table 6.3. *Incremental Percentage of Variance by Blocks (Civic Education Cognitive Total Score, Corrected for Guessing, Population II)*

	Blocks											
	1		2		3		4		5		6	
	Med[a]	Dev[b]	Med	Dev	Med	Dev	Med	Dev	Med	Dev	Med	Dev
FRG	**17.6**			−4.0		+5.6		−0.2		−4.0		−0.3
Finland		+1.4		+0.7		−3.0		+1.7		−0.7		+0.5
Ireland		+1.0		−5.8		+4.9	**5.6**		**10.9**			+2.1
Italy		−9.1	**10.5**			+0.1		+1.2		+3.4		+0.7
Netherlands		−2.3		+9.7		−4.6		−2.1		−5.5	**3.3**	
New Zealand		−3.2		+4.2	**12.1**			−1.8		+2.5		−1.6
United States		+2.8		−3.5		−9.3		+4.3		+8.4		−0.9

Note: For key to blocks, see Table 6.1.

[a] Med=median percentage.

[b] Dev=deviations from the median.

major factor in accounting for differences in Civic Education achievement, the questionnaires for civics gave little attention to such items as Years of instruction, Hours of instruction, and Hours of homework (in the subject), items which figured prominently on the science, English and French questionnaires.

The main emphasis in this discussion of regression results is on Population II where nearly the whole age group is in school and where, in contrast to Population I, there are a fair number of countries to compare. The small amount of variance explained and the differences in selectivity among countries are reasons for giving less attention to Population IV.

Table 6.3 shows how much each block, entered in the standard IEA order, adds to the explanation of differences in cognitive scores among Population II students. The statistic used is the added variance explained by each block. Thus, the contribution of Block 2, for example, is the increase in R^2 that comes about when Block 2 variables are added to the Block 1 variables already entered. Table 6.3 shows this contribution in terms of the median percentage (Med) for the seven countries and the deviations from this median (Dev). Thus in Block 2 the median percentage increase in variance accounted for is 10.5. It occurs in Italy. In the Federal Republic of Germany (FRG), where the percentage increase for Block 2 is 6.5, the deviation is

−4.0. Israel is omitted from this table because variables from the school and teacher questionnaires were answered by only a small subsample.

Block 1 (Home background, Sex and Age) behaves rather consistently, with most countries close to the median of 17.6 percent. Italy is the main exception. The Italian sample, composed solely of students taking English as a Foreign language, was not representative of the nation. Eighty-eight percent of the Italian schools in the Population II sample reported serving only urban areas, and only 7 % of the Population II students reported fathers in agricultural occupations.

Since Block 2 (Type of school or program) was defined differently for different countries, its contribution naturally varies more than Block 1. One might expect the contribution of Block 2 to be large in a highly differentiated school system like the Netherlands and small in less differentiated systems like the United States. However, this explanation does not fit all countries. In the Federal Republic of Germany, for example, attending a *Gymnasium* or *Realschule* as opposed to a *Volksschule* did not make as much difference as one might have expected.

As for Block 3, the median increase in R^2 is sizeable. The results suggest that current Learning conditions are a significant factor in Civic Education. In the United States, however, the contribution of the Learning conditions block is particularly small, accounting for only 2.8 % of the variance.

Among the last three blocks, the contribution of the Word Knowledge score is most important. The measurement of student or parental interests and activities does not add much to the prediction although in the United States its contribution compensates somewhat for the weakness of Block 3. Block 6, the Anti-Authoritarianism attitude score, in spite of the handicap of being entered last, increases the R^2 a little in each country. To account for this contribution, at least three explanations might be given. One would be that this cognitive test is ideologically biased against students with authoritarian values. In other words, students who have equal knowledge, but hold authoritarian values might be more likely to find reason to reject answers considered correct. Another explanation would be that less authoritarian students might be particularly motivated to learn about politics. Still another would be that knowing more about civic affairs makes one less authoritarian. The data do not allow one to say which of these explanations is correct.

THE EFFECT OF CHANGING THE ORDER
OF THE BLOCKS

Given the interest in the contribution of the Learning condition variables in all IEA subjects, especially close examination of their importance is warranted. Since the order of entry of the blocks is critical to the amount of additional variance each explains, it is helpful to examine what happens when the order is changed. To permit the partitioning of explained variance among four blocks of variables taken in each of all possible orders, Gilbert Peaker (1975) has extended a technique originally proposed by R. G. Newton and D. J. Spurrell (1967).[4]

Table 6.4 shows the effect of different orders on two blocks of variables—Learning conditions and Home background, Sex and Age. The first column of figures shows the proportion of variance accounted for by each of these blocks when entered first. The second column shows the increase in R^2 for each block when entered third, preceded by the other and Type of school or program. Likewise, the last column gives the increase when the Kindred block is added to the list of prior blocks.

In all countries except the United States, when Learning conditions are entered first, they better account for variation in Civic Education achievement than do Home background, Sex and Age entered first. The median for Learning conditions entered first is 32 % versus 18 % for Home background entered first. When Home background, Sex and Age are entered third, after Type of school and program and Learning conditions, they add only a median 2 % to the explanation of achievement. The student's antecedent circumstances have very little explanatory power that is independent of school factors. Learning conditions, as we have seen, account for a median 12 % in this, their standard position. When the two blocks are entered fourth, the median for Home background, Sex and Age is still 2 % whereas Learning conditions have a median of 9 %. Thus, in terms of all the variables put up for the first four blocks, the Learning condition variables do make a unique contribution to the explanation of differences in achievement.

---

[4] See Chapter 6, Peaker (1975). The figures reported in this chapter may differ slightly from those in Peaker's report since his analyses show the effect of changing the order of only those variables *entering* the original regressions while the ones reported here used all the variables listed in Table 6.1, whether or not they entered the standard IEA regressions.

This contribution must not be confused with the total effect of schools. Regression analysis uses deviations from the means in predictor variables to predict deviations from the mean in a dependent variable. If the predictors do not vary, they cannot explain variance in the criterion. Nevertheless, constant inputs can have a much greater effect on students than the inputs measured that do vary. In other words, the analyses reported here do not say what young people would be like if they had never gone to school or if they had gone to radically different schools.

Table 6.4 shows the unusually small amount of variance in the United States explained by the Learning conditions block, regardless of block order. Learning conditions entered first in the United States account for 7 % of the variance as compared with a median among the seven countries of 32 %. Entered third, this block accounts for an increase of 3 %, compared to a median 12 %. Entered fourth, its contribution is 2 %, the median 9 %. This difference occurs in spite of the fact that the total variance and the total variance explained in the United States are both above the median for these seven countries. While the Civic Education regression findings are in general rather similar across countries, this exception in the United States demonstrates the risk of generalizing from research conducted in only one country—even when the countries concerned seem similar.

THE VARIABLES OF INTERNATIONAL IMPORTANCE

The next step in the analysis was to look, within blocks, for the individual variables which were most important in explaining the variance in cognitive scores. The approach here was to search for consistency across countries. This method was one way to cope with the possibility that a given variable in a particular country may have been poorly measured and hence unreliable or invalid. For unless a great deal is known about local circumstances and the gathering of the data, it is best not to lean too heavily on variables which entered the regressions in only one country. Relationships which occured in more than one country and which, in this sense, have been replicated merit more confidence.

Tables 6.5 through 6.7 report, separately by population, the results for each of the variables tested for entry into the regressions. Israel is included because these tables make clear which variables were unavailable. Each of the tables is divided into sections. Section

Table 6.4. *Learning Conditions Versus Home Background, Sex and Age When Order of Entry into Regression is Varied (Civic Education Cognitive Total Score, Corrected for Guessing, Population II)*

| Country | Block | Increase in R^2 | | |
		First	Third	Fourth
United States	Home background, Sex and Age	**20**	9	4
	Learning conditions	7	**3**	2
Finland	Home background, Sex and Age	**19**	2	2
	Learning conditions	35	**9**	7
Ireland	Home background, Sex and Age	**19**	4	2
	Learning conditions	34	**17**	12
FRG	Home background, Sex and Age	**18**	2	2
	Learning conditions	38	**18**	13
Netherlands	Home background, Sex and Age	**15**	2	1
	Learning conditions	32	**7**	7
New Zealand	Home background, Sex and Age	**14**	2	1
	Learning conditions	28	**12**	10
Italy	Home background, Sex and Age	**9**	1	2
	Learning conditions	23	**12**	9
Median	Home background, Sex and Age	**18**	2	2
	Learning conditions	32	**12**	9

The bold entries represent regressions run in standard IEA order.

Notes: Key to block order for the figures reported above:

| | Order | | |
	First	Third	Fourth
Prior blocks for Home background, Sex and Age (HBSA) entries	None	TOS LC	TOS LC K
Prior blocks for Learning condition (LC) entries	None	HBSA TOS	HBSA TOS K

TOS=Type of school or program, K=Kindreds.

A is for variables which performed consistently in two or more countries. To be so classified, variables had to meet two conditions. First, the direction of the relationship had to be consistent within a country. In other words, the zero-order correlation and the regression coefficient (after Block 4) had to have the same sign. Sometimes, of course, it is possible to explain changes in sign, but in these regressions many such cases did not make sense. Hence, variables exhibiting these sign changes were classified separately. The second condition for a variable to meet before it could be listed in Section A was that the variable had to enter the regression in at least two countries and had to have the same sign in every country entered.

Section B contains variables which were mostly consistent, that is, which were predominantly positive or negative in two or more countries. For a variable to be included here, the signs in one direction—positive or negative—had to outnumber the sum of signs in the opposite direction plus question marks. Question marks stand for variables whose regression coefficient (at the end of Block 4) and zero-order correlation differed in sign.

Section C lists variables which entered in more than one country, but without consistency in sign. Section D is for variables entering the regression in only one country while section E is for variables which entered in no country. Section E was almost unnecessary; in Population II and IV every variable initially selected for testing entered the regressions in at least one country. The low F-level made entry easy for variables which had passed a preliminary screening for the size of their relationships, both with the criterion and with other predictors.

Population II (Table 6.5). Section A shows that, in Blocks 1 and 2, the Home background cluster, Size of family and either Type of school or Type of program were consistently related to achievement in all the Population II countries. Sex came through consistently in the Federal Republic of Germany, Finland, the United States and the Netherlands: boys generally did better than girls (boys were coded 1 and girls 2, hence the negative sign).

Of the Block 3 variables, only one was consistent in every Population II country, namely, the Student's report on the extent to which freedom of expression was encouraged in his classroom. This variable was in all cases positively related to achievement. Another variable produced consistent negative relationships in every country except Italy. Again a student report, it concerned the extent to which Patriotic rituals were practiced in the classroom or school. The only

Table 6.5. *Variables Entering Regression by the End of Block 4 and Their Signs (Civic Education Cognitive Total Score, Corrected for Guessing, Population II)*

Variables by block	Source	Italy	FRG	Finland	New Zealand	Ireland	United States	Netherlands	Israel
A. *Variables Entering Consistently in Two or More Countries*									
Block 1									
Home background cluster	Q	+	+	+	+	+	+	+	+
Size of family	Q	–	–	–	–	–	–	–	–
Student's sex	Q		–	–			–	–	
Block 2									
Type of school	F	+	+	+		+	+		+
Type of student program	Q	+			+	C	+	+	
Block 3									
Independence of opinion encouraged in classroom	Q	+	+	+	+	+	+	+	+
Patriotic rituals practiced in classroom or school	Q	–	–	–	–	–	–	–	–
Grade in school	Q		+	+	+	+		+	
Teachers' use of printed drill	T	–	–			–			M
Block 4									
Hours of pleasure reading	Q	+	+	+	+	+	+	+	+
Reports making peer group decisions by voting	Q	+	+	+	+	+	+	+	+
Interest in public affairs TV	Q	+	+	+	+	+	+	+	+
Expected education	Q	+		+	+	+	+	+	+
B. *Variables Predominantly Positive or Negative in Two or More Countries*									
Block 1									
Use of dictionary in home	Q	+	+		+			+	–
Block 3									
Stress on facts in civics class	Q	–		+	–	–		?	M
Teachers' emphasis on country's history	T	+	–	?	+	+			M
Teachers' specialization	T	+	+	+		–			M
Teachers' use of lectures	T	–	–					+	M
Teachers' use of standardized tests	T	–	–		?				M
Block 4									
Like school	Q	+	+	+	+		+		–
Participation in civic activities	Q	–	+						+

140

Table 6.5. (Cont.)

Variables by block	Source	Italy	FRG	Finland	New Zealand	Ireland	United States	Netherlands	Israel
C. *Inconsistent Variables*									
Block 1									
Age	Q				?		M	+	−
Block 3									
Amount of teachers' in-service training in the social sciences	T	−	?	?	?	−		+	M
Teachers' preparation for lessons: hours per week	T	−	+	+		?	−	?	M
Teachers' sex (percent female)	T	+	−	?	−	+			M
Amount of teachers' post-secondary education in social sciences	T	+	?	?	+			?	M
Teachers' emphasis on non-political aspects of citizenship	T	−	?	?		?	+		M
Grade at which social studies begun	S	M	+		?	C	?	?	M
Teachers' use of audio-visuals	T	?	?		+		+		M
Teachers' emphasis on non-western cultures	T	?	?	+		−			M
Teachers' readiness to introduce sensitive issues	T	+	−	?			+		M
Teachers' years of full-time post-secondary education	T		?	?	+	?			M
Teachers' use of ability grouping within class	T			?	?	+	−		M
Membership in social science teachers' association	T	−			+	?		?	M
Teachers' use of projects, term papers, etc. in assessment	T		?				−		M
Block 4									
Parental intervention to further learning of language and arts	Q	−	?	−	?	?	?		?
Participation in political discussion with friends	Q		+	?	?		?	+	−
Asserting independence from parental expectations	Q	?	+	+			−		
Urbanization of community served by school	S	C		?		?	?		M

Table 6.5. *(Cont.)*

Variables by block	Source	Italy	FRG	Finland	New Zealand	Ireland	United States	Netherlands	Israel
D. *Variables Entering in Only One Country*									
Use of entry examination by school	S	C	+		C				M
Proportion of school's students belonging to a minority group	S	M	C	C	–	M	M		M

Source
Q=Student questionnaire
T=Teacher questionnaire
S=School questionnaire
F=Sampling frame

Sign of 0-order Correlation and Regression Coefficient after Block IV
+ =Both positive
– =Both negative
? =Differ in sign

Excluded variables
M=No data or too little data collected
C=Insufficient variation

Blanks indicate that variables were tested, but failed to enter step-wise regression ($F=2.0$).

teacher-reported variable to appear in this section, Use of printed drill materials, had a negative relationship in three countries.

In Block 4, four variables were almost always associated with high achievement. Although all involve student attitudes, each appears to tap a somewhat different domain. One, Hours of pleasure reading per week, can be seen as a measure of general intellectual interest. Another is an interest variable specific to Civic Education, namely, Interest in public affairs programs on television. The third is the Amount of education expected by the student, a measure which in varying degrees reflects student aspiration, self-concept, and external constraints. Finally, the fourth variable is the extent to which students reported that they would make Peer group decisions by voting. The decisions in question were changing the rules of a game,

Table 6.6. *Variables Entering Regression by the End of Block 4 and their Signs* (*Civic Education Cognitive Total Score, Corrected for Guessing, Population I*)

Variables by block	Source	Italy	Netherlands	FRG
A. *Variables Entering Consistently in Two or More Countries*				
Block 1				
Home background cluster	Q	+	+	+
Age	Q	+	+	
Size of family	Q		−	−
Block 3				
Independence of opinion encouraged in classroom	Q	+	+	+
Equality among students in classroom	Q	+	+	+
Grade in school	Q		+	+
Teachers' emphasis on non-political aspects of citizenship	T	−	−	M
Teachers' use of lectures	T	−		−
Teachers' use of printed drill	T	−	−	
Block 4				
Hours of pleasure reading	Q	+	+	+
Like school	Q	+	+	+
Reports making peer group decisions by voting	Q	+	+	+
Participation in political discussion with friends, parents and teachers	Q	−	−	−
Asserting independence from parental expectations	Q	−	−	
B. *Variables Predominantly Positive or Negative in Two or More Countries*				
Block 3				
Teachers' years of full-time post-secondary education	T	−	+	+
Patriotic rituals practiced in classroom or school	Q	+	−	−
C. *Inconsistent Variables*				
Block 1				
Use of dictionary in home	Q		+	−
Block 3				
Teachers' use of standardized tests	T	+	−	
Teachers' use of projects, term papers, etc. in assessment	T		+	−
Teachers' use of audio-visuals	T	+		?

Table 6.6. *(Cont.)*

Variables by block	Source	Italy	Netherlands	FRG
Block 4				
Parental intervention to further learning of language and arts	Q		?	–
D. *Variables Entering in Only One Country*				
Block 1				
Student's sex	Q			–
Block 3				
Teachers' sex	T			+
Teachers' preparation for lessons: hrs per week	T	+		
Teachers' use of ability grouping within class	T	+		
Amount of teachers' in-service training in the social sciences	T	+	M	M
Teachers' specialization	T	–		
Stress on facts in civics class	Q	–	M	M
Amount of teachers' post-secondary education in social sciences	Q	–	M	M
Block 4				
Interest in public affairs TV	Q			+
Participation in civic activities	Q		+	
Urbanization of community served by school	S		?	
E. *Variables Not Entering in Any Country*				
Block 2				
Type of school	F			
Block 3				
Teachers' readiness to introduce sensitive issues	T			M
Membership in social science teachers' association	T			M
Use of entry examination by school	S	C	C	
Proportion of school's students belonging to a minority group	S	M	M	C
Grade at which social studies begun	S	M	M	M

Note: For key see Table 6.5.

Table 6.7. *Variables Entering Regression by the End of Block 4 and Their Signs (Civic Education Cognitive Total Score, Corrected for Guessing, Population IV)*

Variables by block	Source	United States	New Zealand	Finland	Sweden	Netherlands	Ireland	FRG
A. *Variables Entering Consistently in Two or More Countries*								
Block 1								
Student's sex	Q	−	−	−	−	−	−	−
Home background cluster	Q	+	+	+	+[a]		+	+
Size of family	Q	−	−	−			−	
Age	Q	−	−	−				−
Block 3								
Patriotic rituals practiced in classroom or school	Q	−	−	−	−	−	−	−
Teachers' years of full-time postsecondary education	T	+	+		+		+	
Stress on facts in civics class	Q	−	M			−	M	
Block 4								
Hours of pleasure reading	Q	+	+	+	+	+	+	+
Expected education	Q	+	+	+	M	+	+	+
Participation in political discussion with friends, parents and teachers	Q	+	+	+	+	+	+	
Interest in public affairs TV	Q	+		+	+	+	+	+
Participation in civic activities	Q		+	+	+	+		
Reports making peer group decisions by voting	Q	+					+	+
B. *Variables Predominantly Positive or Negative in Two or More Countries*								
Block 1								
Use of dictionary in home	Q	+	+	+	+	−		−
Block 2								
Type of student program	Q	+	−	+	+	+	C	C
Type of school	F	+		C		+	+	?
Block 3								
Teachers' preparation for lessons: hrs per week	T	+	+	−	+			
Teachers' use of lectures	T		+	?	−		+	+
Grade at which social studies begun	S	+	+		C		C	?
Teachers' readiness to introduce sensitive issues	T		−	+		+		
Independence of opinion encouraged in classroom	Q	−		−	+			

Table 6.7. *(Cont.)*

Variables by block	Source	United States	New Zealand	Finland	Sweden	Netherlands	Ireland	FRG
Teachers' use of standardized tests	T	−	+					−
Teachers' use of printed drill	T	?			−	−		
Block 4								
Parental intervention to further learning of language and arts	Q	?	?	−	−	−	−	
C. Inconsistent Variables								
Block 3								
Teachers' specialization	T	+	−		+	−		?
Teachers' emphasis on non-western cultures	T	+	+				−	−
Amount of teachers' in-service training in the social sciences	T	−			+	M	−	+
Teachers' emphasis on country's history	T		−	+	−			?
Teachers' sex (% female)	T	−			+	?		−
Teachers' use of projects, term papers, etc. in assessment	T	+			?	−		
Teachers' use of audio-visuals	T		?		?			+
Teachers' use of ability grouping within class	T		?		−	?		
Amount of teachers' post-secondary education in the social sciences	T	?			?	M		
Use of entry examination by school	S	?	C		C		+	
Teachers' emphasis on non-political aspects of citizenship	T	?						+
Block 4								
Like school	Q		−	+	M			
Asserting independence from parental expectations	Q	−						+
Urbanization of community served by school	S	?		+				
D. Variables Entering in Only One Country								
Proportion of school's students belonging to a minority group	S	M	+		C	M	M	C
Membership in social science teachers' association	T				−			

Note: For key see Table 6.5.

[a] The Home background cluster in Sweden consisted of Father's occupation and Number of books in home. Data on Father's education and Mother's education were not available.

deciding where to go on a hike or a trip, and choosing a leader. The analysis has not answered the question whether students who advocated voting were sincerely committed to this norm or whether they were test-wise students who used their skill on both the test and questionnaire.

Section B in Table 6.5 (predominantly consistent variables) contains mostly Block 3 variables, two with predominantly positive relationships and three with negative. In Italy, New Zealand, and Ireland the teacher's Emphasis on teaching the political history of the country was positively related to the cognitive test scores. In the Federal Republic of Germany the relationship was negative. Since the political implications and ideological significance of national history differ from country to country, a change of sign in this case is not surprising.

Students in schools where the civics teachers were specialized generally did better in three countries, but worse in one. Students who reported stress on facts in Civic Education classes were generally less successful in Italy, New Zealand and Ireland, but in Finland they did better than other students. In two of three cases the teachers' reported use of lectures and their reported use of standardized tests had a negative relationship with achievement.

Population I (Table 6.6). In general, the sign tables for Populations I and II are rather similar. The following variables were classified as consistent or predominantly consistent in both populations. In other words, they are found in sections A or B of both tables.

Consistent in a positive direction:
Home background cluster
Independence encouraged
Grade
Hours of pleasure reading
Like school
Peer group decisions by voting

Consistent in a negative direction:
Size of family
Patriotic ritual
Teachers' use of lectures
Teachers' use of printed drill

147

The variable Equality among students was not important enough in Populations II and IV to pass the initial screening. In Population I it entered the regressions in all three countries with a positive sign. This finding supports the belief that the quality of interaction between teacher and student as well as among students is even more important for achievement at the 10-year-old than at the older levels.

Population IV (Table 6.7). Comparison of Populations II and IV also reveals similarities across populations. Classified as consistent or predominantly consistent, with signs in the same direction, were the following:

Consistent in a positive direction:
Home background cluster
Use of dictionary in home
Type of school or program
Hours of pleasure reading
Expected education
Interest in public affairs television
Participation in civic activities
Peer group decisions by voting

Consistent in a negative direction:
Student's sex (female)
Size of family
Patriotic ritual
Stress on facts
Use of standardized tests
Use of printed drill

There are also notable differences between Populations II and IV. Sex, for example, is a more prominent variable in Population IV than in either of the younger populations. In Population I it entered in one of the three countries. In Population II it entered in four of eight countries, but in no case contributed more than 2 % as an increase in R^2. In Population IV Sex entered in every country, with an increase in R^2 of more than 2 % in six countries. In every case in which Sex came into the regressions, boys outscored girls. In this respect, cognitive achievement in Civic Education resembles the IEA Science study rather than Literature where the reverse was true (Comber and Keeves 1973; Purves 1973).

148

Age (in months) also showed up in the regression in more countries at Population IV, the variance in age being much greater in a population not defined as a one-year age group. In four countries the older students did less well, probably because students who have academic difficulty often take longer to finish school.

Two variables in the consistent sections of Tables 6.5 and 6.7 changed signs from one population to the other. The Encouragement of classroom independence, positive in every country at Population II, was negative in two and positive in one at Population IV. Teachers' use of lectures changed from predominantly negative to predominantly positive. In addition, Teachers' years of full-time post-secondary schooling, inconsistent at Population II, turned out uniformly positive at Population IV. Political discussion with friends, used at Population II, was spoiled by a scoring error. It was replaced by a measure of Total discussion with friends, parents and teachers, which ended up positively related to achievement in every country in Population IV except the Federal Republic of Germany.

Inconsistent variables. It is surprising that in all three populations fewer variables were classified under section B than under section A. One might well find many variables to be predominantly consistent and few variables entirely consistent—that, at least, is what the social scientist learns to expect. Such was not the case. Most variables with inconsistencies revealed no predominant pattern and hence were included in section C. Among the poor performers ending up in sections C, D, or E of each of the sign tables were the following: Amount of teachers' in-service training in the social sciences, Teachers' post-secondary education in the social sciences, Use of audio-visuals, and Membership in a social science teachers' association.

THE NEGATIVE SHOWING OF ROTE AND RITUAL

Table 6.8 lists the consistent or predominantly consistent Learning condition variables by country and by sign. In every country the table provides at least some evidence for the following conclusions: students characterized by high exposure to rote or ritual learning generally performed less well than students characterized by low exposure; students who felt that independence of opinion was encouraged generally performed better than students who did not feel this way.

The variables in Table 6.8 have been classified in terms of support for or opposition to the argument that high achievement is associated with free speech and low achievement with rote and ritual. Instances which support the argument have been underscored with a solid line while those which oppose the argument have been singled out with a dashed line. Variables that are irrelevant to this issue have not been marked. In other words, any variable which suggests emphasis on rote, ritual or nonpolitical ideals of citizenship has been underscored with a solid line if its regression coefficient was negative and with a dashed line if the coefficient was positive. In turn, the practices of encouraging independent thought and introducing sensitive issues in the classroom have been marked with a solid line where positive and a dashed line where negative. In each country the results which were consistent with the argument (solid lines) outnumber those which were not (dashed lines).

Nearly all the exceptions denoted by dashed lines occurred in Population IV. Use of lectures was positive in the Federal Republic of Germany, Ireland, and New Zealand, negative in the Netherlands and mixed in Sweden. Independence encouraged was negative in Finland and the United States, but positive in Sweden. Of the countries in Population IV, New Zealand deviated most from the overall pattern. In that country three variables had signs which were exceptional, in terms of the interpretation of rote and ritual offered above, while only one conformed. New Zealand, it might be noted is the country with the highest mean score on the cognitive test at Population IV.

Table 6.8 also shows how much difference the consistent or predominantly consistent variables made. Once again the ordering of variables is of paramount importance. The table shows the effect of order in two ways. First, the effect of the original order is shown as the increase in variance accounted for ($IncR^2$) when the variable in question is added to variables previously in the regression. Within blocks the increase in R^2 for variables entering early is, by nature of the step-wise procedure, larger than the increase in R^2 for variables entering late. The table gives the increase in R^2 for the Learning condition variables when these variables are entered as Block 3.

One can also look at the contribution of a variable in terms of the decrease in R^2 ($DecR^2$) when the variable in question is dropped from the regression, but all other variables through the end of a certain block are left in. The table shows the decrease in R^2 as computed after the first four blocks have been run in standard order. This

Table 6.8. *Country Profiles: Contribution of Consistent and Predominantly Consistent Learning Condition Variables at the End of Block 4* (*Civics Cognitive Total Score, Corrected for Guessing, Populations I, II and IV*)

Country and Population	Positive Variables	IncR^2	DecR^2	Negative Variables	IncR^2	DecR^2
FRG						
Population I	Independence encouraged	2.7	1.3	Patriotic ritual	5.1	2.4
	Student equality	2.5	1.3	Use of lectures	0.4	0.4
	Grade	1.0	1.0			
	Teacher education	0.2	1.0			
Population II	Independence encouraged	2.0	1.0	Use of printed drill	4.5	3.9
	Grade	1.4	1.9	Patriotic ritual	2.6	1.4
	Teacher specialization	0.3	0.0+	Emphasis on country history	1.2	0.6
				Use of standardized tests	0.3	0.4
				Use of lectures	0.1	0.0+
Population IV	Use of lectures	1.1	1.3	Patriotic ritual	1.1	0.5
				Use of standardized tests	0.7	0.5
				Grade social studies begun	0.3[a]	0.3[a]
Finland						
Population II	Grade	3.9	3.2	Patriotic ritual	2.2	1.5
	Teacher specialization	0.4	0.1	Use of printed drill	0.3	0.3
	Stress on facts	0.1	0.0+	Emphasis on country history	0.1[a]	0.1[a]
	Independence encouraged	0.1	0.0			
Population IV	Sensitive issues	0.2	0.1	Patriotic ritual	0.2	0.4
				Independence encouraged	0.2	0.3
				Hours of preparation	0.1	0.2
Ireland						
Population II	Grade	2.3	2.2	Patriotic ritual	4.9	4.0
	Independence encouraged	0.9	0.4	Use of printed drill	1.8	1.1
	Emphasis on country history	0.5	0.5	Stress on facts	0.8	0.8
				Teacher specialization	0.8	0.7
Population IV	Use of lectures	2.4	0.8	Patriotic ritual	1.3	1.9
	Teacher education	1.0	0.6			
	Sensitive issues	0.5	0.6			
Israel						
Population II	Independence encouraged	1.4	1.3	Patriotic ritual	0.4	0.3
Italy						
Population I	Independence encouraged	11.8	5.6	use of lectures	0.5	0.2
	Student equality	7.5	2.0	Teacher education	0.5	0.1
	Patriotic ritual	0.3	0.3	Teacher non-political citizenship	0.2	0.4
				Use of printed drill	0.2	0.3

151

Table 6.8. *(Cont.)*

Country and Population	Positive Variables	IncR²	DecR²	Negative Variables	IncR²	DecR²
Population II	Emphasis on country history	0.8	1.0	Use of standardized tests	0.8	0.2
	Independence encouraged	0.7	0.5	Use of lectures	0.6	0.2
	Teacher specialization	0.5	0.4	Stress on facts	0.3	0.1
Netherlands						
Population I	Grade	4.2	2.9	Patriotic ritual	1.9	1.5
	Independence encouraged	2.1	2.1	Use of printed drill	0.2	0.4
	Student equality	0.4	0.2	Teacher non-political	0.1	0.2
	Teacher education	0.1	0.2	citizenship		
Population II	Grade	2.4	1.6	Patriotic ritual	0.8	1.2
	Use of lectures	1.1	1.0	Stress on facts	0.1[a]	0.1[a]
	Independence encouraged	0.9	0.5			
Population IV				Use of lectures	2.0	0.5
				Stress on facts	0.6	0.3
				Patriotic ritual	0.5	0.6
				Use of printed drill	0.5	0.2
New Zealand						
Population II	Grade	5.7	4.5	Patriotic ritual	2.6	2.3
	Independence encouraged	1.1	0.6	Stress on facts	0.1	0.2
	Emphasis on country history	0.1	0.3	Use of standardized tests	0.1[a]	0.1[a]
Population IV	Teacher education	0.3	0.5	Patriotic ritual	0.4	0.6
	Use of lectures	0.2	0.4	Sensitive issues	0.3	0.4
	Use of standardized tests	0.2	0.3			
	Hours of preparation	0.2	0.2			
	Grade social studies begun	0.2	0.1			
Sweden						
Population IV	Independence encouraged	1.5	0.9	Use of printed drill	0.6	0.2
	Teacher education	0.1	0.1	Use of lectures	0.3[a]	0.4[a]
	Hours of preparation	0.1	0.0+	Patriotic ritual	0.2	0.1
United States						
Population II	Independence encouraged	0.3	0.0+	Patriotic ritual	0.7	0.8
Population IV	Teacher education	0.9	0.7	Patriotic ritual	0.9	0.5
	Hours of preparation	0.2	0.1	Stress on facts	0.5	0.6
	Grade social studies begun	0.1	0.1	Independence encouraged	0.1	0.2
	Use of printed drill	0.1[a]	0.1[a]	Use of standardized tests	0.1	0.1

Note: 0<0.0+ <0.05.

[a] Position in positive or negative column based on regression coefficient. Zero-order correlation is in the opposite direction.

figure is an attempt to measure the unique contribution of a variable, given the other variables which have entered the regression.

Using these figures one finds, for example, that Patriotic ritual was more than a consistent variable. On the whole, it also made a sizeable contribution relative to other Learning condition variables. Moreover, its contribution was somewhat independent of all other variables used in Blocks 1 to 4. The decrease in R^2 was greater than 1 % in two of three Population I countries and five of eight Population II countries (it reached this level in only one of the seven Population IV countries, however). In five of the ten cases where Grade and Patriotic ritual can be compared, Patriotic ritual was a better predictor in terms of the increase or decrease in R^2.

Independence encouraged in the classroom was a strong variable in Population I, particularly in Italy. In that country its zero-order correlation with the criterion was 0.35, enabling it to enter first in Block 3 and thereby increase the R^2 by 11.8 %. The same variable in Population II, though entering in all countries, did not explain much of the variance—in no case more than 2 % either as an increase or decrease in R^2. The individual contribution of the other underscored variables was small, with some exceptions. Use of printed drill made a fair difference in Ireland and the Federal Republic of Germany at Population II. Use of lectures likewise made a strong showing in some countries: Federal Republic of Germany Population IV (+), Ireland Population IV (+), Netherlands Population II (+) and Netherlands Population IV (−). But the differences in sign make one wonder what this variable means.

The negative showing of rote and ritual is consistent with much modern pedagogical thinking, which stresses the active participation of students in learning and the value of students drawing their own conclusions to social and scientific problems. Findings that agree with preconceived ideas should not, however, blind one to the fact that the order of causation is unknown for most of the variables in these regressions. The permissiveness perceived by high achieving students may be, not a cause, but an effect of achievement or some other variable. Similarly, the teacher may stress facts when faced with low-achieving students.

WORD KNOWLEDGE AS A PRETEST PROXY

Since these regressions included no direct measure of student abilities at the beginning of the period of relevant instruction, Block

153

3 variables might have appeared important only because they were correlated with pre-existing student abilities and not because of any independent effect. Therefore, to put Block 3 to the most stringent test with the data available and to produce the most *conservative* estimates of the unique contribution of the Learning conditions block, additional regressions were run with Word Knowledge (rather than Type of school or program) as Block 2. In this instance Word Knowledge was being used as a proxy for a pretest of general verbal competence, a pretest that might have been given before the period covered by the current learning conditions. The Word Knowledge score qualifies as a proxy because, of the measures available, it can plausibly be thought to have the highest correlation with the hypothetical pretest. However, the Word Knowledge test is not just a measure of aptitude; it is also a measure of achievement, of general verbal skills which can themselves be influenced by recent school factors. Therefore, the use of this measure, together with Home background, is likely (if anything) to overestimate the variance explained by pre-existing differences in student ability. If the Block 3 variables survive in such a regression, there is cause for some confidence that they are more than pale reflections of differences in ability.

The variables for these regressions (listed in Table 6.9) are a subset of those found to play a consistent or predominantly consistent role in the earlier regressions. The F-level for the new regressions was set at 7.0, a limit high enough to make it very unlikely that the contribution of a variable in any given country would result solely from sampling variability.

Table 6.10 summarizes the variance explained by blocks. Overall, not a great deal was lost by reducing the list of individual variables from 43 to 15. In the original regressions the median variance accounted for across the seven Population II countries was 60.0%. In the new regressions with Word Knowledge as Block 2 it was 56.8%. Each of the four blocks in these new regressions would have had considerable explanatory power if entered by itself (see columns headed *1st*). In terms of the median, the Word Knowledge score would be most powerful under such conditions, accounting for 39.8%, with Attitudes and interests second, Learning conditions third, and Home background fourth at 13.7%.

What then happened in these regressions when the Learning conditions block was pitted against Home background and Word Knowledge, the latter two blocks being entered first to approximate

154

Table 6.9. *Variables for Regression with Word Knowledge as Block 2 (Civic Education Cognitive Total Score, Corrected for Guessing, Population II)*

Block 1: Home Background Cluster[a]

Block 2: Word Knowledge Score

Block 3: Learning Conditions
  Grade
  Patriotic rituals practiced in school
  Teacher's emphasis on country's history
  Independence of opinion encouraged in classroom
  Stress on facts in civics class
  Teachers' specialization
  Teachers' use of printed drill
  Teachers' use of lectures

Block 4: Attitudes and Interests
  Anti-authoritarianism
  Hours of pleasure reading
  Interest in public affairs TV
  Expected education
  Like school score

[a] Same variables and weights as in Table 6.1.

a pretest? The results are shown in the column headed *3rd*. In five countries Learning conditions ranged in the neighborhood of 4 to 6 % of variance explained, figures which were not large but not negligible either. In Italy the contribution was smaller (2 %) while in the United States, Learning conditions were virtually eliminated when entered third. In these two countries, however, the block was not very powerful when entered first. In the other countries even the entry of the Attitude and interest variables did not completely wipe out the Learning conditions block (see column headed *Last* under Learning conditions).

One other test was carried out with Word Knowledge as Block 2 (Table 6.11). It might be thought that a variable would be more likely to enter in countries where it had a large variance than in countries where its variance was small. A quick check was made of this possibility by classifying the standard deviation of Block 3 and 4 variables in each country as larger or smaller than the corresponding median standard deviation for the seven countries in Population II. The plus signs in the table stand for standard deviations greater than or equal to the median. The median itself is listed at the right along with the range of the standard deviations. The circles in the table show the

Table 6.10. *Incremental Percentage of Variance by Blocks for Regressions with W[o] Knowledge as Block II (Civic Education Cognitive Total Score, Corrected for Guessing, Popu[la]tion II)*

	Home Background		Word Knowledge			Learning Conditions			Attitudes and Interests			Tota[l]
	1st	Last	1st	2nd	Last	1st	3rd	Last	1st	Last	Total	Old Ord[er]
Netherlands	**12.8**		32.4			24.0			33.0			
				23.3			**6.3**				49.5	55.2
		0.5			6.4			4.2		**7.1**		
New Zealand	**12.3**		46.0			25.1			27.6			
				35.9			**5.1**				57.3	60.0
		0.3			15.7			3.9		**4.0**		
Finland	**17.1**		40.7			26.5			41.2			
				27.3			**5.0**				56.8	60.6
		0.4			8.6			2.6		**7.4**		
FRG	**13.7**		39.8			28.2			35.5			
				27.6			**4.6**				51.8	57.2
		0.2			8.2			2.2		**6.0**		
Ireland	**17.7**		39.7			24.6			40.4			
				26.1			**4.0**				57.7	62.2
		−0.1			9.1			2.1		**10.0**		
Italy	**5.5**		37.7			8.0			25.1			
				33.0			**2.0**				45.3	56.3
		0.4			17.9			1.0		**4.8**		
United States	**19.2**		50.0			3.4			35.8			
				33.2			**0.4**				58.8	61.8
		0.5			18.5			0.2		**6.1**		
Median	**13.7**		39.8			24.6			35.5			
				27.6			**4.6**				56.8	60.0
		0.4			9.1			2.2		**6.1**		

Note: The bold figures give the increment in R^2 for the order of prima[r]y interest.

countries in which each variable entered the regression. In general, the table reveals no relation between entering the regression and having a large standard deviation. Of the variables with relatively high standard deviations, 49 % entered the regressions as compared to 50 % of the other variables. Even if one takes the variables one at a time, only Hours of pleasure reading, with perfect correspondence between high standard deviations and entering, might be seen as

156

Table 6.11. *Standard Deviations versus Entry into Regression (Word Knowledge as Block 2, Civic Education Cognitive Total Score, Corrected for Guessing, Population II)*

Variables	Finland	United States	Ireland	FRG	Italy	Netherlands	New Zealand	Israel	SD median	Range
Independence encouraged	⊕	⊕	+	+	+	○	○	○	0.78	0.68–0.83
Grade	⊕	C	⊕	+	○	○	⊕		0.52	0.43–0.73
Emphasis on country history	+	+	+	+		⊕		M	0.32	0.18–0.62
Teacher specialization	⊕	+		+		⊕		M	0.48	0.26–0.63
Use of lectures	+	+	+	⊕		○	○	M	0.31	0.20–0.56
Patriotic ritual	○	⊕	⊕	○	+	○	○	+	0.72	0.60–0.83
Use of printed drill	⊕	+	○	⊕		+		M	0.43	0.30–0.61
Stress on facts		+	+		+	+		M	0.81	0.75–0.83
Anti-Authoritarianism	⊕	○	⊕	○	⊕	○	○	⊕	0.56	0.49–0.64
Hours pleasure reading		⊕	⊕			⊕	⊕		1.34	1.17–1.41
Interest in public affairs TV	⊕	⊕	○	⊕	+		+	+	0.43	0.40–0.46
Expected education	⊕	○		+	+	⊕	○	○	1.04	0.83–1.16
Like school	+	+	+				⊕	○	5.08	4.34–5.42

+ =SD⩾median SD, ○=entered regression, M=insufficient data, C=insufficient variation.

contradicting the overall conclusion drawn from this table. The table also suggests that the low contribution of Block 3 variables in the United States cannot be attributed to low variance in the predictors since, in this country, every Block 3 variable had relatively high variance except Grade.

CONCLUSION

One purpose of the IEA studies has been to see how the importance of the school might vary from subject to subject and from country to country. This question is particularly open to debate in Civic Education. While the school has had its defenders, all agree that out-of-school factors like the home and mass media also play an important role. The data presented in this chapter suggest that the school is important in accounting for differences in Civic Education cognitive achievement. Even after one has allowed for the student's home background, interests and attitudes, knowledge about the school attended makes possible a better prediction of performance on the IEA Civic Education cognitive test. Inasmuch as the other blocks of variables also make a substantial contribution to this prediction, future research must continue to deal with influences both inside and outside the school.

These data also lend some comfort to those who for years have advised teachers to step down from their platforms, get away from the flag, throw away their drill sheets and engage students in a discussion of the issues of the day. Those who disagree with these prescriptions may take equal comfort from the inadequacies of the analysis. Nevertheless, the cross-national consistency of the findings is sufficient reason for schools which administer a large dose of rote and ritual to take stock of their own results and to see if performance might not be improved by a more Socratic approach to Civic Education.

Chapter 7

The Development of Attitudinal Outcome Measures in Civic Education

INTRODUCTION

The assessment of achievement or outcomes in Civic Education cross-nationally is attended by a number of awkward problems: uncertainty about a "common core" of the subject; the need for special attitude measures as well as knowledge tests; conceptualization of the links between knowledge, percepts and attitudes in the growing child; the probability of strong out-of-school influences; and difficulties created by the use of terminology with political overtones. In consequence it was found necessary to engage in a prolonged period of pilot work, both to improve conceptualization and to develop adequate techniques of measurement. The curriculum analysis and the development of the cognitive tests have been described in Chapter 4. The present chapter gives an abridged account of the *attitudinal* techniques which were designed by A. N. Oppenheim and Judith Torney for this study—a fuller description has been published elsewhere in Oppenheim and Torney, *The Measurement of Children's Civic Attitudes in Different Nations*, Stockholm: Almqvist & Wiksell, 1974. Also included here is a description of scales developed for collecting background information and of a new technique for assessing the student's perceptions of institutions and values (How Society Works).

The particular need to develop attitudinal outcome measures arose from the fact—much stressed both in the curriculum objectives and by the teachers themselves—that Civic Education does not merely consist in the transmission of a body of *knowledge*, but that it aims at inculcating certain common *attitudes* and values, such as a liberal and democratic outlook, political responsibility, the ideals of tolerance and social justice, respect for authority, and so on. Behind the need to teach pupils certain fundamentals about political,

159

economic and social activities and institutions lies the desire to turn them into effective and responsible citizens of their society. Indeed the cognitive content of the curriculum is frequently used in order to highlight the underlying principles and ideology; thus, information about electoral systems could be utilized to bring out fundamental ideas about equality and majority rule.

The members of the International Civic Education Committee of I.E.A. which met in Rome in April 1967, had before them a series of documents produced by the National Centers of the Federal Republic of Germany, Italy, Finland, Iran, Sweden, England and Wales, and the United States. These documents contained a digest, for each country, of the curricular aims and contents in Civic Education for different age groups, of text-books used, and of examination contents. Although the country documents differed widely, it was obvious from the start that, in addition to knowledge, all countries laid considerable emphasis on values and attitudes. Here, for instance, is section (1) of article 26 of the constitution of the West German State of Bremen:

> "Children should be brought up in a community spirit based on respect for the dignitiy of all men and on desire for social justice and political responsibility, and should be taught to regard the opinions of others with objectiveness and toleration and work peacefully with other people and nations."

A detailed analysis of the *affective* contents of the country documents showed, perhaps a little unexpectedly, that there was a common core of basic values which are stressed in all seven countries concerned. This common core consisted of the political ideology of equality (freedom and civil liberties, tolerance of diversity, majority rule, non-violent conflict resolution, etc.) and citizenship values (such as informed participation, being law-abiding, interest in welfare of fellow citizens, love of country). These values were set out in detail, and were in due course incorporated in the conceptual framework and in the measuring instruments.

In consequence the focus gradually changed from a concern with Civic Education as a school subject, to a study of certain aspects of political socialization. Initially the approach of most previous I.E.A. surveys—an input-output model of the educational system in each country and focussed on the school—was followed. While this approach could be justified for subjects such as Mathematics or a foreign language, where the school is the main source of relevant knowledge, it was soon found that for a subject such as Civic Education there was a need to go *beyond* the school. From an educational assessment framework the design moved more towards social psychology and political science, and in particular to the handful of political socialization studies which were available at the start of this study. Since that time, research in the field of political socialization has grown rapidly, with an increased emphasis on the *implications* which the findings have for the political processes within a given system, and the uses to which they might be put. The IEA emphasis, since it had to work through existing institutions in different countries, will inevitably be regarded by some as too supportive of the status quo, and as failing to give sufficient attention to alternatives. On the other hand, it has been useful to accept as an initial task a study of the extent to which countries or nations achieve the civic education goals which they themselves have set, utilizing the conceptualization and methods of political socialization.

At every stage the limitations set by the use of large-scale cross-national surveys in schools had to be borne in mind. Apart from prodigious sampling problems this meant, for example, that there was constant pressure to keep the test battery short; that, in the end, no projective or open-ended techniques could be used (although some of these were developed); and that there was constant concern about the problems of comparability, both between the three chosen age-groups and across countries. Translation had been a problem in previous I.E.A. studies, but in this study it became of special importance because of the increased focus on attitudinal and perceptual variables, which are notoriously sensitive (especially where children are concerned) to slight fluctuations in meaning, such as readily occur in even the best translations. In addition to careful checking of translation, factor analysis was used to demonstrate the comparability of the affective measures across countries. The same method was used to achieve approximate comparability across age-levels, but here two additional problems arose: first, it was difficult to design a set of questionnaires or scales which would be equally applicable to 10-year-olds and 18-year-olds; second, some of the important attitudes and percepts to be measured were, as yet, unformed or only partly formed among the younger children. It was possible to show this quite clearly in the projective techniques, and link this to the child's stage of conceptual development; the factor analyses also demonstrated this, becoming more articulated and clear-cut with increasing age. Since the child is not yet an adult citizen, some of his attitudes and thoughts about citizenship must relate to some time in his own future: it became very important *not* to believe something had been measured which was not yet present in the child, and not to impose a preconceived framework on his responses. Abundant opportunities were offered to the student to say "I don't know," "I am uncertain," "I have not thought about this" or "I do not understand the question;" indeed, IEA would have liked to have done a special study of the many qualities of the children's ignorance or misunderstanding in this complex area.

In short, the task of designing a battery of scales and questionnaires to measure the child's civic percepts and attitudes, at different ages and in different countries, presented a series of unusual conceptual and technical problems.

THE AFFECTIVE DOMAIN: CONCEPTUAL FRAMEWORK AND OVERVIEW OF PILOT WORK

As has been seen, the analysis of the content of the country documents showed that all the countries concerned emphasized education for *citizenship* and the broad ideological area of *equality*, egalitarianism or democratic values. A number of pilot interviews were therefore carried out in England, Sweden, Germany and Italy, to give a more detailed conceptual framework and a better understanding of children's developing thought processes in these areas.

The pilot interviews however, showed very vividly that political awareness and perception of the community develop only gradually. The young child tends to focus on himself and the people he knows, and does not perceive the community as an organized whole, with its services, economy, education system, and its many competing interest groups. He trusts adults and does not question why or how things are provided; he lacks a sense of historical development and future progress; and he cannot conceive of adult conflict. His cognitive style is such that he tends to *personalize* and *"concretize,"* i.e., to see political events in familiar personal terms rather than as broad principles or institutions: if the British government made a mistake, the landlord of the House of Commons would evict them. Everything is seen in simple, stereotyped, good/bad terms at first, with little awareness of finer differentiations or of the possibility of criticism and improvement. Politicians, elections, fellow citizens, his own and other countries are all seen by the child in very simplistic terms;

162

only later does he become aware of broader issues such as individual freedom versus the rights of others, civil liberties, majority rule, social justice, or the functions of the State.

In addition, therefore, to measures of our own broader areas of concern (citizenship and egalitarianism), measures were developed which—hopefully—would serve to demonstrate children's growing *perceptual awareness* of their communities. For instance, a number of questions were asked which allowed the child to answer in personal or in community-oriented terms, to show his perception of politicians and of elections, his awareness of historical development, or his feeling of closeness/distance in relation to the national government. The analysis of pretests proceeded with a view to improving and shortening these measures and turning open-ended questions into closed ones.

The above examples will by implication have brought out another important point: that great care is needed in developing measures of values and percepts in children, because these are subtle processes which are easily biased by instruments which are too highly structured or which impose a preconceived, adult framework. For this reason, a variety of techniques were employed: projective, forced-choice, graphic, etc. and many areas were covered more than once. Thus, attempts were made to develop methods suitable for each age-level.

The development of the measures for the two main affective areas (democratic values and citizenship) followed parallel stages. First, a detailed conceptual framework was drawn up, based on the content analysis of the country documents and on the pilot interviews; next, a variety of instruments was designed using different techniques (projective questions, attitude statements, check lists, forced choice items), which were tried out in the Federal Republic of Germany, the United Kingdom and the United States in 1968; as the result of pre-testing and analysis, a shortened and improved set of questionnaires was prepared for a second pilot of questionnaire items conducted in 1968 in the United Kingdom, the Federal Republic of Germany, Finland, Sweden, and the United States. Finally a "Dry Run" of semi-final instruments took place in 1970 in all countries listed above except in the Federal Republic of Germany and with the addition of Italy, the Netherlands and New Zealand. With each successive pilot it was possible, by virtue of larger and more representative samples, to conduct more detailed statistical analyses. With the exception of Ireland, Israel, and Iran every country in the final testing had participated in at least one pilot testing of the instruments.

The detailed conceptual framework—and hence the measures related to it—dealing with *democratic values* covered principles of equality, civil liberties, majority rule, women's rights, tolerance of diversity, racial equality, etc. The analysis subsequently showed the factor structure of these measures, the degree of inter-correlation between them, and their suitability at different age levels. It is perhaps worth stressing that in these instruments the emphasis is not on the correctness of the child's knowledge, but on his values and attitudes, on his own developing political ideology.

The conceptual framework regarding *citizenship values* covered such areas as political participation, willingness to serve the community, obedience of the law, loyalty, the functions of government criticism, interest in fellow citizens, interest in other countries, etc. From the pilot interviews it was already known that different aspects of the citizen role are stressed in different countries, and so initially an inventory dealing with the child's percepts of the components and width of the good citizen role, in terms of stated ideals, was designed. For example, the child was asked to indicate whether any of the following are included in "what *you* mean by a good citizen:"
A good citizen:

> obeys the law
> is always polite
> loves his parents
> votes in every election
> works hard
> has good table manners
> and so on (34 items).

It should be stressed that these items were not scored for "correctness," but for variations in the degree of endorsement from country to country and for children of different ages and backgrounds.

Next, several attempts were made to design a suitable instrument to measure the child's own adherence to citizenship values. There are difficulties here, since the child is not yet old enough to take on all aspects of the role of a citizen, and so he had to be asked what he would do, whom he would support, how he would react, and so forth. This inevitably entailed elements of unreality, and it could certainly not be assumed that the instruments would have predictive validity for the child's behavior as a grown-up; the only hope was to

164

find out what his attitudes are now, in anticipation of his role of citizen. To this end, several instruments were designed employing different techniques (forced-choice, open-ended questions, attitude statements) but covering much the same ground: voting and political participation in general; sense of political efficacy; standing up for citizens' rights; interest in national and in foreign affairs; recognition and resolution of conflicts; law enforcement; loyalty to country; interest in welfare of fellow citizens; etc.

The instruments were intended to produce not merely quantitative scores to make cross-country comparisons possible and meaningful, but also qualitative scores or profiles which would show differences in the way children see their communities at different age-levels in different countries, the different emphasis they place on certain sub-areas and so on. The problem of *comparability* or equivalence was never far from the minds of the IEA Civic Education International Committee. If a technique worked well with younger children but appeared to be too simple for the older ones, or *vice versa*, then a dilemma would have to be resolved: either take the risk of using the same technique throughout knowing that the scores might have somewhat different meanings at different age levels (or in different countries); or use different techniques for different populations, as appropriate, losing the opportunity of making accurate comparisons. The reader who is interested in the details of pilot studies (including tables of item factor loadings) is referred to Oppenheim and Torney (1974). A few examples of the type of items which were used in the first two pilot runs, however, are given below.

Two sets of 10 "projective" items dealing with democratic values and with citizenship values were developed for the youngest age group. The child was given a sentence of direct speech by a hypothetical person, and asked whether he would think likewise, or support such a person, when he grows up. (For example: "Some newspapers go too far in criticizing our government," said Mr. D., "and if I were a judge I'd close them down or send their editors to prison for being disloyal.") The child could answer Yes, No, or Can't decide; this made the instrument readily scorable. In some versions of this technique the child was also asked to explain his response ("Why is that? It is because . . ."). These explanations showed not only whether the item was understood or not, but also something of the child's political comprehension. The above item, for instance, was intended to show awareness of freedom of the press as a basic democratic right. Looking over the responses of some of the 10-year-old children of low ability level no awareness of this principle was found; mostly they said "No" because "the people need to see what's going on in this country," while some referred to the non-political functions of newspapers, e.g., "If there was a disaster the people who are injured their mothers or fathers won't know if it was their child or not."

At the conclusion of the second pilot testing the situation could be summarized as follows:

1. For Populations II and IV suitable attitude scales had been developed which showed adequate factorial equivalence across countries and between these two populations; this meant that score differences could be used to show that one group of children is more tolerant or more nationalistic than another group.

2. For Population I it was possible to show on these same scales that their attitudes are less clear or less formed than those of older children.

3. The projective items could, in closed form, be used to show much the same difference in articulation or development between Population I and Population II (the items were hardly suitable for Population IV); in addition, in open-ended form, where the child was asked to explain his responses, this technique could throw a good deal of light on the child's developing political awareness—but this made the technique more time-consuming, and more laborious to process.

Since the May 1970 Dry Run would only include Population II children, it was therefore decided that the projective and open-ended items would be left out of the battery. Those who might wish to use this technique will find the items in Appendix I of Oppenheim and Torney (1974).

THE RESULTS OF THE DRY RUN OF MAY, 1970 AND THE CONSTRUCTION OF THE FINAL ATTITUDINAL INSTRUMENTS AND BACKGROUND QUESTIONNAIRE

There was one more opportunity to try out these instruments before the main fieldwork stage, namely by incorporating them in the 1970 Dry Run. The IEA has found it useful, in the case of most of their major surveys, to conduct a Dry Run for the fieldwork, to make sure that the National Technical Officers in each country knew how to draw samples, how to contact and brief the schools, how to do the initial data processing, and how to deal with the many other problems that arise, such as translation, printing, distribution and collection, dealing with missing data, getting estimates of the timing of the work in the classroom, and so on. All this benefits the organization of the main fieldwork stage the following year.

Seven countries took part in the May, 1970, Dry Run for Civic Education. Each country was asked to draw a judgment sample of around 200–300 pupils in about 10 schools, for Population II only. The following numbers were actually obtained

England	101
Finland	272
Italy	227
Netherlands	179
New Zealand	123
Sweden	278
United States	157
Total	1 337

Several countries had not seen these instruments before, and numerous translation problems had to be resolved. This was the first time that each child was given *all* the instruments (Cognitive Tests, Perceptual and Affective Scales, and Background Questionnaire), making for a time-consuming battery.

The results of the Dry Run are best summarized with direct reference to the scales and items incorporated into the final field work. Table 7.1 lists the scales from the affective Civic Education questionnaire utilized in the analysis reported in this volume. A complete copy of the affective scales and the Background Questionnaire is included as Appendix II of Oppenheim and Torney (1974).

The first four listed scores come from a series of semantic differential-type items designed to measure the image of the national and local governments. Each item is also of interest in itself, and shows how children differentiate between the national and the local levels. The factor-analyses at the pilot phase showed adequate to good congruence across countries: generally, the younger children tended to show a structure indicating unclear percepts or else the whole instrument was swamped by a General Evaluation (Good/Bad) factor; among the older children, two clear factors emerged at first: General Evaluation, and Perception of Power; further analysis showed a Responsiveness factor (its opposite being distant, hard to influence). See Table 7.2.

Table 7.1. *Items Included in Scales and Direction of Scoring (Affective Outcomes and Student Predcitor Scales)*

Local Government Evaluation—Semantic Differential

High score indicates the student rates the town council as "friendly," "warm-hearted," "popular," and "can be trusted."

Local Government Responsiveness—Semantic Differential

High score indicates that student rates the town council as having the following characteristics—"cares about me and my family," "does things for the good of the whole area," "pays attention to complaints," "can have their decisions changed by ordinary people," "run by people just like ourselves."

National Government Evaluation—Semantic Differential

High score indicates the student rates the national government on the same scales as in Local Government Evaluation

National Government Responsiveness—Semantic Differential

High score indicates the student rates the national government on the same scales as in Local Government Responsiveness

Anti-Authoritarianism—Attitude Scale

High score indicates that student agrees with the following statement:

1. Talking things over with another nation is better than fighting.

And disagrees:

2. Hotels are right in refusing to admit people of certain races or nationalities
3. Regular elections in our country are unnecessary.
4. People of certain races or religions should be kept out of important positions in our nation.
5. War is sometimes the only way in which a nation can save its self respect.
6. The people in power know best.
7. So many people vote in a general election that when I grow up, it will not matter much whether I vote or not.
8. It is wrong to criticize our government.
9. I don't really care what happens to others so long as I am all right.
10. People should not criticize the government, it only interrupts the government's work.

Tolerance and Support for Civil Liberties—Attitude Scale

High score indicates that student agrees with the following:

1. Newspapers and magazines should be allowed to print anything they want except military secrets.
2. No matter what a man's color, religion, or nationality, if he is qualified for a job he should get it.
3. People should be allowed to come together whenever they like.
4. Swimming pools should admit people of all races and nationalities to swim together in the same pool.
5. Citizens must always be free to criticize the government.

Table 7.1. *(Cont.)*

6. People who disagree with the government should be allowed to meet and hold public protests.
7. When something is wrong, it is better to complain to the government about it than to keep quiet.
8. It is good for a government to be frequently criticized.
9. Our nation has its faults just like other nations.

Sense of Political Efficacy—Attitude Scale

High score indicates that student agrees with the following:

1. The government cares a lot about what all of us think of any new laws.
2. The government is doing its best to find out what ordinary people want.

And disagrees:

3. Government decisions are like the weather; there is nothing people can do about them.
4. There are some powerful men in the government who are running the whole country and they do not care about the opinions of ordinary people.
5. The government does not try to understand ordinary people.
6. Most politicians are too selfish to care about ordinary people.

Support for Women's Rights—Attitude Scale

High score indicates that the student agrees with the following:

1. Women should run for public office and take part in the government much the same as men do.
2. Women should have the same rights as men in every way.

And disagrees:

3. Women should stay out of politics.
4. Most women do not need the right to vote.

Belief in Value of Criticism of Government—Attitude Scale

High score indicates that the student agrees with the following:

1. Citizens must always be free to criticize the government.
2. People who disagree with the government should be allowed to meet and hold public protests.
3. It is good for a government to be frequently criticized.

And disagrees:

4. It is wrong to criticize our government.
5. People should not criticize the government, it only interrupts the government's work.

Don't Know Score from Influence on Laws Questions

Count of number of "Don't Know" responses given to ten items.

Pressure Group Influence on Laws

High score indicates that student believes that Union Leaders and Rich People have influence on laws made for the country.

169

Table 7.1. *(Cont.)*

Support for Equality for All Social Groups

High score indicates student feels that the following groups should have "exactly the same" (rights and freedoms) as everyone else:

1. Lawyers.
2. Religious leaders.
3. Discharged prisoners.
4. Black people.
5. Artists.
6. Communists.
7. Factory workers.
8. Leaders of big business corporations.
9. Military leaders.
10. Tramps.
11. People with anti-mother-country views.
12. Doctors.

Tendency to Avoid Perceiving Adult Conflict

High score indicates student feels that the following groups "mostly agree about what the government should do":

1. Men and women.
2. Business leaders and union leaders.
3. The newspapers and people in legislature.
4. Middle class people and working class people.
5. Older people and younger people.
6. People of different religions.
7. Well-to-do people and poor people.
8. Different political parties.
9. Radio or TV commentators and the people in legislature.

Active Perception of Citizenship

High score indicates student feels that the following "help to explain what a good citizen is":

1. Votes in every election.
2. Joins a political party.
3. Knows a good deal about how our tax money is spent.
4. Tries to change things in the government.
5. Gets other people to vote in elections.
6. Belongs to a labor union.

Non-political Perception of Citizenship

High score indicates student feels that the following "help to explain what a good citizen is":

1. Is always polite.
2. Is loyal to his family.
3. Works hard.
4. Has good table manners.
5. Studies hard to pass an examination.
6. Shows respect for a funeral.

170

Table 7.1. *(Cont.)*

Personalized Egocentric Reasoning

High score indicates that student has chosen the following:

1. Birth/deaths recorded so you can prove who you are.
2. Deciding to vote should be on the candidate who will do his best for me and my family.
3. Each nation has own flag to show which nation we belong to.
4. People go into politics to become popular and have more money.

Sociocentric Reasoning

High score indicates that student has chosen the following:

1. Birth/deaths recorded so that the government will know how many people have been born.
2. Deciding to vote should be on principles best for the nation as a whole.
3. Each nation has own flag to be a symbol of being different from other nations,.
4. People go into politics because they want to make changes and improve things in the nation.

Interest in Public Affairs T.V.

High score indicates that student likes to watch programs dealing with current events, how factories work, people in other countries, social problems in community, how the legislature and the government do their job, news.

Participation in Political Discussion with Friends, Parents, Teachers

High score indicates that student often discusses the following with friends, parents and teachers:

1. What is going on in government and politics.
2. What is happening in other countries.
3. A particular political party or a particular political candidate.

Unawareness of Political Opinion

High score indicates that student has chosen "I don't know what their political ideas are" in connection with father, mother, best friends, and civics/social studies teacher.

Agreement with Family

High score indicates that student agrees with both parents' political ideas.

Agreement with Friends

Same for friends.

Agreement with Teachers

Same for teachers.

Participation in Civic Activities

High score indicates that student reports frequent participation as follows: listening to political broadcasts, trying to be elected at school, helping to collect money for good cause, borrowing a book from library about current affairs, reading a book about the UN, finding out about how town or city council does its work, asking parents about political parties.

Table 7.1. *(Cont.)*

Reports Making Peer Group Decisions by Voting

High score indicates that student chooses "we would talk about it and then take a vote" in response to four peer group decision dilemmas.

Rejection of Parental Values

High score indicates that student has done or thought about: being rude to parents, playing truant from school, hurting parents' feelings, deliberately doing things which older people don't approve of.

Asserting Independence from Parental Expectations

High score indicates that student has done or thought about: smoking cigarettes, leaving the house in the evening without permission, getting into trouble with the police, betting or gambling for money, going out drinking, being independent of family, staying out late with a group of older boys or girls.

Equality Among Students in Classroom

High score indicates that student does not perceive his classroom as having the following qualities:

1. Certain students work only with their friends in class.
2. Certain students stick together in small groups.
3. The better students get special favors from teachers.
4. The teachers seem to run down our best ideas.
5. Certain students are favored by the teachers more than the rest.

Independence of Opinion Encouraged in Classroom

High score indicates that students perceives his classroom as having the following qualities:

1. Teachers try to get students to speak freely and openly in class.
2. Students can feel free to disagree openly with their teachers.
3. Students are encouraged to make up their own minds.
4. Our teachers respect our opinions and encourage us to express them.

Patriotic Rituals Practiced in School

High score indicates that student reports the following activities:

1. We sing songs about our country in class.
2. We sing our national anthem in school.
3. We participate in a flag ceremony,
4. There are pictures of national leaders in our classroom.

Stress on Factual Knowledge in Civics Class

High score indicates that student perceives his civics, social studies, history or current events classes in the following way.

1. There is great stress in civics and history classes on learning facts.
2. In history or civics classes we must memorize dates or definitions.

172

Table 7.1. *(Cont.)*

Interest in Civics Class

High score indicates that student perceives classes in the following way:

1. The students like the courses where civics and history are discussed.
And disagrees:
2. Students are not interested in civics and history.

Total Don't Know Score from How Society Works—Count of Number of Don't Know responses given to 120 items.

Perceived Conflict in Society (How Society Works)

High score indicates that student sees Elections, Congress, and Political Parties as "not settling arguments and disagreements," "not creating better understanding ....," "creating disagreements."

Democratic System—Business Differentiation (How Society Works)

High score indicates that student believes that the Democratic System does more to realize the values of "giving people a right to write or say what they think" and "helping people to take part in important decisions about their own lives" than do Large Business Organizations.

Note: The translations in each country were carefully checked. In some questions in addition to translating the stem of an item, an institution or group appropriate to the country was specified. For example, in the United States "Congress" was the institution specified in questions dealing with the legislature, while in Germany the "*Bundestag*" was specified. Likewise, instead of referring to "Black people" in Israel "national or ethnic minorities" was substituted.

Table 7.2. *Format of Semantic Differential*

General Evaluation (Good/Bad) Factor

Friendly :___:___:___:___:___:___:___:	Unfriendly
Warm-hearted :___:___:___:___:___:___:___:	Cold-hearted
Popular :___:___:___:___:___:___:___:	Unpopular
Foolish :___:___:___:___:___:___:___:	Sensible
Can be trusted :___:___:___:___:___:___:___:	CanNOT be trusted

Responsiveness Factor

Cares about me and my family :___:___:___:___:___:___:___:	Doesn't care about me and my family
Does things for selfish reasons :___:___:___:___:___:___:___:	Does things for the good of the whole area
Pays attention to complaints :___:___:___:___:___:___:___:	Doesn't pay attention to complaints
Can have their decisions changed by ordinary people :___:___:___:___:___:___:___:	Can only have their decisions changed by powerful people
Run by a few big powerful groups :___:___:___:___:___:___:___:	Run by people just like ourselves

173

The four-items indexing power which had appeared as a factor in some countries were scored but not used in the final analysis due to overlap and poor reliability.

One of the most important sets of items in the final instrument was that designed to measure various aspects of democratic and citizenship values by obtaining the student's agreement or disagreement with various attitudinal statements. These were the instructions:

"In the following questions there are some statements about the way our country should be governed. You may agree with some of them and disagree with others, sometimes you will agree or disagree strongly, at other times you will feel uncertain or have no opinion. Please look at each statement, and then indicate whether you strongly agree, agree, have no opinion, disagree or strongly disagree."

Initially, these *political ideology* attitude statements were factor-analysed for each of the seven countries separately; after that, a combined factor-analysis was undertaken based on all 1 337 pilot cases (results reported in Oppenheim & Torney, 1974). The basic pattern which emerged from the majority of the samples was a 4-factor structure, with some variations in the different countries. The four factors were provisionally labelled as follows:

1. Anti-Authoritarianism;
2. Tolerance and Civil Liberties;
3. Sense of Political Efficacy;
4. Women's Rights.

The results were quite similar to the earlier pilot factor-analyses, and showed acceptable congruence between countries.

Due to the extensive pilot work it was possible to be reasonably satisfied that the items retained in the scales were comprehensible and meaningful to the children, and dealt with issues on which the majority had formed an opinion. Nonetheless, it was noted that this 4-factor structure accounted for no more than 26.5 % of the common variance; it would be expected that a stronger factor structure would emerge among older pupils.

Bearing in mind the generalized and highly complex issues in the political sphere, the fact that these attitudes are not yet stable or fully formed in children of this age group, the radically different composition of the item pools, the problems of translation and of cultural differences, the smallness of the samples, and the fact that several countries were involved for the first time in the Dry Run—the striking finding is the clarity and consistency of the results of these factor analyses. As before, however, there were variations in the item loading; the factors emerged in different orders in different countries, while in most countries additional weak factors showed up, or the same factors were in part defined by different items. This is not surprising, given the nature and smallness of the samples, and their varying compositions (see Oppenheim and Torney, 1974).

The items included on each factor and scored on the scales derived from the attitudinal endorsements are listed in Table 7.1: Anti-Authoritarianism, Tolerance and Support for Civil Liberties, Sense of Political Efficacy, Support for Women's Rights. The scale Value of Criticism was formed to augment the other scorings, on the basis of a supplementary factor analysis, done on the final field work data for New Zealand and the United States. Some of the items on this scale overlap with items already included in Anti-Authoritarianism and in Tolerance and Support for Civil Liberties. The Value of Criticism Scale has not been extensively used because of this overlap.

A series of items indicating the student's perception of which individuals or groups have an influence upon the laws made for the country was taken relatively directly from Hess and Torney (1967). A Don't Know score was formed but otherwise these were used only as individual items.

Also produced was a short set of items dealing specifically with the child's *egalitarianism:*

There are lots of different people in our country. Do you think they should all have the same rights and freedoms as everyone else or should they be treated differently?

	More rights and freedoms than every-one else	Exactly the same as every-one else	Fewer rights and freedoms than every-one else	I don't know
They should have:				
Lawyers				
Religious leaders				
Communists . . .				

and so on for 12 groups (see list in Table 7.1).

These items, scored for the number of choices of "exactly the same as everyone else" produced the Support for Equality Scale. A Don't Know score was also calculated.

The specially designed set of items dealing with equality or *egalitarianism* worked well in the Dry Run. Item-total correlations ranged from 0.32 to 0.47, and the Score (i.e., the number of times the child chose the option "should have exactly the same rights as everyone else") correlated 0.44 with the Total Cognitive Score, 0.49 with Anti-Authoritarianism, and 0.33 with Tolerance and Civil Liberties.

It will be recalled that the early pilot interviews had shown that younger children have but a limited awareness of political processes or institutions, of conflicts between interest groups, of historical development, and so on. They tend to be in an earlier stage of cognitive development, so that they see everything in highly personal and concrete terms and find it difficult to use abstractions. The conceptual framework called for the measurement of a number of these percepts, most of which were approached in the first stage of the pilot work by means of open-ended questions; in the second stage, the more successful ones were retained, and some of these had been turned into multiple-choice items.

To measure the child's perception of *adult conflict* a set of items was developed, along the following lines:

How united are we?

Do all grown-ups generally agree about what our government should do or do they sometimes disagree? Below you will find different groups of people in each question; please tell us how well *you* think they agree with each other about what the government should do.

	Mostly agree	Agree about half of the time	Disagree most of the time	I don't know
		about what the government should do		
Men and women . . .				
Business leaders and trade union leaders . .				
The newspapers and the people in parliament . .				

and so on for nine groups (see list in Table 7.1). The item-total correlations for this scale as administered in the Dry Run ranged from 0.44 to 0.53.

Also developed was a Perception of Good Citizenship scale, to show how children perceive the citizen role.

"Imagine that you had to explain what a good citizen is, or what a good citizen ought to do. Please read each sentence, then put a tick ($\checkmark$) under the heading 'Good Citizen' if that is what *you* mean by a good citizen. If the sentence does NOT help to explain what you mean by a good citizen, put a tick under 'No'. If you are not sure, put a tick under the question-mark '?'."

The Active Good Citizenship factor highlighted characteristics such as joining a political party and getting other people to vote in elections. A separate factor could be described as a Non-political Perception of Citizenship (having good table manners, studying hard to pass examinations). Scales were formed to measure these perceptions of good citizenship, and the items are listed in Table 7.1. A factor which indicated a less fully engaged perception of citizenship (obeying the law, paying taxes) was scored but not used in the analysis as a scale (though some individual items results are cited). All of these citizenship perception items were also included in the Teacher Questionnaire.

There was a small group of items derived from the projective, open-ended questions, which dealt with the child's *egocentric versus sociocentric* thought processes, and with his tendency to use *concrete versus abstract* concepts. Four multiple choice items were designed, with a pre-determined scoring scheme. After improving the scoring categories the items were included in the final fieldwork, to enable us to distinguish between children at different stages of social development, making a score for Personalized-Egocentric reasoning and another for Sociocentric reasoning (see Table 7.1).

The following type of items was included:

Why do all births, deaths, and marriages have to be officially recorded?

A. To make it easier to find people who have disappeared
B. So that you can prove who you are, or prove that you are married or not
C. So that the government will know how many people have been born, married, or have died
D. I don't know

What is the most important thing to know when deciding how to vote
   in an election?

A. What principles are best for the nation as a whole
B. The candidate will do his best for me and my family
C. What the candidate will do for the community
D. I don't know

The next sets of items listed in Table 7.1 were included in what is
called the Background Questionnaire, though some of them were
used both as predictor and as outcome variables in the analysis. They
all had some relationship to political interest and participation. The
scale indexing student Interest in Public Affairs Television was derived from a list of 14 types of television programs of which half
had a political or public affairs content and half were distractors.
The Participation in Political Discussion scale was a fairly straight-
forward inquiry about how frequently domestic and international
political issues were discussed with family, friends and teachers.
Four scales showing the student's awareness of the political opinion
of his family, friends and teachers as well as his level of agreement
with these opinions were also included. In addition a number of
civic activities were listed, and the student was asked to indicate
participation.

Three scales were designed to assess the personal relationship of
the students to family and to peer group. This included reports that
peer group decisions were made by voting (rather than by consensus
or appeal to authority). The others were factor-derived measures
indicating the extent to which students accepted or rejected parental
values and the extent to which they were actively asserting independence from parental expectations. These items are also listed in
Table 7.1.

Two measures of classroom climate were factored from a set of
statements in which the students described experiences in their
classrooms. The original set of items from which these were chosen is
similar to that developed by Walberg and Anderson (1968). The
specific items showing Equality among Students and the degree of
Independence of Opinion Encouraged in Classroom are listed in
Table 7.1. In each case the student reported on his or her classroom
as described by the statement "Always, Often, Sometimes, Rarely or
Never." A similar set of five response options was used to allow the
students to describe the frequency of patriotic observances in their
school or classroom.

One set of questions was answered only by students enrolled in civics, history, social studies or current events classes. One two-item set indicates the degree to which the student believes that the learning of facts, dates or definitions is important in these classes. The second indicates the expressed level of interest in these classes (see Table 7.1).

In contrast to the cognitive tests which consisted of different items for each Population, the affective questions, background questions, and the instrument described in the following section (How Society Works) were administered in identical form to all students.

CHILDREN'S PERCEPTIONS OF THE POLITICAL SYSTEM: HOW SOCIETY WORKS

The Need for a New Technique

From the earliest stages of the Civic Education study it had been anticipated that, in addition to cognitive and affective measures, techniques would be needed for studying the child's *perceptions* of social and political processes and institutions. Some of the Committee's hypotheses related to the child's awareness of conflict or disagreement among groups of adults, such as political parties or labor/management. In addition, much experimentation with projective and free-response techniques had shown the ways in which perceptual processes were related to the stage of the child's cognitive and attitudinal development. During the early stages of the project the design of cognitive and affective instruments proceeded somewhat independently, and ways were sought whereby these two aspects of political understanding could be brought together. A technique requiring the integration of knowledge and attitudes might meet these needs. Also, because of the multi-national nature of the study, a method was sought which would be based neither on agreement/disagreement with attitude statements nor on the choice of a single correct answer from among several incorrect ones.

The affective and cognitive pilot work—though not without problems—had proceeded along fairly orthodox lines of scaling and item analysis. After much of this work had already been completed it was decided to try to design another instrument which would integrate cognitive and affective approaches and which would attempt to obtain information on social perception. Moreover, the new method had to be capable of easy translation into many languages, and be equally suitable for Populations I, II and IV.

179

The Development of the How Society Works Instrument [1]

Basically, the problem concerned the child's perception and understanding of political and social processes and institutions within and beyond the State. A convenient way of conceptualizing these areas would be the following:

1. *Values* and attitudes, e.g., justice, freedom of speech, minority rights.
2. *Concepts,* descriptive definitions of basic principles, e.g., democracy, rule of law.
3. *Institutions,* such as political parties, the Church, the Police.
4. *Macro processes,* which show how values and concepts are turned into compromise decisions by the relevant institutions, e.g., taxation.
5. *Micro processes,* which show the citizen coping with his needs vis-a-vis the state bureaucracy: as a child, and as an adult.

It was tempting to think of a continuous line through these five levels, thus:

Value:	justice
Concept:	rule of law
Institutions:	the Courts
Macro processes:	trials, appeals, open courts, etc.
Micro processes:	standing trial, instituting proceedings, jury service, being put on probation as a child.

However, this relatively simple continuity rarely applies. Most values require several institutions, and most institutions deal with several value areas—indeed, frequently it is the function of institutions to deal with *conflicting* values, needs and principles, and to make rules and decisions which will be seen as congruent with majority societal values.

The central question thus became: how to measure the child's understanding of the interaction between values and institutions? To this might be added some understanding of concepts, and of the micro processes mentioned above. A simple grid approach showing possible links between institutions and values might result in the following:

---

[1] The new technique was developed jointly with Mr. Leslie A. Smith, of the Curriculum Laboratory, Goldsmith College, University of London.

180

INSTITUTIONS

VALUES	Constitution	Courts	Unions	Education	Taxes	Welfare agencies	Elections	Police
Freedom of speech								
Justice								
Prevention of poverty								
Property rights								
Economic stability								
Minority rights								
Equality of opportunity								
Sovereignty								
Government authority								
Public service								

Questions could go either from institutions to values, or from values to institutions. Here is an example of the former approach:

"In our country, why do we have laws? What do they *do* and what are they for?"

We have laws:

to punish us
to educate us
to prevent people from harming others
to let each of us get more of what he needs
to oppress the people
to make sure we all do the same thing
to show the power of the government
to make silly rules and regulations
to guard our liberties
to settle our arguments
because otherwise there would be chaos.

Questions of this kind are capable of a variety of ways of scoring, concentrate on *understanding* of the links between institutions and values rather than on factual knowledge, provide a *range* of possible responses, and do not use any correct/incorrect criterion.

Initially attempts were made to design a set of items to test the child's understanding of the functions of 18 institutions, by confronting him each time with the same set of 24 value statements (in random order). The value statements had originally been grouped under sub-headings of broader value areas, e.g., civil liberties. There were four items under each area heading, three reinforcing that value area and one in opposition to it. These main value areas were selected on *a priori* grounds but corresponded to some of the attitudes being measured in the affective domain.

A good deal of trouble was taken over the wording of the value statements. The language was kept as simple as possible for the sake of Population I and of the translators, but it was also sufficiently broad to make each statement of possible relevance to a variety institutions. Thus, after applying these value statements to a variety of domestic institutions, a child might well find that the following ones could be relevant also to, for example, the United Nations.

"Make sure there are fair shares for everyone

Help more people to take part in important decisions about their own lives

Give help to the needy

Help the strong to rule the weak

Prevent people from harming others

Show who is the strongest

Settle arguments and disagreements

Create a better understanding so that people can live and work together

Help one side in a dispute against the other

Help our national security"

It was expected that several types of scores would be developed:

1. *profiles* for each institution, for comparison across countries, populations and sexes. These would show the "image" of each institution, and the child's quality of understanding, on a *relative* rather than an absolute (correct/incorrect) basis;

2. a *complexity* or sophistication score, indicating awareness of overlapping or conflicting values;

182

3. a *"value realization"* score, showing the extent to which different values were being generated, or not, across a number of institutions;
4. a *don't know* score.

After some preliminary try-outs the new technique ("How Society Works") was incorporated in the 1970 Population II Dry Run. The 24 statements were repeated each time for 18 institutions, including elections, laws, the prime minister, taxes, welfare agencies, the UN, advertising, military conscription, protest meetings, labor unions, etc. Three frequency categories: Do this a lot/Sometimes/Almost never, and two non-frequency categories: Don't Know, and Don't Understand were used. To study age-differences the instrument was also given to a specially selected sample in England which included Populations I and IV as well as Population II.

As a result of the Dry Run, the How Society Works instrument was much shortened, a number of improvements were made to item wording, the Don't Understand category was dropped and in its place another frequency category was added, making a 4-point range. It was also found that the introductory rubric at the head of each page needed improvement, for as it stood it might have been taken to refer either to the functions each institution ought to have, or to what it actually did in practice. It would have been useful to obtain both sets of data in order to compare and contrast them, but this would have doubled the length of the instrument, so in the end the rubric was strengthened firmly towards realism: i.e., in practice, what do they actually do. The total number of items for each institution was reduced from 24 to 12 on the basis of their discrimination power, and the number of institutions from 18 to 10, making a total of 120 items. For each institution there was also an optional open-ended question allowing the child a free response: e.g., "What else do political parties *really* do? Please write your answer here."

The instrument was finalized and used in the field work in the following format:

In (insert name of nation), why do we have the POLICE? In practice, what do they actually do and what effects do they *really* have? Please read each of the sentences below, then put your check marks to show what you think.

THE POLICE do this

	Almost always	Fairly often	Sometimes	Almost never	Don't know
1. Make sure there are fair shares for everyone . . .					
2. Settle arguments and disagreements					
3. Give help to rich people .					
4. Show who is the strongest					
5. Create better understanding so that people can live and work together					
6. Force people to obey the rules					
7. Create disagreements . .					
8. Give people a chance to write or say what they think					
9. Help people to take part in important decisions about their own lives					
10. Make people afraid to say what they think					
11. Prevent people from harming others					
12. Make prices go up					

In addition to the Police[2] the institutions included were the following: Elections, Laws, Parliament (Congress, Bundestag, etc.), Democratic System of Government, United Nations, Political Parties, Welfare Agencies, Labor Unions, Large Business Organizations.

[2] Two countries (Sweden and Ireland) encountered serious printing errors which could only partly be rectified, resulting in loss of cases. Inspection indicates that errors in both countries were randomly distributed: remaining cases seem reasonably representative. "Welfare Agencies" produced some translation or adaptation problems; in Ireland it was made to read "Social Services (old age pensions, health services, children's allowances)" while in Finland it was translated as "Social relief organizations."

In the response system finally adopted for the How Society Works instrument there were four frequency categories (ranging from Almost Always to Almost Never) and a separate category for Don't Know. A Don't Know response implies that the child understands the question but lacks the knowledge to answer it. As such, it is, in a sense, a cognitive response although it deals with less "factual"-type contents. An omit may have a different meaning. Besides lack of knowledge, the child may omit the item because of an inadvertent oversight, because of some misunderstanding or uncertainty, or he may be recorded as having omitted the item because of failure of the marking technique or because of a punching error.

Throughout the Civic Education project, special attention has been paid to the Don't Know responses, especially in the affective domain. In the various stages of the pilot work a variety of non-responses categories were used to distinguish, for example, between children who did not understand the question, and children who did not know the answer. Since there was special interest in the developmental stages through which a child may pass in acquiring civic knowledge and attitudes, and since Don't Know responses are unlikely to suffer greatly from guessing or social desirability-type errors, special attention was paid to them as responses in their own right ("the quality of ignorance") rather than dismissing them as errors or non-responses. For each institution a separate Don't Know score was calculated for each child (for 12 items), and these Don't Know scores for all 10 institutions in the instrument were added to give a total How Society Works Don't Know score for each child. This score has been incorporated in various correlation analyses and is listed in Table 7.1.

Earlier it was stated that such a Don't Know score represents, in a sense, a negative cognitive score—except, of course, that it deals with items that are more perceptual and attitudinal than factual. At the level of the Dry Run the moderate level of negative correlation with the Civic Education cognitive test encouraged the continued use of this score. Likewise, in the final field work the correlations between How Society Works Don't Know and Civic Education Cognitive total ranged at Population II from -0.133 (Ireland) to -0.322 (Italy). At Population IV the correlations were lower, probably due to decreased variance in the How Society Works Don't Know at that age level.

Whereas the Civic Education Cognitive total score has a substantial general intellectual component as measured by the Word Knowledge Test (correlation of around 0.65 in Population II), the How Society Works Don't Know scores were somewhat less strongly related to general Word Knowledge (correlation ranging from -0.078 in Ireland to -0.292 in Italy). These findings indicate that the How Society Works instrument fulfilled one of its purposes, namely, to build a perceptual, understanding-type instrument which would overlap only partly with knowledge of Civic Education and with verbal ability.

The How Society Works instrument was designed to permit the calculation of a number of other scores which go beyond the perception of values and institutions and tell something about the perceptual process itself. It is possible to calculate scores on groups of items across institutions to show more generalized perceptual features, much like attitudinal scales listed in the early part of this chapter. For example, three items dealing with disagreement were taken ("settle arguments and disagreements," "create better understanding so that people can live and work together," and "create disagreements") and the score for each child across three institutions was calculated, thus composing a score for Political Conflict Perception. For the first two items, only the number of "Sometimes" and "Almost Never" responses were counted, while for the third item "Almost Always" and "Fairly Often" were counted and these scores were added for each child over three institutions: elections, the legislature, and political parties. This score reflects the amount or degree of conflict the child perceived in the domestic political process (see Table 7.1).

It is also possible to take specific sets of items and use them to explore the contrast between certain pairs of institutions; for example, the scores of two items ("Gives people a chance to write or say what they think" and "Help people to take part in important decisions about their own lives") for the Democratic System of Government were compared with those for a number of institutions such as Labor Unions, Big Business, Welfare Agencies, and the Police, in order to see which institution was, according to the children, more likely to produce participation and freedom of expression. This involved the calculation of *signed difference scores* (referred to in Table 7.1 as a Differentiation score) for each child on those items and institutions. Finally, unsigned difference scores were experimented with briefly; these measure not which institution is "better," but rather the degree of "different-ness" between percepts of institutions (reflecting perceptual complexity).

The calculation of difference scores is complex and laborious, because each score has to be calculated for each individual child (rather than using group means). Scores could not be calculated unless a given child had responded to all the items contributing to a particular score. For these reasons a relatively small number of such scores have been calculated. Moreover, the composition of these scores had to be specified *before* the univariates tabulations for the How Society Works instrument were received. As a result, the use of group means based on individual items had to be relied upon in later stages of the analysis.

The primary purpose of the How Society Works instrument is to draw country profiles of the perceptions of institutions and of value realization through these institutions. This is done comprehensively with the use of single item mean values in Chapter 11. In addition three scores from this instrument: Don't Know, Perception of Political Conflict, and Big Business-Democratic System Differentiation were included in other analyses and so are listed in Table 7.1.

SUMMARY

1. Analysis of the country documents showed that Civic Education has important attitudinal and perceptual components, in addition to cognitive ones.

2. Bearing in mind the need for measures which would be comparable across age-groups and countries, yet subtle enough to show emergent attitudes and concepts in school children, a flexible and varied series of techniques was designed and piloted in several stages and in different countries. This work has been extensively and separately reported in Oppenheim & Torney (1974) for the affective scales and is included in this chapter for the instrument How Society Works.

3. Projective and open-ended techniques, though subtle and sensitive, proved too time-consuming to be included in the final battery. Attitude scales were used to measure political ideology and citizenship values, while a number of other techniques were used to measure egalitarianism, perception of adult conflict, perception of municipal and national government, and concepts of the "Good Citizen."

4. Despite translation problems, sampling differences, political and cultural diversity, and the relative youth of the children taking

part, a series of factor analyses showed a remarkably consistent set of underlying dimensions for these affective outcome measures and a compilation of these measures was used by all countries participating in final field testing.

5. An instrument called "How Society Works" was successfully developed to show the child's perceptions of social values and institutions.

Chapter 8

The Psychometric Characteristics and Factor Structures of the Civics Attitudinal Instruments

Although the IEA Civic Education Attitudinal Questionnaire used some items taken from previous research in political socialization, this instrument covered a broader range of topics than previous studies. In addition to measures such as sense of political efficacy, cynicism about the government, generalized support for democratic values, and interest in political issues (frequently used in political socialization research), the IEA affective questionnaire included items investigating the support for equality, support for women's rights, and perceptions of the local as well as the national government. To these attitudinal items, this study also added an assessment of perceptions of institution-value linkages in the instrument How Society Works. These items, taken as a whole, covered quite intensively the attitudes and values which had been listed by the National Centers as aims of their curricula.

Although the attitudinal measures had been pilot tested and used in a Dry Run in several countries, data from the final field testing were required to compute reliabilities for the scales and intercorrelations between them. This lengthy and very careful piloting process in the construction of the attitudinal instruments is described in considerable detail in Oppenheim and Torney (1974).

Even in the period between the selection of items for the final instrument and the choice of scales to be presented in this final report some items have had to be laid aside for later individual consideration or, in a few cases, for rescaling. This is primarily because it has been necessary to focus attention on a manageable number of civic attitudinal outcomes for the purpose of regression analysis and between-country comparisons. Table 7.1 listed the items included in each of the major attitudinal outcome and predictor scales.

RELIABILITY OF ATTITUDE SCALES

Following the scoring of responses to form scale scores for all student respondents, reliabilities were computed on those attitudinal scales which were planned for major analysis. Table 8.1 presents the median alpha coefficients for the attitudinal variables by Population. Kuder-Richardson Formula 20 values are presented for those scales which were the sum of a series of dichotomous choices. Reliability figures are not available for some variables reported in later analysis. "Don't Know" responses, for example, appeared with some consistency.

A series of 120 item-total correlations for the total Don't Know score was not feasible. The Differentiation score, indicating the amount of distinctiveness the student sees between the concept of a Large Business Organization and the Democratic System, does not have an unequivocal reliability computation, since it is a difference score.

The reported reliabilities are adequate for purposes of the analysis proposed; the four years of pilot work and factor analysis of items in the pilot instruments paid off in producing civic attitude scales with reasonable degrees of internal consistency. In general the reliabilities are slightly lower for the 10-year-olds than for the older students (as one might expect).

Some predictors of cognitive achievement or attitudes had been used in other subject areas (e.g., a measure of Liking for school), others were developed particularly for the Civic Education study, including the two measures of classroom climate based on students' perceptions (Independence of opinion encouraged in classroom, Equality among students in classroom). A similar scale was used to obtain an estimate of the frequency of Patriotic rituals in the classroom. These scales also show substantial inter-item consistency.

In summary, the reliabilities of the scales developed as measures of both outcomes and inputs in Civic Education are adequate for the purposes of the proposed analysis in spite of considerable differences in the political systems referred to in the questions, problems of translation, and limited tryouts in some nations.

	Population I		Population II		Population IV		Num. Items
	Range	Median	Range	Median	Range	Median	
Local Government Evaluation—Sem. Diff.	.487–699	.544	.523–644	.620	.661–799	.719	4
Local Government Responsiveness—Sem. Diff.	.233–575	.323	.320–578	.498	.611–746	.663	5
Nat'l Government Evaluation—Sem. Diff.	.489–637	.570	.465–694	.673	.660–810	.774	4
Nat'l Government Responsiveness—Sem. Diff.	.083–558	.419	.199–601	.485	.612–736	.670	5
Anti-Authoritarian Attitude Scale	.640–661	.647	.547–739	.677	.525–741	.638	10
Tolerance and Support for Civil Liberties–Attitude Sc.	.451–620	.576	.524–658	.585	.539–563	.649	9
Sense of Political Efficacy–Attitude Sc.	.490–531	.498	.666–737	.698	.747–800	.778	6
Support for Women's Rights–Attitude Sc.	.463–553	.524	.544–745	.676	.635–747	.694	4
Belief in Value of Criticism of Government–Attit. Sc,	.400–531	.482	.613–704	.687	.581–875	.719	5
*Support for Equality for all Social Groups	.735–827	.789	.638–829	.785	.722–857	.774	12
*Tendency to Avoid Perceiving Adult Conflict–Choice	.382–688	.478	.438–679	.579	.404–687	.534	9
Active Perception of Citizenship	.474–637	.539	.502–724	.567	.483–692	.602	6
Non-Political Perception of Citizenship	.553–726	.566	.641–833	.718	.705–777	.727	6
Interest in Public Affairs TV	.505–596	.548	.632–730	.693	.642–743	.674	6
Participation in Political Discussion with Friends, Parents, Teachers	.737–816	.756	.705–791	.763	.719–838	.794	9
Rejection of Parental Values	.565–780	.620	.515–687	.617	.542–659	.598	4
Asserting Independence from Parental Expectations	.690–801	.718	.702–770	.714	.612–748	.711	7
Participation in Civic Activities	.257–314	.278	.288–433	.363	.323–489	.423	7
Equality among Students in Classroom	.379–540	.490	.374–669	.581	.461–697	.648	5
Independence of Opinion Encouraged in Classroom	.539–634	.624	.487–738	.650	.652–800	.776	4
Patriotic Rituals Practised in Classroom	.379–540	.490	.451–627	.533	.331–771	.595	4
*Word Knowledge	.789–926	.870	.764–873	.831	.695–866	.774	40
	4 countries		9 countries		8 countries		

Note: Those marked * are KR20 reliability coefficients for item analysis of dichotomous or keyed item choices; all others are alpha coefficients for continuous scales.

RATIONALE FOR FACTOR ANALYSIS OF CIVIC EDUCATION OUTCOMES

Although there was considerable overlap in the specifications of the desirable qualities of good citizens by participating educational centers of different countries, the processes by which these qualities were to be achieved were seldom articulated. It was not clear whether the curriculum designers in fact believed that these outcomes were independent of each other and differentially effected by different educational practices or whether good civic education practice was expected to increase diverse kinds of civic outcomes fairly equally. Might one assume, for example, that an instructional unit on government structure in so far as it realizes the ideals of democracy would have an equal effect upon support for democratic values, upon loyalty to country, and upon the individual's desire to be an active citizen?

Before it is possible, therefore, to assess the relationship between various Civic Education practices and outcomes, it is necessary to determine whether it is appropriate to view the results of Civic Education as unidimensional or as multidimensional. Does the good-citizen student product of Civic Education in a given country rank high on all dimensions which educators would define as part of citizenship? Or are there different types of citizenship which when taken together contribute to a prepared citizenry but are not equally characteristic of all individuals within the system? For example, does active participation in influencing government always accompany other components of citizenship? A multidimensional view of citizenship attitude development might be considerably more appropriate than a unidimensional one.

It is important to determine whether there are separate and independent dimensions of good citizenship within a single country and whether the same dimensions of attitudinal outcomes of civic education exist in different countries. Do the students of Finland, for example, show patterns in their civic attitudes which are very different from those of the students in Italy or the United States? Does cognitive knowledge in civics relate to a variety of attitudinal outcomes, or to only a few? Is the relationship the same in different countries? In an international study of the kind reported here, one finds that the emergence of similarities becomes almost as intriguing as the detection of differences.

In addition to establishing the multidimensional or unidimensional nature of citizenship, the plotting of independent dimensions of citizenship attitudes would, from the point of view of instrument construction, further strengthen the IEA Civic Education scales. Campbell and Fiske (1959) have pointed to the importance of method factors in psychological measurement, arguing that there should be stronger relationships between the same trait measured by different methods than those which exist between different traits measured with the same type of item or instrument. It was hoped that the IEA Civic Education instrument would avoid the all too frequent case in attitude measurement in which method factors predominate—e.g., all the agree–disagree items clustering together regardless of content and all the semantic differential ratings, independent of content, loading by themselves on another factor.

Therefore, to check both the content and the method dimensions of the instrument and in order to ascertain the multidimensional or unidimensional nature of the outcomes of civic education, an early step in the IEA Civic Education analysis was to construct a series of correlation matrices including major student outcome variables. Following that, a selection of twenty-one outcome variables was made to represent all the major outcomes, excluding scales where item overlap would produce artifactual correlations. Factor analysis with varimax rotation was carried out separately for each age-population and country. No attempt was made to rotate the factors to a common structure although the same criteria for factor extraction and rotation were used for each problem (e.g., rotating factors with eigen values greater than 1.0).

GENERAL RESULTS OF FACTOR ANALYSIS

In the analysis reported here the twenty-one scales which were factor analyzed were each composed of a number of items (reliabilities have been previously noted). These scales may be viewed as representing the outcomes of Civic Education—knowledge, attitudes, and reported perceptions and behaviors.

The variables included in the factor analysis are listed in the left hand margin of Tables 8.2 through 8.4 and will be described more completely as the factors are described. The percentage of common variance accounted for is listed across the top of these tables. The loadings, the figures in the body of the tables, indicate the height of projection of each variable upon each factor after rotation. A factor was generally assigned a name based upon the items which were highly loaded.

Table 8.2. *Rotated Factor Structures—Civic Education Outcomes (Population I)*

Factor …	Federal Republic of Germany					Italy					
	1	2	3	4	5	1	2	3	4	5	6
% Unrotated Variance	14.5	11.6	8.9	6.1	5.9	19.0	11.1	8.0	6.6	6.0	4.9
Cognitive Total	.675		-.177	-.113	.138	.744					
Democratic System—Business	.299		.788			.475					
How Society Works—Don't Know	.290	-.159	-.355			-.226	-.115	-.170	.634		
Perceived Conflicts					.171			-.124	-.317		.103
Local Government Evaluation	.167	.568					.713				
Local Government Responsiveness		.487		.139			.737				
National Government Evaluation		.652		.181			.667				.103
National Government Responsiveness		.600				.119	.707				
Anti-Authoritarianism	.791				-.155	.669					
Tolerance Civil Liberties	.261	.167	-.141	.147	.418	.539	.107	.165	-.115		-.151
Efficacy	.415				-.185	.462	.372				-.155
Support Women's Rights	.486				.134	.516	.150				-.107
Influence on Laws—Don't Know	-.164		.661	-.128		-.150		-.180	.624		
Pressure Group Influence			-.231						-.105		.509
Support for Equality	.581			.236	.104	.626	.101	.188	-.151		-.160
Active Good Citizenship	-.175	.182		.110				.562			
Non-Political Good Citizenship		.154	-.122	.357	.261			.647			
Interest in Public Affairs TV	.315			.629	.126	-.158				.338	
Participation Discussion	-.197		-.115	-.128		-.302				.361	
Unaware Political Opinion					.274					-.201	
Civic Activities			-.205	.489		.134				.671	

194

Table 8.2. (*Cont.*)

Factor ...	Netherlands				
	1	2	3	4	5
% Unrotated Variance	15.1	9.5	8.6	6.7	5.8
Cognitive Total	*.714*				
Democratic System–Business	.222				
How Society Works—Don't Know	-.102		*.810*	-.152	
Perceived Conflicts			-.340		
Local Government Evaluation	-.132	*.506*			.299
Local Government Responsiveness	.136	*.520*			
National Government Evaluation		*.503*			.265
National Government Responsiveness		*.478*			
Anti-Authoritarianism	*.720*	.178			-.111
Tolerance Civil Liberties	.325	*.392*	-.130		.251
Efficacy	*.361*				
Support Womens' Rights	*.389*	.121	-.105		
Influence on Laws—Don't Know	-.101		*.638*		-.148
Pressure Group Influence	-.216		-.187		.101
Support for Equality	*.642*		-.156		
Active Good Citizenship					.342
Non-Political Good Citizenship	.209	.158			*.414*
Interest in Public Affairs TV		.140		*.435*	
Participation Discussion				*.723*	
Unaware Political Opinion	.114			-.153	
Civic Activities	.137			*.566*	

Note: Factor loadings higher than 0.35 are printed in italics; factor loadings between 0.34 and 0.11 are printed in roman type; factor loadings less than 0.10 are not listed.

Table 8.3. Rotated Factor Structures—Civic Education Outcomes (Population II)

Factor ...	Federal Republic of Germany						Finland					
	1	2	3	4	5	6	1	2	3	4	5	6
% Unrotated Variance	18.2	11.2	8.5	6.3	5.5	4.9	16.4	12.6	8.7	6.5	6.4	4.9
Cognitive Total	.439	.118			.244	.731	.707			-.230		.287
Democratic System—Business	.178					.449	.467					.182
How Society Works—Don't Know		-.114	-.136		-.785		-.127		-.123	.752		
Perceived Conflicts	.231	.114			.341	.202	.110	-.277		-.234	-.137	-.106
Local Government Evaluation			.136	.872				.585				
Local Government Responsiveness			.292	.549				.580				
National Government Evaluation			.573	.246				.641				
National Government Responsiveness			.735	.109				.639				.110
Anti-Authoritarianism	.721	.148			.123		.189	.787		.111		-.106
Tolerance Civil Liberties	.502	.113			.158	.274	.616			-.118		-.253
Efficacy	.242	.107	.503			.113	.603	.540				.286
Support Women's Rights	.595		.129					.136				-.207
Influence on Laws—Don't Know	-.158				-.482		-.114	-.248	-.126			-.267
Pressure Group Influence	-.132	.165		-.129	.202					.583		
Support for Equality	.518				.128	.128	.588			-.108		.129
Active Good Citizenship		.152	.113						.132		.726	
Non-Political Good Citizenship	-.379					-.258					.726	
Interest in Public Affairs TV	.299	.530			.119	.120	.241	.107	.464			
Participation Discussion		.689							.678			
Unaware Political Opinion		-.218				-.108			-.277			
Civic Activities		.633					.105		.677			

Table 8.3. (Cont.)

Factor …	Iran					Ireland						
	1	2	3	4	5	1	2	3	4	5	6	7
% Unrotated Variance	13.0	11.6	10.2	6.6	6.1	15.9	12.6	9.4	6.4	5.9	5.1	4.9
Cognitive Total		.579	.106			.747			-.103			.226
Democratic System—Business	.114	.258				.331					-.120	
How Society Works—Don't Know	-.199	-.586	-.210	.242				-.153	.648		-.104	-.104
Perceived Conflicts	-.143		.232		-.317	.255	-.362	.169				.456
Local Government Evaluation	.621	-.121	.114		.199	-.209	.295			.829		
Local Government Responsiveness	.593	.181					.329			.510		
National Government Evaluation	.646					-.175	.674			.245		
National Government Responsiveness	.568	.241			.213		.681			.147		.124
Anti-Authoritarianism		.590				.764						
Tolerance Civil Liberties	.120	.242	.257		.166	.564	.671				.108	
Efficacy	Not	scored				.507	-.109					
Support Women's Rights		.430				.119						
Influence on Laws—Don't Know		-.146	-.688	-.225		-.243		-.132	.708			.157
Pressure Group Influence		-.148	.398	.105	.121		-.125	.113				-.308
Support for Equality		.530	.271			.577			-.121			
Active Good Citizenship	.129	-.159			.402	-.177		.145			.463	-.184
Non-Political Good Citizenship					.440						.737	
Interest in Public Affairs TV	.161	-.121	.152	.205	.307	.198		.430			.159	.124
Participation Discussion				.571				.732				
Unaware Political Opinion				-.388				-.228				
Civic Activities		.100		.605	.122			.582				.113

Table 8.3. (Cont.)

	Israel					Italy					
Factor ...	1	2	3	4	5	1	2	3	4	5	6
% Unrotated Variance	18.7	9.6	8.0	6.3	6.2	16.9	12.6	9.0	7.1	5.7	4.9
Cognitive Total	.636			-.168		.656			-.135	-.201	
Democratic System—Business	.393	-.110	-.122			.376	-.118			-.172	
How Society Works—Don't Know	-.260			.642		-.269	-.121		-.106	.593	
Perceived Conflicts		-.202		-.248	.131	-.113	-.191	-.118		-.242	
Local Government Evaluation		.565					.652				
Local Government Responsiveness		.539	.109	-.132			.649				
National Government Evaluation	.182	.421				.105	.704				
National Government Responsiveness	.159	.445					.707				
Anti-Authoritarianism	.773					.745					
Tolerance Civil Liberties	.654	.490		-.111	.185	.568	.523				-.103
Efficacy	.440	.175				.290					
Support Women's Rights	.623					.543		-.115		-.144	.231
Influence on Laws—Don't Know	-.129			.574		-.196				.581	
Pressure Group Influence					.270						-.259
Support for Equality	.676	.151		-.128		.612					
Active Good Citizenship					.546				.712	-.153	.288
Non-Political Good Citizenship	-.302				.476	-.203			.699		
Interest in Public Affairs TV	.119	.124	.390	-.103	.125	.372		.432			.234
Participation Discussion	-.152		.698		.133			.600		-.137	
Unaware Political Opinion			-.257					-.357			
Civic Activities			.544					.669			-.144

Table 8.3. (*Cont.*)

Factor ...	Netherlands					New Zealand					
	1	2	3	4	5	1	2	3	4	5	6
% Unrotated Variance	16.6	10.8	8.6	6.4	5.8	14.0	12.5	9.2	6.2	5.6	4.8
Cognitive Total	.587			.339	-.310		.468		-.206	.619	
Democratic System—Business	.396			.220	-.237		.188			.357	-.118
How Society Works—Don't Know	-.134			-.795			-.152	-.141	.566		
Perceived Conflicts	.146			.335	-.120	-.264				.136	
Local Governmental Evaluation		.504			.162	.587	.116			.210	
Local Government Responsiveness	.151	.512				.539	.218				
National Government Evaluation	-.115	.627				.697	-.118				
National Government Responsiveness		.583			-.103	.633				.194	
Anti-Authoritarianism	.743		.104			-.111	.684			.160	-.123
Tolerance Civil Liberties	.565	.587		.113	.103	.603	.556				.113
Efficacy	.211	.126				.115	.431			.280	
Support Women's Rights	.448										
Influence on Laws—Don't Know	-.133		-.130	-.442	-.113	-.138	-.116	-.106	.649		
Pressure Group Influence				.249				.212			
Support for Equality	.567	.103		.172	-.124		.456		-.168	.223	
Active Good Citizenship					.283			.118			.632
Non-Political Good Citizenship					.490	.134				-.117	.484
Interest in Public Affairs TV	.168		.523			.176	.110	.456			.119
Participation Discussion			.660					.675			
Unaware Political Opinion			-.355					-.323			
Civic Activities	.129	.135	.619			.101		.611			

199

Table 8.3. (*Cont.*)

Factor ...	United States			
	1	2	3	4
% Unrotated Variance	17.6	12.8	8.4	6.1
Cognitive Total	.108	.628		.406
Democratic System—Business Diff.		.399		.245
How Society Works—Don't Know		-.112	-.180	-.609
Perceived Conflicts	-.200	.192	.138	.232
Local Government Evaluation	.558			
Local Government Responsiveness	.578			
National Government Evaluation	.698			
National Government Responsiveness	.711			
Anti-Authoritarianism		.754		
Tolerance Civil Liberties		.590	.131	
Efficacy	.666	.148		.125
Support Women's Rights		.476	.175	
Influence on Laws—Don't Know		-.135	-.172	-.498
Pressure Group Influence	-.164		.148	.138
Support for Equality		.531		.136
Active Good Citizenship	.195		.168	
Non-Political Good Citizenship	.191	-.320	.100	
Interest in Public Affairs TV	.191	.191	.448	
Participation Discussion			.709	
Unaware Political Opinion			-.322	-.129
Civic Activities	.108		.615	

Note: Factor loadings higher than 0.35 are printed in italics; factor loadings between 0.34 and 0.11 are printed in roman type; factor loadings less than 0.10 are not listed.

Table 8.4. *Rotated Factor Structures—Civic Education Outcomes (Population IV)*

Factor ...	Federal Republic of Germany					Finland					
	1	2	3	4	5	1	2	3	4	5	6
% Unrotated Variance	15.1	13.3	7.3	6.9	5.6	15.3	13.4	8.1	6.6	5.5	5.1
Cognitive Total		.164			-.196		.335				-.119
Democratic System—Business	.166	.172				.110		.186			
How Society Works—Don't Know			-.103		.676		-.144			.638	
Perceived Conflicts					-.620	-.349			-.168	-.192	
Local Government Evaluation	.250			.727		.312			.565		
Local Government Responsiveness	.229			.855		.257			.809		
National Government Evaluation	.664					.764	-.101				
National Government Responsiveness	.850			.158		.725			.184		
Anti-Authoritarianism		.754	.210				.211	.708			
Tolerance Civil Liberties		.638	.193				.174	.566		-.109	
Efficacy	.668	.109	.108	.248		.572	.139	.126	.217		-.102
Support Women's Rights		.553	.207		.247			.638			
Influence on Laws—Don't Know		-.193	-.167	-.206			-.173			.601	
Pressure Group Influence	-.215		.148			-.165	.175	.105	-.210		.225
Support for Equality	.160	.441			-.125	.101		.413		-.117	
Active Good Citizenship		.173	.285				.312	.154			.652
Non-Political Good Citizenship		-.257			.116			-.236	-.133		.393
Interest in Public Affairs TV	.104	.221	.422				.538	.145			.152
Participation Discussion			.681				.717				
Unaware Political Opinion			-.285		.121		-.254			.107	
Civic Activities			.635				.655	.133			

Table 8.4. (Cont.)

Factor ...	Iran						Ireland					
	1	2	3	4	5	6	1	2	3	4	5	6
% Unrotated Variance	15.6	13.1	8.5	6.5	5.5	5.1	16.6	12.6	8.8	6.6	6.1	5.3
Cognitive Total		.499						.548		-.137	-.123	
Democratic System—Business		.296					.223	.471			-.114	
How Society Works—Don't Know	-.293	-.340	-.103	-.330		.185		-.112	-.182	.642		
Perceived Conflicts	.123	.268		.164	-.253	-.367	-.369		-.104		-.261	-.122
Local Government Evaluation			.540		.338	.140	.306	-.203			.718	
Local Government Responsiveness			.909		.174		.345				.721	
National Government Evaluation		.114	.147		.788	.151	.765	-.146			.138	
National Government Responsiveness			.309	-.112	.564	.176	.781				.192	
Anti-Authoritarianism	.154	.610					-.177	.582				
Tolerance Civil Liberties	.132	.507		.211	-.226		-.211	.549				.204
Efficacy		Not scored					.736	.101			.120	
Support Women's Rights	.116	.276	.175		.151	.166		.404				
Influence on Laws—Don't Know	-.303	-.225		-.672				-.172		.746	-.183	
Pressure Group Influence	.128	-.104		.465		.142	-.258			-.122		.225
Support for Equality		.481		.160				.494		-.105		
Active Good Citizenship						.466		.122				.612
Non-Political Good Citizenship						.425		-.199				.518
Interest in Public Affairs TV	.120	.115			.134			.116	.451			
Participation Discussion	.674	.124		.194					.703			
Unaware Political Opinion	-.437								-.237			
Civic Activities	.666	.111				.139	.102		.656			

Table 8.4. (*Cont.*)

Factor ...	Netherlands							New Zealand						
	1	2	3	4	5	6	7	1	2	3	4	5	6	7
% Unrotated Variance	15.2	12.9	8.2	7.0	5.9	5.3	5.0	14.7	13.0	8.3	6.5	5.6	5.3	4.8
Cognitive Total	-.117	.146	-.133	.178			*.631*		.154	.164			*.726*	-.159
Democratic System—Business	.129	.188					.211		.158				.188	
How Society Works—Don't Know			*.936*								-.116			*.435*
Perceived Conflicts	-.175	.109	-.393		-.102		.106	-.345			-.106	-.134	.181	
Local Government Evaluation	.230				*.696*			.241			*.737*			
Local Government Responsiveness	.308				*.758*			.330			*.735*			
National Government Evaluation	*.738*	-.123			.104		-.130	*.745*			.126			
National Government Responsiveness	*.771*				.171			*.754*			.127			
Anti-Authoritarianism	-.114	*.788*		.142				-.114	*.731*	.133				
Tolerance Civil Liberties	-.102	*.692*	-.107				.163		.560	.101				
Efficacy	*.674*	.557		.113	.155		.128	*.764*	.588	.133	.157		.140	
Support Women's Rights														*.636*
Influence on Laws—Don't Know			*.473*							-.148				
Pressure Group Influence	-.288		-.130	.133	-.147			-.298		.159	.103			-.140
Support for Equality		.453		.138					.417				.135	
Active Good Citizenship						*.499*			.151	.111		*.587*		
Non-Political Good Citizenship		-.118				*.627*		.108	-.191			*.557*	-.133	
Interest in Public Affairs TV		.179		*.463*	.100	.128	.132	.155	.251	*.425*		.114		
Participation Discussion				*.692*						*.733*			.107	
Unaware Political Opinion				-.323			-.123			-.299				
Civic Activities				*.591*						*.629*				.129

203

Table 8.4. (Cont.)

Factor ...	Sweden						United States				
	1	2	3	4	5	6	1	2	3	4	5
% Unrotated Variance	18.2	14.7	8.1	6.8	5.9	4.9	18.1	14.2	7.8	6.1	5.4
Cognitive Total	.194	.207	.246	-.147			.529	.189		-.105	.464
Democratic System—Business	.274						.356				.232
How Society Works—Don't Know	-.151		-.166	.857					-.156		-.558
Perceived Conflicts		-.230		-.325	-.101		.187	-.234		-.161	.296
Local Government Evaluation		.342			.586			.261		.931	
Local Government Responsiveness		.286			.901			.373		.488	
National Government Evaluation	.111	.753			.126		-.117	.720			
National Government Responsiveness		.806			.211		-.103	.781		.210	
Anti-Authoritarianism	.798		.193				.745		.160		
Tolerance Civil Liberties	.747	.722	.150				.632	-.163	.122		
Efficacy	.178	.145	.124		.206			.743	.177	.154	
Support Women's Rights	.724						.539				
Influence on Laws—Don't Know	-.250		-.194	.438			-.165				-.386
Pressure Group Influence		-.223		-.104	-.195		.235	-.250	.119		.277
Support for Equality	.633	.167		-.230			.544				.187
Active Good Citizenship			.113			.589		.124	.138		.195
Non-Political Good Citizenship						.770		.133			
Interest in Public Affairs TV	.181	.112	.543				-.363	.111	.432		
Participation Discussion			.717				.222		.660		.134
Unaware Political Opinion			-.255						-.360		
Civic Activities			.659						.689		.118

Note: Factor loadings higher than 0.35 are printed in italics; factor loadings between 0.34 and 0.11 are printed in roman type; factor loadings less than 0.100 are not listed.

204

It is important to consider at the outset questions concerning what factor analysis can tell about the adequacy of the measuring instrument. First, are the factors similar in different countries, suggesting that the attitude instrument was operating similarly when translated from English into languages as diverse as German, Dutch, Italian, Finnish and Hebrew? Second, do the factors tend to include items of similar content but different format or do they tend to be made up only of items of a single format irrespective of content?

At the Population II (14-year-old) level the number of factors successfully rotated according to the citerion ranged from four in the United States (five actually met the criterion but convergence in the rotation was possible only with four), through five in Iran, Israel and the Netherlands, six in the Federal Republic of Germany, New Zealand, Finland, and Italy, to seven in Ireland. The items which load on these four factors in all countries are very similar. This occurs in spite of the fact that the factor-analysis procedure actually was done without any particular effort to rotate to similar factor structures. In countries where six or seven factors were extracted, the later factors tend to account for small amounts of variance and to a little like "leftover" pockets of common variance.

At Population IV, the pre-university student groups, five factors were extracted in the United States and the Federal Republic of Germany; six in Finland, Sweden, Ireland, and Iran; and seven in the Netherlands and New Zealand. In this population also the five factors extracted in the United States and the Federal Republic of Germany can be matched with the first five factors in all the other nations.

Among the 10-year-olds (Population I), as might be expected, the factors were a little less clear-cut and accounted for smaller amounts of variance. The factor structures, however, were still very similar in the three countries which tested at this early age level (the Federal Republic of Germany and the Netherlands five factors; Italy, six factors). Israel was not analyzed at this level because the cognitive test was not administered.

The factor structures in Iran were quite similar to those in the other nations, with the same basic factors described in the following section. Since the Efficacy scale was not administered in Iran, the loading patterns for the first two factors differ somewhat. Therefore, the actual loadings for Iran are included in the tables but not in the summary which follows.

FACTOR RESULTS BY COUNTRY AND POPULATION

Support for Democratic Values Factor

The Population II and Population IV results for each of the countries show two relatively large factors, each of which contains items and scales in at least two different formats. One of these factors, which accounts for between 8.8 and 18.7 % of the common variance in the different countries, may be titled Support for Democratic Values factor (on the basis of an examination of the items showing high loadings on it). From the items in the agree–disagree attitude format, the following show consistently high loadings in the Population II and IV groups: Anti-Authoritarianism (loadings all above 0.582); Tolerance and Support for Civil Liberties (loadings all above 0.502); Support for Women's Rights (loadings all above 0.404). The Support for Equality Scale, consisting of the number of times the respondent chose from a multiple choice format the option, "Should have the same rights as everyone else," for groups as diverse as "lawyers" and "hoboes and bums," had factor loadings in all countries which were 0.413 or higher.

In addition to these attitudinal measures in two different formats, the total Civic Education Cognitive score showed loadings ranging from 0.146 to 0.747 on the Democratic Values factor. All the Population II loadings for this knowledge variable were greater than 0.430; only two of the Population IV loadings (out of seven) were so high. This age difference in loading pattern is probably due to restricted variance in the Population IV cognitive test, particularly in the countries with more selective school systems.

A fourth type of scale which had relatively consistent loadings on the Support for Democratic Values factor was that which measured the students' ability to perceive certain differences between the values espoused by large business organizations and those inherent in the democratic system itself. This difference score comes from the How Society Works instrument, which asked the student which political institutions serve to realize certain values. The loadings of this differentiation score on the factor were not strikingly high (0.158 to 0.471) but appeared consistently in all countries testing at Population II and IV. This scale was an attempt to measure the complexity of the students' perceptions rather than their content; it is thus a somewhat different type of ability than is measured by the other outcome variables. Another item which appeared on this factor in several but not in all of the countries (and generally with a negative loading) was the student's concept that citizenship involved primarily politeness, hard work and studiousness, in other words, the Non-political perception of citizenship.

At Population I the pattern of item loadings on the Democratic Values factor is similar to that presented above, with two exceptions. First, the Sense of Political efficacy (the other agree–disagree attitude scale) shows relatively high loadings (0.361 to 0.462). This suggests that for the younger age group this first factor is somewhat more of a method- or format-based cluster of items rather than a content-based cluster. Secondly, the loading of Civic Education Cognitive total is very high (0.675 or higher) at this age level. This may indicate that among younger students a certain minimum level of civic knowledge is necessary for the individual to support democratic values. It should be borne in mind that while the attitudinal measures were identical at every Population level, there was relatively little carry-over in the cognitive items.

Support for National Government Factor

A second factor of substantial size in all of the samples may be labeled Support for National Government, including Positive evaluation of government and Sense of political efficacy. This factor shows an interesting developmental pattern.

At Population I in the three countries where full testing took place at this age, this factor accounted for between 9.5 and 11.6 % of the common variance; it included all four of the semantic differential ratings. National government evaluation, National government responsiveness, Local government evaluation, Local government responsiveness all loaded 0.478 or higher and Sense of political efficacy (an agree–disagree attitude scale) loaded 0.167, 0.372, and 0.392 on this factor in the three countries among the 10-year-olds. However, at this age level Efficacy showed a higher loading on the Democratic Values factor with attitude statements of similar format. At the 10-year-old level, therefore, this second factor is a very generalized positive support for government factor rather than a clear evaluation of any particular level of government or government responsiveness norm.

A Population II factor with similar items accounts for between 9.6 and 17.6 % of the common variance. In six of the eight countries where 14-year-olds were tested, the scales of the semantic differential type, measuring Local Government Evaluation, Local Government Responsiveness, National Government Evaluation, National

Government Responsiveness were loaded 0.421 or higher on this factor. In this 14-year-old group, Sense of Political Efficacy was clearly part of this cluster (loading 0.490 or higher) and not a part of the Democratic Values cluster as at Population I. In this case the factor may be interpreted a indicating positive support for national and local government and a sense of political efficacy (or perhaps more accurately as general non-cynicism factor). It might be mentioned also that among 14-year-olds items in two different formats both appear with high loadings.

In two of the Population II countries (the Federal Republic of Germany and Ireland) and in all of the Population IV countries a major factor accounting for 8.5 to 16.6 % of the variance includes two of the same semantic differential scales listed above—National Government Evaluation and National Government Responsiveness (loaded 0.573 or higher) and Sense of Political Efficacy (loaded 0.503 or higher). In contrast to the general Population I and II results, however, Local Government ratings for Evaluation and Responsiveness did not show high loadings on this factor in these older groups. Rather, a separate and somewhat smaller factor (accounting for 5.9 to 6.9 % of the variance) included both of the Local Government Scales.

Showing a consistent but not high loading of opposite sign on the National Government factor is a scale indicating that the student perceived considerable conflict within the operations of government (i.e., elections, congress, and political parties creating disagreement rather than better understanding between people). This further confirms the interpretation of this factor as one of cynicism—or lack of cynicism. At Population IV (and in two of the countries tested at Population II) general support for the national government and belief in its responsiveness seem to accompany a sense of political efficacy (or non-cynicism) and the belief that unresolvable conflict is not a major part of the system's operation. Belief in the good intentions and responsiveness of local government is an independent factor by the pre-university years. That is not to say that students believe less (or more) in their local government, only that they are more able to make a distinction between local and national government and may feel positively about one and negatively about the other.

Civic Education Cognitive Total, a measure of the respondent's knowledge about civics, does not show an appreciable loading on the factor with items indicating support for the national government.

This attitude of support appears to be relatively separate from one's knowledge about governmental operations. Even children who know very little about the particulars of government operation may feel confidence in it, or *vice versa.*

Civic Interest/Participation Factor

Another important factor may be labelled the Civic Interest/Participation factor. This shows similar patterns of loadings at the Population II and IV levels in all countries—accounting for between 7.0 and 13.4 % of the variance. Variables loading on this factor were Interest in public affairs T.V. (0.390 or higher); Participation in political discussion with friends, parents and teachers (0.600 loadings or higher) and Participation in civic activities (loading 0.544 or higher). Unawareness of the political opinions of parents, teachers and peers was loaded in a negative direction in a consistent but less strong fashion (loadings ranging from −0.218 to −0.360). There were no other outcomes consistently loaded on this factor. In particular it is of interest to note that Sense of political efficacy is not part of this factor. The belief that the government will pay attention to the opinions and actions of citizens does not seem to be a major motivation toward expressing civic interest through participation in political discussion or activities. It may be that the meaning of political activity undergoes a qualitative change at the time when one is recognized as a voting and taxpaying adult; or it may be that researchers have presumed that what are commonly defined as political efficacy items in many studies of the political behavior of adults and children are little more than a differently phrased measure of positive government evaluation or the lack of cynicism regarding the system. In other words, the belief that "all is well" in government may include the belief that in case something does go wrong, it will be possible for citizens to make their beliefs heard and felt. The evidence in this study is that a sense of political efficacy is not a sufficient condition for citizens to attempt to be active monitors of governmental action on a continuous basis.

The finding that the Sense of political efficacy and political participation load on different factors is similar to the findings regarding the dimensions of political competence and participant citizenship reported in two cross-national studies of adults (Muller, 1970 and Inkeles, 1969). Muller used the Survey Research Center efficacy items as an index of acceptance of the norm of political efficacy—the belief that the government is responsive to citizens in general and not specifically the respondent's desire or wish to act in relation to the government. Muller factor-analyzed results from adult samples of 900 from each of the following countries: Federal Republic of Germany, Italy, Mexico, the United Kingdom and the United States. The factor structures in these different countries were very similar.

The first factor included discussion of political issues, report of attention the respondent paid to political campaigns, and the like. (Many of these adult items were similar to items IEA used at the adolescent level.) The second factor included the belief in a personal ability to influence local and national government. IEA did not include items of this sort. Muller's third factor closely resembled the Support for National Government factor, including items which indicated support for the norm of efficacy, or the belief in responsiveness of the government to citizens in general. Muller maintained that belief in the responsiveness of the government (including efficacy) and political involvement (similar to interest-participation) function *prior* to attempts to influence the government. He found evidence for this in the United States and the Federal Republic of Germany, but not in Italy. The IEA Support for National Government factor includes more global positive evaluations of the national government (an area in which Muller had no items). His work is important, however, as it further confirms that responses to the efficacy items show a belief in the norm of government responsiveness; there is no necessary relationship between this belief and active participation.

Inkeles (1969) has also considered the relationship between efficacy and involvement among adult males in six developing countries (including Israel). He concluded, from an analysis of inter-correlations, that participant citizenship is an independent dimension which is "context-free." Whether he approves or disapproves of government action, the active citizen will be informed and participate in civic life.

Inkeles' participant citizenship scales showed a low level of relationship to positive government evaluation scales. For example, no correlations in Israel reached the 0.01 level of significance.

The responses of adolescents in the IEA survey show factors such as Support for the National Government (including political efficacy) and Civic Interest/Participation which are very similar to the factors derived from cross-national adult studies of political attitudes and behavior.

The Cognitive Civic Education score was not strongly loaded on the Civic Interest/Participation factor in any of the Population II groups; in the Population IV samples the loading was slightly stronger but still quite weak. The Population I results also show a Civic Interest Participation factor (with the same items loaded) but one which accounts for less variance (6.0 to 6.7 %) and which shows no appreciable loadings for the Civics Cognitive test.

Don't Know Factor

A factor including several measures of the absence or presence of attitudes, as indicated by Don't Know scores, also appears at every age level in every country, accounting for between 4.8 and 8.9 % of the variance.

Citizenship Perception Factor

A slightly smaller factor which appears in some but not all of the countries includes both the citizenship perception scales. The score indicating that a good citizen is one who is active in public matters is loaded in the same direction on this factor as the score indicating that the good citizen is polite, hard-working and studious. The original intent of these scales was to discriminate between those who had an active citizen orientation and those with a non-political or merely "good person" conception of citizenship. Apparently many students either endorsed both or neither of these aspects of citizenship.

Other Factors

Factors still smaller than this (the 5th and 6th factors) seem to account for little more than left-over variance. There are small factors where only one item shows a substantial loading. In a few countries Civic Education Cognitive total appeared on a late factor, either by itself or with the differentiation score. It is not clear why this is so in those countries and not in others.

SUMMARY

The similarity of factor structures in different countries and, to a somewhat lesser extent, at different age levels is striking. It strongly supports the power, reliability, and validity of the instruments as a cross-national measuring device in the area of affective outcomes of Civic Education.

The results are also encouraging with respect to the multi-method nature of the items represented on the three major content factors. At least in Population II and IV the Democratic Values Factor includes attitudinal items in two formats, the Civic Education Cognitive total score and a Differentiation score. The Support for National Government factor includes semantic differential scores, one agree–disagree attitude score, and a value-institution rating difference score. The Civic Interest/Participation factor includes two distinctly different formats of items. Overall, the substantive content of items, rather than the response format seems to determine their loading patterns.

The factor structure also suggests that the outcomes of Civic Education in the affective domain are multi-dimensional. There are at least three, and at the older levels four, clusters of such outcomes which are relatively independent of each other. The first is a general support for democratic values—tolerance, anti-authoritarianism, equal rights for minorities and women. This cluster at the younger ages is related relatively strongly to cognitive Civic Education achievement. The second important factor includes positive support for national government and lack of cynicism regarding its responsiveness to citizen demands. Items usually regarded as forming an Efficacy scale appear with high loadings on this factor among 14-year-olds and pre-university students. The scales loading on this factor, however, may best be interpreted as expressing a general positive evaluation of the goverment and its responsiveness. This is similar to what Muller has called the efficacy norm. For the oldest students the local government is differentiated from the national government and forms another distinguishable independent factor. The final major factor includes scales indicating that the individual participates (or fails to participate) in various activities having civic relevance. There is little evidence that this activity has any very direct relationship to the perception that the government requires monitoring by a concerned citizenry. This analysis of adolescent attitudes shows a lack of relationship between active interest/participation and perception of responsiveness which is very similar to that found by Muller (1970) and Inkeles (1969) in cross-national samples of adults.

Other factors (the Don't Know factor, the Citizenship Perception factors, and others which appear in only one country) are of limited interest in the assessment of outcomes. The three or four large factors will guide the further presentation in an attempt to map between-country differences and to determine the familial and educational antecedents of between-student differences in the major components of civic attitudinal outcomes—first, Support for Democratic Values; second, Support for the National Government, and third, Civic Interest/Participation. Support for the Local Government scales, which factor slightly differently at different ages, will be less deeply analyzed.

Chapter 9

Patterns of Between-Country Differences in the Attitudinal Outcomes of Civic Education

It is self evident that the governmental and educational systems of the nations participating in the IEA Civic Education study are diverse; if a political or a social scientist were to try to delineate the characteristics of the citizenry required for optimal governmental functioning in each country, these profiles would be markedly different in many respects. In some of the political systems, support for civil liberties might be the most important of the democratic values a child could learn; in other countries important qualities might include unswerving positive support for the national government or for the local government. The role of Civic Education in preparing students to fulfill citizenship roles may also vary in different nations: in some countries in-school Civic Education may be most important; in others mass media or youth organizations may play a larger role.

The appropriateness of analyzing patterns of Civic Education outcomes has been indicated in the preceding chapter. Evidence was presented there for at least three (and in the case of pre-university students, four) major factors of Civic Education outcomes which show sufficient orthogonality to form independent clusters of scales. But there is no single prototype future citizen in all the countries tested, even though the major components of citizenship are the same. The empirical evidence of the existence of the independent factors, which express the similarity of the relationship of scale scores to each other in different nations, does not mean that the levels at which these various dispositions toward politics exist is the same in the students in these nations. In fact, the analysis in this chapter comparing the mean attitudinal scores of students in each country indicates that *different patterns* of citizenship attitudes (arrayed along these three or four major dimensions) exist in the different nations studied.

Since the questionnaires were originally constructed to measure the attitudinal outcomes which had been listed as important by the IEA National Centers, let us briefly review these reports. There was considerable similarity in the topics emphasized and the attitudinal outcomes considered desirable by those who reported on the content of national Civic Education curricula. At the 14-year old age level *every value* out of the 23 on which ratings were obtained was taught in some form in more than half of the 10 responding countries. There was considerable similarity in the kinds of outcomes considered important in these 10 nations—democratic values ("respect for others," "equality before the law," "belief in the freedom of the individual," "the right to vote," "the right to be represented"); positive feeling about one's country and its government (appreciation both of the "traditions of one's own nation" and "the interdependence of peoples"); political interest as a form of participation ("maintenance of active interest in political activities" and "establishing of interest in current events"). These qualities of the good citizen are presented above in categories which parallel those obtained from the factor analysis; all are clearly important in Western-type Civic Education. In noting the nearly unanimous agreement among the National Technical Officers that these are important qualities of the good citizen it should also be realized that none of these respondents was asked to make mutually exclusive choices between values. No National Center respondent was asked, for example, which was more important—"support for civil liberties as reflected in respect for others" or "respect for and defense of the traditions of one's own nation." It would have been possible in the method used to rate all 23 values as equally important.

There is some evidence concerning the limitations of an input-output model in providing direct cause-effect linkages between curriculum and student outcomes even in subjects which have relatively clear cognitive objectives like science and mathematics (Comber and Keeves, 1973; Husén, 1967). It would not be surprising if the linkage between nationally adopted civics curriculum objectives and attitudinal outcomes were even less strong. In the area of civic and political attitudes, there may well be as much input from the realities of the governmental structure and events in the political realm as there is from the school system; there may well be as much influence from parents, peers and mass media programs as from classroom experiences. The known complexity of fostering social attitudes and the existence of unintended as well as intended consequences of educational activities, would lead to the expectation that no educational system could be equally successful in fostering all 23 of these values (or any others).

Success or failure in promoting certain attitudes must be seen as resulting from an interaction between the structure of the governmental system, particular historical and political circumstances, adult public opinion, agencies outside the school which influence attitude formation, and a variety of other factors. So it is unlikely that the relationship between curriculum objectives and attitudinal outcomes will be pure and direct.

A further consideration in the area of civic attitudes is the problem of underlying assumptions about "good attitudes" and "bad attitudes" which may be implied in these scales. In subject areas like science it is relatively easy to assert that achievement, number of items correct on a keyed test, is "good." Even in the domain of Civic Education it could be expected that knowledge of civics (measured in this study by the Civic Education Cognitive Test) would be widely considered to be a positive outcome. From the point of view of many citizens and educators, it might also be possible to determine a correct answer to certain questions of attitudes and values.

Limitation of space makes it difficult to deal adequately with the numerous dilemmas regarding values which are posed by the civics attitudinal instruments. However, in the case of several scales described in Chapter 8 as comprising the Democratic Values factor there is a relatively clear directional implication. The large majority of democratic systems place positive stress upon citizen support for equality of treatment regardless of social or political position, support for civil liberties, tolerance and respect for other persons; they place negative stress upon what has come to be known as authoritarianism—i.e., belief that certain groups should be denied political power and belief that "might makes right."

There is little doubt that Civic Education in the large majority of those countries surveyed is intended to increase Support for Equality, Anti-Authoritarian Attitudes, and Tolerance and Support for Civil Liberties—all of which are scales on the Democratic Values factor. Some countries, because of external or internal factors, however, may choose to be selective in their teaching of democratic values—stressing some rather than others. For example, the value placed upon increasing the Support for Women's Rights among students is less clear in the curricular statements. In some countries it might be considered as an extension of equality and respect for the rights of every citizen. In other countries women's rights have become an issue with further political and non-political implications. However, the items on the Support for Women's Rights scale deal primarily with the political rights of women (e.g., to hold public office).

Although it may be argued that the attitude scales which have been used to measure support for Democratic Values are not the most appropriate representatives of the particular values stressed in some countries, care was taken to measure, in all of the participating nations, democratic values which represented a common core of the content of the civics curriculum.

With regard to interest and participation there exists an even less clear-cut criterion for defining the type of civic behavior to be positively valued. The National Centers endorsed objectives which placed some stress upon developing political interest, participation in discussion and similar activities—particularly at the 14-year-old and pre-university levels. The questions which could be included in the attitudinal instrument were limited to those activities which were likely to be common among adolescents and pre-adolescents. These include: watching television programs which are concerned with current events, participation in discussions about politics, participation in a rather narrow range of "civic activities," which of course does not include voting. There is some evidence in the factor analysis that an individual who demonstrates interest in one aspect of political life will also be participant in other phases. Our research does not permit us to say, of course, whether those who discuss politics are more or less likely to vote 10 years in the future or to hold political office 20 years in the future.

Finally, there are the scales which comprise the factor labelled Support for the National Government. These include the ratings on the semantic differential scales for evaluation and responsiveness of the national government and also attitude statements concerning political efficacy. On this dimension civic educators and social scientists may disagree concerning the most appropriate direction for Civic Education. However, most would probably agree that a certain amount of positive regard for one's government is valuable. Many would argue, however, that the citizen needs to retain some skepticism and vigilance concerning governmental actions, particularly where performance may fall short of the ideal. Some would be likely also to maintain that some sense of political efficacy is a critical and distinct component of the citizen's reaction to government—a feeling

217

Table 9.1. *Description of Process by which z Scores Obtained for Three Major Dimensions*

Student scale scores	Mean scale scores by country	z Score for scales by country	Averaged z scores for factors
Ten agree–disagree ratings on Anti-Authoritarian items averaged, after appropriate reversal, to form scale score for each student	Mean Anti-Authoritarian scale score for each country computed (based on weighted sample of students)	z score for Anti-Authoritarian computed for each country by subtracting each mean scale score from the mean for all countries and dividing by standard deviation of country means	z score for Support for Democratic Values dimension computed for each country by averaging the country's z scores for Anti-Authoritarian, Tolerance and civil liberties, Support for women's rights, Support for equality
Nine agree–disagree ratings on tolerance and civil liberties items averaged as above	Mean Tolerance and civil liberties scale computed for each country as above	z score for Civil liberties computed for each country as above	
Four agree–disagree ratings on Support for women's rights items averaged as above	Mean Support for women's rights scale computed for each country as above	z score for Support for women's rights computed for each country as above	
Twelve possible choices of equal rights counted to form Support for equality scale score for each student	Mean Support for equality scale score for each country computed as above	z score for Support for equality computed for each country as above	

218

... semantic differential ratings on National government evaluation averaged after appropriate reversal to form scale score for each student	Mean National government evaluation scale score for each country computed (based on weighted sample of students)	z score for National government evaluation computed for each country by subtracting each mean scale score from the mean for all countries and dividing by standard deviation of country means	z score for Support for National Government factor computed for each country by averaging the country's z scores for National government evaluation, National government responsiveness and Sense of political efficacy[a]
Five semantic differential ratings on National government responsiveness averaged as above	Mean National government responsiveness scale score for each country computed as above	z score for National government responsiveness computed for each country as above	
Six agree–disagree ratings on Sense of political efficacy averaged as above	Mean Sense of political efficacy scale score for each country computed as above	z score for Sense of political efficacy computed for each country as above	
Six ratings of Interest in public affairs TV programs averaged to form scale score for each student	Mean Interest in public affairs TV scale score for each country computed (based on weighted sample of students)	z score for Interest in public affairs TV computed for each country by subtracting each mean scale score from the mean for all countries and dividing by the standard deviation of country means	z score for Civic Interest/Participation factor computed for each country by averaging the country's z scores for Interest in public affairs TV, Participation in discussion, Civic activities
Nine ratings of frequency of Discussion with friends, parents, and teachers averaged as above	Mean Participation in discussion scale score computed for each country as above	z score for Participation in discussion computed for each country as above	
Seven possible activities for participation counted to form Civic activities scale score for each student	Mean Civic activities scale score computed for each country as above	z score for Civic activities computed for each country as above	

[a] Local government evaluation was not included because of somewhat different factor patterns in populations II and IV.

that if things go wrong the citizen has a recourse to set them right. In the analysis presented in Chapter 8 it seems that for the students tested by IEA there is a strong relationship between positive evaluation of the government in general and a sense of political efficacy, lending some credence to the interpretation of efficacy as support for a norm of government responsiveness. Particular care must therefore be taken with the interpretation of this scale.

The critical question is whether different *patterns* of citizenship are characteristic of the students in different nations and whether these can be interpreted in the light of what is known about Civic Education, governmental structure, political history, educational practices, and parent or adult opinion in these countries. *The purpose of between-country comparisons, therefore, is not to proclaim the winner of the comparison but to identify groups of countries which are alike in their attitude configurations, to indicate how these configurations are congruent with structures and practices, and to indicate what processes of attitude development seem to be operating.* The results in the section which follows focus on differences and patterns of differences. Although the students in some countries do tend to agree or disagree with some statements more than the students in other countries, the attitudes and interests expressed by the large majority in all the nations indicate considerable Support for Democratic Values, Support for the National Government, and Civic Interest/Participation. The variations which exist by country are large enough and consistent enough to inform our view of political socialization and Civic Education. In no case are they so large as to cause alarm regarding the future of democracy or citizen support in these nations.

POPULATION II—
MEAN ATTITUDE SCORE COMPARISONS

The results which are graphed in Figure 9.1 represent a comparison of the 14-year-old students in each of the countries on their averaged z-scores with respect to the three major attitudinal dimensions. Table 9.1 describes the procedure by which these scores were computed. The first step is computing scale scores averaged over items for each student; the second step is computing country mean scale scores. In the third step mean scale scores of the eight countries in which 14-year-olds were tested were arrayed, the overall mean and standard deviation of these country means calculated, and a z-score representing the ranking of each country relative to the other seven

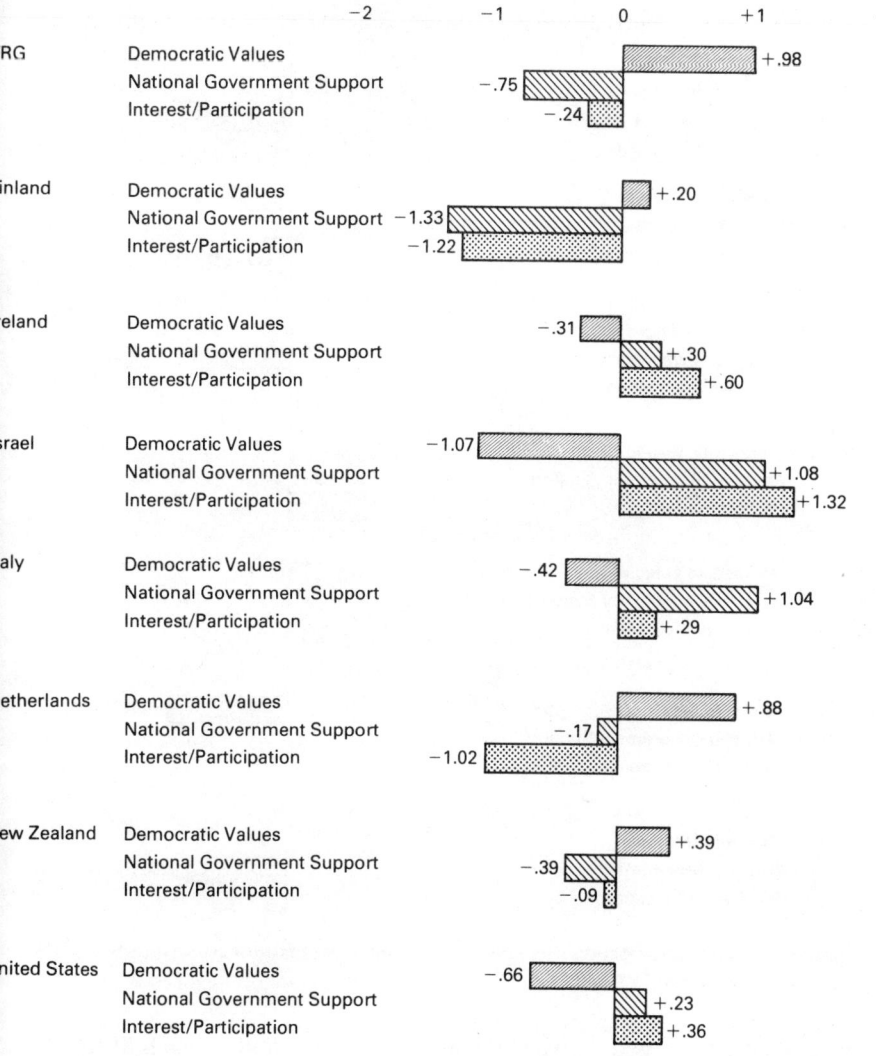

Figure 9.1. Averaged z-Scores Representing Country Means on Civic Attitude Dimensions (Population II).

countries on this scale was calculated. This technique was employed in order to make scales in different metrics comparable and to give some graphical indication of how far above or below the mean attitude for 14-year-olds in all countries the mean in each country fell. This is similar to a technique used in the IEA Science volume (Comber and Keeves, 1973) to determine the countries in which an individual item was especially difficult or especially easy. These z-

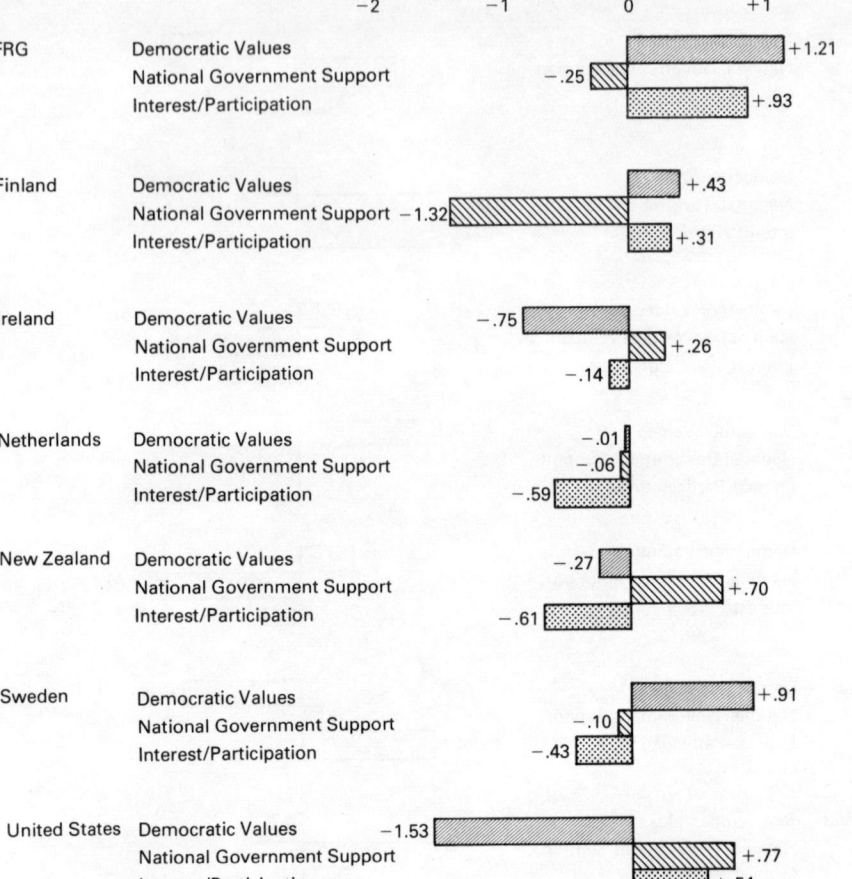

Figure 9.2. Averaged z-Scores Representing Country Means on Civic Attitude Dimensions (Population IV).

scores were averaged across the major scales included on each of the three major dimensions. Thus, for example, the z-scores for Anti-Authoritarian, Tolerance and Civil Liberties, Support for Women's Rights, and Support for Equality were averaged to yield an estimate of the z-score on the cluster of scales of Support for Democratic Values in each country where 14-year-olds had been tested. The patterns of these averaged z-scores appear in Figure 9.1. The z-scores are not intended to imply tests of significance, only to indicate the relationship of a given country's mean to the mean for all countries. The z-scores based on the scales (before averaging by dimension) and in some cases the relative position of the countries on individual items (before the formation of scale scores for students) will be presented as supplementary material in the text.

The same type of averaged z-scores appears for the pre-university students in Figure 9.2 in the subsequent section. Since only four countries were tested at Population I, a similar figure might be misleading. It is appropriate to make comparisons between countries only within age population, since the countries which tested 14-year-olds were not identical with the countries which tested pre-university students.

Several things are striking about the pattern of z-scores among the 14-year-olds. First, those countries where students are above the mean of all countries in their Support for Democratic Values are without exception countries where mean scores on Support for the National Government and Civic Interest/Participation are below the mean for all countries. Furthermore countries which are above the mean for all countries on Support for the National Government and Civic Interest/Participation are without exception below the mean for all countries on Support for Democratic Values. This result gives further support to the conception of the multi-dimensionality of civic educational outcomes. A program which effectively educates students toward support for democratic values may not also be able to promote interest in political participation and positive support for the national government.

Attitudinal Pattern in Israel, Ireland, Italy and the United States—
Government Support and Interest/Participation Countries
at Population II

Democratic values. The pattern of below average Support for Democratic Values, above average Interest/Participation and above average National Government Support is most characteristic of Israel. Three other countries—Italy, the United States, and Ireland—present similar patterns but with scores closer to the mean scores for all countries. At some points these countries are referred to as the Government Support and Interest/Participation countries at the Population II level.

Looking at the items making up the composite scores it will be noted that the low z-score on the Democratic Values dimension in Israel is primarily due to low scores on Anti-Authoritarianism and on Support for equality; in the United States it is Tolerance and support for civil liberties and Support for women's rights which tend to be

223

Table 9.2. *Percentage of Students Who Would Grant Differing Rights and Freedoms to Selected Social Groups by Country (Population II)*

	Religious leaders			Colored people			Communists			Leaders of big business			Tramps		
	More	Same	Fewer	More	Same	Fewer	More	Same	Fewer	More	Same	Fewer	More	Same	Fewer
FRG	14.6	79.3	6.0	1.9	84.0	14.1	2.0	73.1	24.9	15.8	81.0	3.2			
Finland	7.9	85.3	6.8	2.7	89.2	8.1	3.2	73.5	23.2	10.9	81.5	7.5	3.6	82.4	14.0
Ireland	21.6	73.0	5.4	1.9	91.0	7.1	1.8	66.6	31.7	9.6	85.6	4.8	3.3	83.5	13.2
Israel	10.1	80.9	9.1	6.9	75.8	17.3	4.1	50.2	45.7	8.7	85.3	6.0	8.6	75.6	15.8
Italy	15.6	75.4	9.0	4.4	91.7	3.9	3.4	78.3	18.3	6.5	84.6	9.0	1.7	60.6	37.7
Netherlands	6.3	88.9	4.7	1.9	93.3	4.9	2.6	79.4	18.0	9.6	85.4	5.0	1.5	79.2	19.2
New Zealand	8.0	86.6	5.4	1.3	93.2	5.5	2.2	65.2	32.6	8.5	88.9	2.6	2.1	83.5	14.4
United States	7.0	89.5	3.5	3.0	90.0	7.0	1.8	45.2	53.1	5.6	91.0	3.4	1.7	76.1	22.2

	Military leaders			People with anti-mother country views			Doctors			Sum of weights
	More	Same	Fewer	More	Same	Fewer	More	Same	Fewer	
FRG	13.8	83.1	3.1							1 316
Finland	18.3	76.2	5.5	3.4	66.5	30.1	18.5	78.1	3.4	2 402
Ireland	21.0	74.2	4.7	2.8	59.3	37.9	23.8	74.3	1.9	847
Israel	30.4	64.1	5.5	5.5	47.8	46.7	15.8	75.5	8.7	1 047
Italy	15.3	77.3	7.4	1.8	60.1	38.1	9.1	87.7	3.2	937
Netherlands	17.7	77.7	4.6	1.7	71.1	27.2	20.5	76.7	2.8	1 697
New Zealand	18.1	79.4	2.6	1.6	72.1	26.3	17.4	80.5	2.1	2 007
United States	15.6	80.8	3.6	1.6	61.9	36.5	10.8	87.1	2.1	3 208

Notes: The Federal Republic of Germany is omitted from this table for some items because an omission of one item from their questionnaire led to realignment of subsequent columns. Support for equality score has been corrected for this omission. In Israel "national or ethnic minorities" was substituted for "Colored people."

low. Italy and Ireland are slightly below the mean for all countries on these four component scores.

There are also interesting between-country differences in the particular item responses which combine to form these general patterns. To achieve the maximum score on the Support for equality scale, an individual would have chosen the response "should have exactly the same rights and freedoms as everyone else" for all of the 12 groups listed in this scale. However, there is a tendency among the Israeli 14-year-olds to prescribe fewer rights and freedoms for "colored people[1]," "Communists," and "people with anti-Mother Country views" and more rights for "military leaders" than do the 14-year-olds in other countries (Table 9.2). These responses help to account for the low overall score on Democratic Values in Israel. In all the countries the denial of equal rights and freedoms was most frequently prescribed for "people with anti-Mother Country views." This response characterized more than 35 % of the 14-year-old students in Italy, Ireland, and the United States, as well as in Israel; it was less characteristic in other countries. "Communists" as a group were also frequently singled out for fewer rights, especially by students in the United States and Israel.

The major purpose of the Support for equality scale, however, is to assay the position of 14-year-olds in these countries on *generalized* Support for Democratic Values and only secondarily to determine which particular groups are seen as deserving enhanced or inhibited rights. Percentage response by item do, however, give a sense of particularity otherwise lost. For example, on some attitude statements scored as part of the Democratic Values scales, the Israeli students were more likely to agree that "people of certain races or religions should be kept out of important positions in our country," "hotels are right in refusing to admit people of certain races or nationalities," "war is sometimes the only way a nation can save its self respect" and less likely to agree with the statements "no matter what a man's color, religion, nationality, if he is qualified for a job, he should get it," "people should be allowed to come together whenever they like," "talking things over with another nation is better than fighting." These are the particular items which seem to account for relatively lower scores on Democratic Values in Israel (and to some extent also in the United States, Ireland, and Italy). Of course the

---

[1] The authors recognise the sensitivity associated with the use of this term. The intention had always been that individual countries would translate the words in a manner which was nationally appropriate.

Table 9.3. *Percentage of Students Who Strongly Agree with Three Items in the Scale of Support for Women's Rights by Country (Population II)*

	Women should run for political office and take part in government much the same as men do	Women should have same rights as men in every way	Women should stay out of politics	Sum of weights
	% strongly agree	% strongly agree	% strongly agree	
FRG	57.3	52.0	4.0	1 316
Finland	53.7	51.9	3.9	2 402
Ireland	42.9	32.8	7.8	847
Israel	45.6	55.1	6.0	1 047
Italy	44.3	43.5	5.3	937
Netherlands	46.1	47.1	2.9	1 697
New Zealand	37.5	22.3	4.0	2 007
United States	27.2	17.3	8.0	3 208

existing political and military situation in Israel where certain national minorities are classified as threats to national security and may in fact be specially regulated or prohibited from holding certain jobs must be important in the formation of these attitudes.

The percentages of students in different countries agreeing and disagreeing with the items measuring Support for women's rights appear in Table 9.3. The mean score on this four-item scale was especially low in the United States, due to a lower tendency for students to agree with the following statements: "women should run for public office and take part in the government much the same as men do," "women should have the same rights as men in every way." There is an increased tendency to agree that "women should stay out of politics." In fact, the percentages of 14-year-olds in the United States who strongly support equal rights in the first two listed items is only about half that in the Federal Republic of Germany and in Finland, while the proportion who strongly agree that women should stay out of politics is about twice as large in the United States as it is in the Federal Republic of Germany and Finland. (These latter countries are chosen for comparison because of their high scores on Support for women's rights. The scores of other nations lie in between.)

National Government and Perceptions of Local Government. The meaning
of the relatively low standing of the students in Israel (and to some
extent Ireland, Italy, and the United States) on Support for Democratic Values can only be understood in the context of scores on the
two other dimensions which are high in these countries; Support for
the National Government and Civic Interest/Participation. The
scores on all three of the components of the Support for National
Government factor—that is National government evaluation, National government responsiveness and Sense of political efficacy—
are uniformly high in Israel and Italy. In Ireland and the United
States the z-scores on Political efficacy are relatively lower than
those on the two scales from the semantic differential ratings of the
national government.

For this reason the *item* responses which account for these score
patterns in these four countries merit examination. In Italy and
Israel the students were especially likely to agree "the government
cares a lot about what all of us think about any new laws" and "the
government is doing its best to find out what ordinary people want,"
and less likely to agree "government decisions are like the weather;
there is nothing people can do about them" and "there are some big
powerful men in the government who are running the whole thing
and they do not care about the opinions of ordinary people," from
among the items on the Political efficacy scale. In the semantic
differential ratings the students in Israel and Italy were also especially likely to *disagree* with the term "run by a few big, powerful
groups" to describe the national government. Fourteen-year-olds
in Ireland, Israel, Italy, and the United States were all more likely to
rate the *national* governments as "warm-hearted," "friendly," "popular," "cares about me and my family," and "can be trusted" on the
semantic differential. The students in all four of these countries
have a non-cynical view of a national government and place great
faith in it; in Israel and Italy this includes the belief that the government solicits and pays attention to citizen needs and demands.

Students in Italy and Ireland are likely to have a view of the local
government which is not only more positive than the mean ratings of
"town council" in all the other countries but is also as positive as the
corresponding rating of the national government. Italian and Irish
14-year-olds are likely to view their local government as "friendly,"
"warm-hearted," and "popular". Italian and Irish 14-year-olds are
positive, supportive and non-cynical in their response to both local
and national levels of government.

Table 9.4. *Reported Participation in Discussion—Percentage Reporting Discussions "Once a Week or More Often" by Country (Population II)*

	With friends			With parents			With teachers			Sum of weights—respondents
	Politics	Other nations	Political candidates	Politics	Other nations	Political candidates	Politics	Other nations	Political candidates	
FRG	14.2	27.8	5.2	20.5	33.5	11.8	31.3	41.6	14.5	1 316
Finland	18.6	25.8	7.8	19.1	24.9	9.0	11.6	17.4	4.8	2 402
Ireland	15.7	15.1	6.5	26.0	18.1	14.3	25.9	26.2	11.2	847
Israel	41.4	38.8	16.4	52.2	47.2	20.1	30.9	23.3	14.1	1 047
Italy	28.8	34.1	21.5	32.8	30.8	21.2	33.7	42.1	15.6	937
Netherlands	7.1	17.3	3.5	18.8	32.6	9.2	15.5	28.7	7.7	1 697
New Zealand	9.2	14.5	3.8	19.0	24.2	9.6	27.9	46.0	12.0	2 007
United States	19.7	13.5	11.3	29.0	18.7	16.5	41.5	41.3	22.2	3 208

Civic Interest/Participation. These four nations may also be characterized according to their reports of behavior on those scales included in the Interest/Participation dimension; Israel is high on all three components (Interest in public affairs T.V., Participation in political discussion, and Civic activities). The high scores in the other three countries are more diverse reflecting particularly high Interest in public affairs T.V. and high Civic activities in Ireland, high Discussion participation in Italy, and high Civic activities in the United States.

The high Participation in political discussion scores in Israel are the result of particular frequency of talking with parents and friends and a moderately high frequency of talking with teachers (see Table 9.4). In Italy students report moderately high levels of discussion with all three groups. In the United States discussion of political matters, international relations and candidates is more likely to take place with teachers than it is with either parents or friends—in fact frequent discussion is twice as likely to take place with teachers as with friends in the United States; these percentages are much closer in Italy while in Israel frequent discussions with friends are actually reported by more students than report frequent discussions with teachers. These results suggest that for 14-year-old American students, the focus of political discussion is more likely to be within the school context than within the more informal peer social milieu in contrast to Israel and Italy. The regression analysis to predict the Total Discussion scores (Chapter 10) will indicate the variations in school environments which predict individual variations in discussion participation within a given country.

Summary and Discussion. The 14-year-olds in Ireland, Israel, Italy and the United States are similar to each other in being relatively low in their support for Democratic Values, while they are relatively high in their Support for National Government and Civic Interest/Participation. Within these factors there is some variation. But the differences within these countries on the civic predispositions mentioned are considerably less than the differences between these countries and the other four countries which can be characterized by the contrasting pattern.

How then may we understand the precursors of the National Government Support and Participation Pattern in Israel, Ireland, Italy, and the United States? What aspects of their Civic Education (or their educational systems in general), of the type of national government, of particular historical circumstances are related to this pattern of civic attitudes? The distinction between dependent and independent variables in these analyses is not a clear-cut one. In regression analyses where the purpose is to account for maximum between-student variability within country the decision was to use as many variables as possible as predictors. This usually included student reports of classroom practices, teachers' reports of methods, student reports of related attitudes and principal's or headmaster's report of school characteristics. In accounting for between-country differences there are some additional data available—indices of the overall character of an educational, political, or social system. Unfortunately the methodology to provide statistical evaluation of the relative importance of these factors in accounting for variations between countries has not been applied. Our inferences from this analysis can therefore be only tentative and must await further confirmation from evidence concerning important predictors in the between-student regression analysis (Chapter 10). Since a major purpose of the IEA studies is to pinpoint the educational inputs which have greater variation between countries than within any single country, the search for correlates of observed between-country differences in outcomes is important, even if it is tentative in its conclusions.

The four countries considered in depth in this section are very diverse in many respects. As clues to the meaning of these between-country differences there are characteristics which distinguish the educational system in Israel and the United States based on our data. Among these are reports of the extensive use of patriotic ritual and national observances in the classroom in these nations. In fact, the four countries characterized by low Democratic Values Support, high Support for National Government, and high Civic Interest/Participation are ranked first, third, fourth and fifth on reports of singing patriotic songs in class and first, second, fourth and fifth on reports of participating in ceremonials with the flag. (Table 9.5.)[2] A further indication of the patriotic and nationalistic focus of civics in these countries is provided in the summaries by National Centers of what is stressed in the affective domain of civics curricula. Here we also find emphasis in the Israeli and Italian civics curriculum upon "defense of the nation." "Appreciation of national traditions" is reported to be an emphasis at one or more levels in Italy, the United States, Ireland, and Israel (and in no other countries). The pattern of civic attitudes with highly positive national regard, high civic activity, and low support for democratic values is most common in systems where great stress is placed upon national traditions and defense of the nation and where patriotic rituals are a common part of school practice. The existence of this pattern in Ireland among adolescents is similar to data from adults analyzed by Raven (1973).

A further interesting facet of the Israeli data from 14-year-old students is the relative unanimity which characterizes the climate of political opinion to which they are exposed. One of the questions asked was whether, on the whole, the students' political opinions agreed with those of parents, friends, and teachers. The students in Israel were very much aware of these opinions and reported "close" agreement with fathers in 55 % of the cases; with mothers in 47 %; with friends in 31 %; and with teachers of civics or social studies in 34 % of the cases. The means summarizing these ratings of agreement indicate clearly that Israeli 14-year-olds agree with these four groups of people to a greater extent than the students of any other nation. Still further evidence of the lack of perceived conflict in

[2] In Israel the questions were worded to ask "when there is a school ceremonial, how often is the flag . . ."; also "patriotic songs" included "motherland songs."

230

Table 9.5. *Percentage of Students Who Report Participating in Patriotic Rituals* "*Always*" *or* "*Often*" *by Country (Population II)*

	Sum of weights	Singing national anthem in class		Patriotic ceremonial with flag	
		%	Ranking	%	Ranking
FRG	1 316	3.2	7	4.3	8
Finland	2 402	5.9	6	8.0	7
Ireland	847	13.4	3	10.5	5
Israel	1 047	31.1	1	66.7	1
Italy	937	11.5	5	15.1	4
Netherlands	1 697	1.9	8	17.8	3
New Zealand	2 007	13.5	2	8.8	6
United States	3 208	12.8	4	32.3	2

Israel comes from a scale which asked students to what extent nine pairs of groups in the society agreed on what course of action the government should take (e.g., middle class and working class, different political parties). Fourteen-year-olds in Israel chose the alternative "mostly agree about what the government should do" more than the students in any other country. As might be expected, wars increase the perception of cohesiveness in the society, even among adolescents.

The climate of civic education in Israel for 14-year-olds may be characterized as one which places considerable stress on national unity and patriotism. The other countries do not ignore patriotism but spend less time in attempts to foster it. Unfortunately since the questionnaire for teachers was not administered in Israel, it is not possible to supplement the analysis with teacher reports.

Student reports of the practices in their classroom indicate little difference in the equality of treatment of students in Ireland, Israel, Italy, the United States and the other four countries. There is, however, a tendency for 14-year-old students in Ireland, Israel, and the United States to report that "there is a great stress in civics and history classes on learning facts" and "in history or civics classes we must memorize dates or definitions," more than is the case with students in the other nations tested. A low factual stress was reported in Italy, however. This stress on facts does not appear to rule out more informal discussions. The United States, Italy, and Ireland rank first, second, and third in the frequency with which

231

students bring up current political events for discussion in civics class. (Israel and New Zealand were tied for rank 4.)

Teacher reports (where available) place stress upon discussion and active participation in the United States. American teachers are far more likely than the teachers in other nations to believe that students should be provided with political experiences in school: working for a political party in an election campaign as part of a school project (71.3 %), taking one side of a political issue in a school debate (89.6 %). They also agree more to student participation in school decision making.

American civic education, as it is reflected in reports of both inputs and outcomes, is in some respects similar to that in Israel. In particular the stress on patriotism and on factual learning is similar; however, students in the United States seem to have much of their Civic Education focussed in the classroom (in political participation related to the national governmental system and to the school system) and in discussion of political issues with teachers. The political activity in the American school situation seems to foster a relatively general interest in participation among Population II students.

Although the pattern of attitudinal outcomes in the United States is similar to that in Israel, the average scores of United States 14-year-olds are considerably closer to the mean for all nations than are those in Israel. Italian and Irish Population II students are quite close to the mean on the attitudinal outcome dimensions; the local level of government is very important to them; like Israel and the United States they report relatively high levels of patriotic observances. In some respects Civic Education in Italy and Ireland appears to be quite traditional, e.g., teachers stress non-political definitions of citizenship and homework performance is a primary source of evaluation in both of these countries. Fortunately in this analysis of between-country differences it is possible to look not only at student and teacher reports, but also at some characteristics of the national government system. For example, in the United States and Israel 18-year-olds are allowed to vote; young people in all the other nations must wait until they are twenty-one. Anticipation of the act of voting may help to account for the strength of the participation in discussion and civic activities in these two nations. Israel, Ireland, Italy, and the United States represent in other respects a wide variety of level of urbanization, economic structure, level of support for education in general, type of government, and size of population.

It is easier to account for the high scores on Support for the National Government and Civic Interest/Participation than it is to account for the low score on Democratic Values in these four nations. It is impossible to infer direct influence from any single source. The between-student regressions may be of some help in that they allow for the partialling out of some variables to examine the unique contribution of other variables. One possibility, which the regression analysis did not address, is that this pattern of low support for Democratic Values and high Support for the National Government and Civic Interest/Participation may exist because Civic Education systems are unable to devote sufficient resources or time to promote high levels in all three of the aspects of citizenship which have been defined in this study. None of these eight educational systems produce students who are equally qualified on all three of the dimensions of Civic Education identified. A second possibility is that the Civic Education practices which promote support for the national government and interest in participation are those which have the additional but unintended effect of slighting democratic values. Participation in patriotic ritual may be necessary to promote nationalistic feeling, but these rituals may have the additional result of making certain democratic values seem less important to students.

A third possibility is that in certain situations the inculcation of a high level of support for one's national government in some way lessens the support for democratic values because the values associated with nationalism and democratic values are incompatible. If preserving the nation and the citizens' high regard for it is an essential national goal, and further, if powerful hostile forces are perceived to exist inside or outside the nation, educational mechanisms may result which tend to justify the denial of rights to certain groups, to present war as a very plausible national alternative, and may promote nationalistic rituals.

When one is discussing the agents of political socialization or Civic Education it is as important to consider the degree of agreement or disagreement which exists among them as it is to consider the content of their input. The outcomes of Civic Education are known to be multidimensional; the inputs must be regarded in the same fashion, and the interaction between various agents within a national setting must be considered. The singleness of purpose which seems to characterize the Israeli political climate for socialization is an instance of one end of this continuum of congruence, and may intensify certain of the effects seen in that country.

Attitudinal Pattern in the Federal Republic of Germany, the Netherlands, Finland, and New Zealand—Democratic Value Support Countries at Population II

A quite different pattern from the four countries we have described up to this point is represented in those countries which show support for Democratic Values above the mean for all countries and National Government Support and Civic Interest/Participation below the mean for all countries. Fourteen-year-olds in the Federal Republic of Germany and the Netherlands may be characterized as especially high on Support for Democratic Values. Both countries are below the mean in Support for the National Government and Civic Interest/Participation (with the Netherlands especially low on the latter). Finland is slightly above the mean on Democratic Values but has a very low score on Support for the National Government and Civic Interest/Participation. The scores of New Zealand are all quite near the mean though they follow the same directional z-score pattern.

Democratic Values. As with the countries classified as Government Support and Participation countries, the particular scales and items which contribute to the Democratic Value Support pattern will be examined. In the Federal Republic of Germany and the Netherlands all four of the components of the Democratic Values dimension are high. The high score of Finnish Population II students on Democratic Values is largely due to their very high score on Support for Women's Rights. Between 50 % and 60 % of the students in Finland and the Federal Republic of Germany strongly agree that "women should take part in the government much the same as men do" and "women should have the same rights as men in every way;" this percentage is considerably higher than in other countries (Table 9.3). The position of New Zealand above the mean on Democratic Values is due especially to scores above the mean for all countries on Anti-Authoritarianism and the highest score of any country on Support for Equality.

The generally high ranking of students in the Netherlands, New Zealand, and the Federal Republic of Germany on Anti-Authoritarianism and of the Netherlands and the Federal Republic of Germany on Tolerance and Civil Liberties may be accounted for by the following answering patterns. Students in the Federal Republic of Germany, the Netherlands (and also in Finland) were more likely than those in other countries to agree with items such as these: "citizens must always be free to criticize the government," and "peo-

234

ple who disagree with the government should be allowed to meet and hold public protests." Fourteen-year-old students in the Federal Republic of Germany, New Zealand and the Netherlands were more likely than the students of other nations to agree that "talking things over with another nation is better than fighting," (also endorsed in Finland) and to disagree that "war is sometimes the only way in which a nation can save its self respect," and "the people in power know best." These were the items which seem to account for the relatively high scores of these countries on Democratic Values. Other items on these scales showed more varied patterns.

National Government and Perception of Local Government. The relatively high support for Democratic Values in these nations needs to be placed in the context of scores on the other two factors— National Government Support and Civic Interest/Participation. Students in Finland, the country with the most extreme negative scores on Support for National Government, are negative in their general evaluation, in their perception of the government's responsiveness, and in their sense of political efficacy. The students in New Zealand are slightly below the mean on all three components. Students in the Federal Republic of Germany are similarly unfavourable toward the national government but have sense of political efficacy which is slightly above the mean for all countries. A similar pattern is characteristic of the Netherlands.

What are the details of the content of these negative perceptions of the national government? The government is seen by students in Finland, the Federal Republic of Germany, the Netherlands and New Zealand as less "friendly," less "warm-hearted," "weaker," less "popular," "doesn't care about me and my family," and less deserving of "trust" than by the students of other countries. These differences are remarkably consistent and are in contrast to the more positive ratings in Israel, Italy, Ireland, and the United States.

With respect to perceptions of the local government, Population II students in the Federal Republic of Germany and New Zealand tended to rate their city or town council at a moderately positive level on all the semantic differential scales. Their views of the level of government closest to them were considerably more positive than their views of the national government on these same ratings. Students in the Netherlands had given relatively low ratings to the national government but gave especially high ratings to the local government on items indexing responsiveness; Dutch students were very likely to rate the local council as "paying attention to complaints," and "run by people just like ourselves." Population II students in New Zealand also perceived responsiveness in local government. Finnish students, in contrast, were equally negative about local and national government.

Sense of Political Efficacy is a very complex variable; it is very low among the 14-year-olds in Finland and moderately low in New Zealand. The students in these two countries, for example, are in fact likely to disagree with items like the following: "the government is doing its best to find out what ordinary people want" and to agree "there are some big powerful men running the whole country, and they do not care about the opinions of ordinary people." This results in a very low efficacy score in Finland and a rather low score in New Zealand (as well as in the United States and Ireland, previously discussed). Understanding of the growth and patterning of the sense of citizen efficacy requires considerably more comparative investigation. At some levels of analysis it seems to represent a lack of cynicism about the government or a belief in the norm of citizen efficacy. At other times it reflects a particular distinction between national and local government or between governmental leaders and institutions.

As a result of the analysis of the various components of National Government Support, we can say that the Finnish 14-year-olds are clearly the most cynical and negative about their government. Fourteen-year-old students in the Federal Republic of Germany and the Netherlands combine a generally negative evaluation of the national government with some Sense of political efficacy (at both the national and local government level). New Zealand is slightly below the average of all other countries with respect to National government evaluation, Responsiveness and Sense of political efficacy.

Civic Interest/Participation. Finland and the Netherlands are also characterized on the Civic Interest/Participation dimension by scores considerably below the mean on Interest in public affairs T.V., Participation in political discussion, and Civic activities. Scores from the Federal Republic of Germany on these three components are only slightly below the mean for all countries; the scores for New Zealand are mixed, being below the mean on the T.V. interest measure and Discussion participation and above the mean on Civic activities.

The data on Participation in discussion may be found in Table 9.4.

236

The low scores for Population II in the Netherlands and Finland may be accounted for by the report of relatively less frequent discussion with parents and teachers on two out of the three topics—on "what is going on in government" and "a particular political party or a particular political candidate." The students in the Netherlands also reported relatively lower levels of discussion with friends than students in Finland, who indicated that they discussed political issues at least as often with friends as with parents and teachers. The other topic of discussion that was included—"what is happening in other countries"—was talked about more often with friends and parents by Finnish and Dutch 14-year-olds than was the case with 14-year-olds in countries which have higher participation scores in general (the United States and Ireland, for example). It may be tentatively concluded that at least to some extent the low level of participation in discussion by 14-year-olds in Finland and the Netherlands may be attributed to general cynicism about the national government. The apathy displayed here appears to be connected with issues involving political parties and candidates rather than with international topics.

In some respects the four Democratic Value Support countries are even more diverse than the Government Support and Interest/ Participation countries previously considered. Population II students in Finland may be characterized as consistently cynical about their national government, and relatively inactive in discussion and other participation; they rank high in Support for Democratic Values primarily due to their high level of Support for women's rights. High scores on all the scales of democratic values are characteristic of students in the Netherlands and the Federal Republic of Germany where, however, Support for National Government and Civic Interest/Participation are below the mean for all countries. New Zealand is very close to the mean for all countries.

Some of the characteristics of these Democratic Values Support countries are the reverse of those noted for the countries expressing high Support for National Government and high Interest/Participation (Israel, the United States, Ireland and Italy). Taking observance of patriotic ritual as an example, it is noted that Population II students in the Federal Republic of Germany, the Netherlands, and Finland participate in the smallest amount of such activity; New Zealand is near the mean. Lack of reported stress on factual material and memorization in Civic Education is quite characteristic of the Federal Republic of Germany and the Netherlands; in contrast, emphasis on facts was characteristic of the two countries (Israel and the United States) where attitudinal patterns were most different from the Federal Republic of Germany and the Netherlands. Current political events are less likely to be brought up by students in the classrooms of Finland, the Netherlands, the Federal Republic of Germany and New Zealand than in Italy, Israel, the United States and Ireland.

The degree of emphasis on particular topics as reported by teachers, is quite similar in all the countries tested even though the attitudinal outcomes are different (Table 3.15). Finnish, Dutch and German teachers rated few topics as of great importance; it is for that reason especially difficult to make a profile for these teachers. In contrast, the teachers in Italy rated nearly all topics as very important. If one ranks the importance topics within each country there is relatively little between-country variation in this ordering and almost none that could be related in any very direct sense to the difference observed in attitudinal outcomes. International problems (over-population), social problems (racial tension and crime), ideology of democracy and the working of local government and social services are commonly ranked as the most important topics. It is a little ironic that students in the United States, where ideology of democracy is ranked first and social problems second by teachers, do not score higher on Democratic Values; likewise the Finnish teachers, who rank the local government as first in importance, have Population II students who give less positive evaluations of local government than those in any other country. There is little support in these data for a model of direct inculcation of values by teachers.

The aspects of the social and political system as a whole which might account for these between-country differences in outcomes are also relatively difficult to find. This may reflect the multi-faceted nature of Democratic Values and the subtle fashion in which they are apparently transmitted. There are a variety of historical as well as contemporary social factors which influence the particular patterning within these values which exists within a country. The West German students' responses to the attitude questions reflect a denial of war as a national instrument—in fact almost an anti-nationalistic position. The attitudinal z-score pattern in Israel is almost opposite to that in the Federal Republic of Germany; the past and present political and historical context of both nations are critical to an understanding of their levels of nationalism.

The source of the relatively negative picture of the national government which characterizes the students in Finland, the Federal

Republic of Germany, and the Netherlands is difficult to pinpoint. These 14-year-olds see a great deal of disagreement between groups in society—businessmen and unions, Parliament and the Premier, newspapers and Parliament, rich and poor—in contrast to students in Israel who pictured the political world in a relatively unified fashion and lacking extensive internal political conflict; whether such conflict is actually more characteristic of these three countries than of the others is a problem requiring social indicators beyond the data collected here.

It would be possible to speculate further on the role of geographic isolation in determining the attitudinal pattern in New Zealand or concerning the existence of an external political threat in Finland. Each of those speculations (as well as those made concerning Israel and the Federal Republic of Germany) requires a great deal more solid data about the nations than is available here. Suffice it to say that data such as these, which represent national stratified probability samples of students answering carefully constructed questionnaires, merit equally strong data at the national level on social, historical, and economic indicators, as well as educational ones, to help in unravelling the complex factors contributing to the growth of contrasting patterns of civic attitudes.

POPULATION I—
MEAN ATTITUDE SCORE COMPARISONS

It was decided to consider the 14-year-old students in the previous section before the 10-year-old students, because Population II is sampled from eight (rather than four) nations and because, according to the reports of National Centers, the sampling at the younger age was more problematic. The analysis of between-country results for 10-year-olds consists primarily of a comparison of the between-country differences from Population I with those of the Population II group already described. Because of some differences of sampling at the two age levels, the description of developmental differences must await analysis which controls for factors such as socio-economic status.

Italy and Israel tested 10-year-olds and were also two of the countries which fell into the Government Support and Interest/Participation grouping in the previous section—low in Support for Democratic Values, high in National Government Support and in Civic Interest/Participation; the Federal Republic of Germany and the Netherlands also tested 10-year-olds and were characterized by the second pattern—high in Support for Democratic Values, low in National Government Support and Civic Interest/Participation.

Having data from only four countries makes z-scores misleading; it is nevertheless possible to determine whether the differential pattern of attitudes observed at 14 is already in existence at 10. This will help to determine whether the critical period for development of nationally differentiated attitude patterns comes before the age of 10 or between 10 and 14. It is particularly fortunate, of course, that those countries which tested 10-year-olds include those which show the most differentiated patterns at later stages.

With regard to Democratic Values the rankings of the four Population I groups by country are very similar to those for Population II on Anti-Authoritarianism, Tolerance and civic liberties, Support for equality and Support for women's rights. Support for Democratic Values among Israeli 10-year-olds was lower than in Federal Republic of Germany and the Netherlands on all four of the scales. The exception was Italy, which relative to the other countries, had higher Population I rankings than Population II ranking on two of the four Democratic Values scales.

Support for the National Government scale rankings of countries were also similar for 10-year-olds and for 14-year-olds. For National government evaluation, the country ranks for Population I were identical to those observed at Population II. Italian 10-year-olds rated the government as more responsive than other 10-year-olds and expressed the greatest sense of Political efficacy. The 10-year-olds from the Federal Republic of Germany ranked lowest on the three scales which composed this factor.

Two components of the Civic Interest/Participation Factor showed very similar rankings for 10- and 14-year-olds (with Israel and Italy higher than the Federal Republic of Germany and the Netherlands). Civic Activities rankings are somewhat different, however; the Israeli 10-year-olds (like the older students) report more participation than those in the other three countries.

Between-country differences in the variables describing the Civic Education process at the 10-year-old level are also similar to those noted at the 14-year-old level. Rankings of the countries on Participation in Patriotic Ritual, for example, are identical as are rankings on amount of agreement with family. The inferences made concerning the direct or indirect influence of Patriotic ritual upon National Government Support, Civic Interest/Participation, and Support for

Democratic Values would appear to apply equally to 10-year-olds and 14-year-olds, at least in these four countries. Very small samples of Population I teachers answered a complete questionnaire in the Federal Republic of Germany, Israel and the Netherlands, so comparisons of teacher inputs between age levels cannot be made.

It may be concluded at least in the Federal Republic of Germany, Israel, Italy and the Netherlands that the process of socializing civic and political attitudes is well under way by the age of 10. The intention here is not to imply that no important changes take place after the age of 10. However, it may be concluded that there are striking differences in patterns of attitudes between Israeli 10-year-olds and West German 10-year-olds and that these patterns persist into the later years relatively unchanged (at least when compared on a group basis). Therefore it may be concluded that the critical period for the channeling of the three major aspects of civic attitudes occurs before the age of 10. Further investigation of the changes which take place with age within country will help to clarify the status of the developmental processes involved.

POPULATION IV—
MEAN ATTITUDE SCORE COMPARISONS

The results of the averaged z-score comparisons for the three major attitudinal factors for the pre-university students in seven countries are graphically represented in Figure 9.2. These are not all the same countries which tested 14-year-olds; Israel and Italy tested the younger group (Population II) but did not test pre-university students (Population IV); Sweden tested only pre-university students. Comparisons of z-scores are justified, therefore, only within age population and must further take into account the differential selectivity of the school systems involved and the different ages of the pre-university students in these nations.

If one makes comparisons of the six countries which tested both 14-year-olds and pre-university students (the Federal Republic of Germany, Finland, Ireland, Netherlands, New Zealand and the United States), the rankings of these countries are quite similar at the two age levels on the Support for Democratic Values dimension and the Support for National Government dimension. It is not appropriate to use z-scores to compare them. The greatest variation in country rankings, if one compares them for Population II and Population IV is on the scales which make up the Civic Interest/

Participation dimension. The full range of political activities is available only to adults, and the items used in this questionnaire refer more to interest in such participation than to actual activity. Since pre-university students are closer to adulthood than 14-year-olds, they will be more likely to express interest in participating in such activity. It is also reasonable to assume that some political systems will provide more impetus and opportunity for that activity than will others; the results in fact are that the pre-university students in some nations express considerably more interest in civic participation than 14-year-olds, while students in other nations show very similar levels of participation at Population II and Population IV.

In particular, pre-university students in the Federal Republic of Germany and Finland ranked above the mean for all countries on Civic Interest/Participation (while the 14-year-olds had ranked below this mean). Pre-university students in Ireland and New Zealand were *less* participant relative to other nations than their 14-year-old colleagues. Students in the United States and the Netherlands had similar rankings at the two age levels. One possible explanation of enhanced participation scores in the Federal Republic of Germany and Finland is the following. The average ages of the West German and Finnish Population IV students were between 18 and 19 years; the average ages of the Irish and New Zealand Population IV students were closer to 17 years. Since the political activity scores tend to change with age more than do basic attitudes it may be that in fact the differences in Civic Interest/Participation reflect the additional year or two of age of the German and Finnish students. However, this cannot account for the difference completely, since students of Population IV in Sweden were also relatively old but had rather low Interest/Participation scores.

Keeping the differences in age in mind, it is still interesting to note the attitudinal patterning (See Figure 9.2, page 222). Among the 14-year-olds, every country which was above the mean on Support for Democratic Values was below the mean on Support for National Government and Civic Interest/Participation. Among the pre-university students it is also the case that countries indicating Support for the National Government above the mean for all countries show Support for Democratic Values which is below the mean for all countries; those countries whose Support for Democratic Values is above the mean for all countries show Support for the National Government which is below the mean for all countries (with one exception). In contrast to the 14-year-old data, at the pre-university level Civic Interest/Participation is high in some countries which are below the mean on National Government Support as well as in some countries which are above the mean in that support. This results in more diversity in attitudinal patterns at the Population IV level than existed at Population II.

The Federal Republic of Germany and Finland are both high on democratic values support, low on national government support, and high on Civic Interest/Participation. Sweden is similar to these two countries except that the Civic Interest/Participation scores are below rather than above the mean for all countries. These three countries will be grouped and discussed together as Democratic Values Support Countries at Population IV with the variations in civic interest noted.

Of the Population IV students tested, the United States is the lowest on Democratic Values Support, and the highest on Support for the National Government. Pre-university students in the United States also have a relatively high level of interest/participation. Ireland is similar to the United States in pattern of attitude except that Civic Interest/Participation is slightly below the mean for all countries and the other two dimensions somewhat closer to the mean. The Irish and United States data will be presented in a section as exemplifying National Government Support countries.

Finally, there are two countries which fall into neither of these two patterns. In the Netherlands and New Zealand, Support for Democratic Values is at or very slightly below the mean for all countries; Support for the National Government is at or slightly above the mean; Civic Interest/Participation is below the mean for all countries. These students are also characterized by the highest scores on Sense of Political efficacy among the pre-university students tested and by perception of the local government as responsive to the needs of citizens. The pattern of attitudes in these two countries is sufficiently different from the other two patterns to justify their separate discussion.

Attitudinal Patterns in the Federal Republic of Germany, Finland, and Sweden—Democratic Value Support Countries at Population IV

Democratic Values. The high level of Support for Democratic Values in these countries results from high scale scores on all the components of this dimension among West German and Swedish Population IV students and moderately high scores in Finland.

Pre-university students from the Federal Republic of Germany and Sweden were more likely than those in other countries to disagree with the following statements from the Anti-Authoritarianism scale: "hotels are right in refusing to admit people of certain races or nationalities"; "regular elections in our country are unnecessary"; and "so many people vote in a general election that when I grow up, it will not matter much whether I vote or not"; "war is sometimes the only way in which a nation can save its self respect"; "the people in power know best"; and "it is wrong to criticize our government."

Support for women's rights is the strongest among students in Sweden, the Federal Republic of Germany, and Finland (in that order). The gap is quite wide between these three countries and the United States, where equal political rights for women receive the least support. This is very similar to the Population II results previously noted.

Support for National Government and Perceptions of Local Government. With a few exceptions it may therefore be concluded that students in Sweden, the Federal Republic of Germany, and Finland are especially likely to subscribe to high levels of what has been called democratic values though the precise pattern in each country differs somewhat. These are also the countries which are characterized as having relatively low support for the national government. Finnish Population IV students see their national government in a uniformly more negative fashion than do the students in the other countries: it is not an especially popular or trustworthy institution, nor does it very adequately respond to citizens, nor do citizens feel a strong sense of political efficacy. The patterning of scales on this dimension among pre-university students in the other countries is a little less consistent. In the Federal Republic of Germany general positive evaluation of the government is above the mean for all countries while responsiveness and efficacy are below the mean—resulting in a slightly negative averaged z-score. The pattern for Swedish pre-university students is a series of z-scores on the components of Support for the National Government which are all within half a standard deviation of the mean for all countries and are only slightly more negative than positive. Swedish students, however, are less positive in their ratings of the attributes of the local government (town council) than are the Population IV students in any other country.

In summary, patterns of democratic values and support for the national government among pre-university students were quite similar to those of the 14-year-olds. Support for Democratic Values above the mean for all countries accompanied National Government Support which was below the mean for all countries.

Civic Interest/Participation. Among the Population IV students, however, when Support for the National Government fell below the mean for all countries, this was not always accompanied by Civic Interest/Participation at a similar low level (as it had been in Population II). In particular the pre-university students in the Federal Republic of Germany had the highest Civic Interest/Participation scores of any country, and the Finnish students were also moderately high. Among West German students it was Interest in public affairs T.V. and Participation in discussion which contributed to these high rankings; in Finland, Interest in public affairs T.V. was especially high with other components near the mean. In Sweden, Civic activities were reported very infrequently, although T.V. interest and discussion were near the mean for all countries; this resulted in an averaged z below the mean for all countries on Civic Interest/Participation.

An inspection of the discussion participation data (Table 9.6) yields the information that the West German and Finnish pre-university students report participation in discussions of politics, of other nations, and of candidates with friends and with parents more frequently than do the students in any of the other countries. Students in the United States discuss political matters more often with their teachers than do the pre-university students in other countries; West German students rank second in their reports of such discussion, however. (Note: Italy and Israel, where discussion with friends and parents was frequent at Population II, are not included in the Population IV countries. This results in a different context for the z-score comparisons at the older level.) The pre-university student in Finland, is less likely to discuss any aspect of politics with his teacher than is the pre-university student in any of the other countries tested at that level.

Summary and Discussion. In attempting to understand the pattern of civic attitudes among Population IV students in these three nations the factors which were suggested as correlates at the Population II level will be examined. Patriotic observances are considerably less frequent at the pre-university level than they were at age 14. However, countries where pre-university students participate in

245

Table 9.6. *Reported Participation in Discussion—Percentage Reporting Discussion "Once a Week or More Often" by Country (Population IV)*

	With friends			With parents			With teachers			Sum of weights—Respondents
	Politics	Other nations	Political candidates	Politics	Other nations	Political candidates	Politics	Other nations	Political candidates	
FRG	52.3	53.6	28.0	42.4	37.2	22.1	41.9	36.2	12.9	1 188
Finland	39.3	46.6	30.5	31.8	32.7	27.0	7.2	9.7	3.2	2 357
Ireland	21.6	15.7	9.2	26.7	17.3	13.9	18.1	18.4	4.2	802
Netherlands	25.2	32.0	12.2	26.9	33.1	14.9	20.4	27.4	11.7	1 315
New Zealand	29.3	28.5	13.1	30.4	28.8	15.5	12.8	18.0	4.1	1 696
Sweden	32.8	40.8	19.8	26.2	31.0	16.5	14.0	19.6	5.3	1 867
United States	33.8	17.7	14.1	30.8	17.0	16.1	60.0	42.1	28.0	3 045

patriotic rituals at Population IV are more likely to have instilled positive feeling for the nation and less likely to have been effective in implanting democratic values.

There is no systematic difference between the reports of students in the Federal Republic of Germany, Finland, and Sweden and the reports of students in the other nations concerning other classroom practices (teachers' giving students opportunities to express opinions and teachers' treating students equitably). It is apparent, however, that the civic education system in Finland encourages the smallest amount of participation in the classroom. (These countries represent a range of selectivity at Population IV—from nine percent of the age cohort still in school in the Federal Republic of Germany to 45 percent still in school in Sweden.)

The national system differences for which concrete data exist at the country level are most striking with respect to women's rights. Those countries (Federal Republic of Germany, Sweden, and Finland) in which students give women's rights the most enthusiastic support are also the countries which have the largest proportion of females elected to the legislature; they are also more likely to have a woman serving in a high judicial post or as a cabinet member (U.N. Secretary General's Report on the Political Rights of Women, 1968 and 1970). Countries like Finland, where more than

20 % of the members of Parliament are female, clearly present a different image of the political rights and abilities of women than does the United States or New Zealand where less than 5 % of such high offices are filled by women. It is impossible to say, of course, whether adolescent support for women's rights reflects and is the result of the visible presence of women in governmental and political decision making. It may either be that when women are seen performing in high governmental positions they are thought of as deserving equal political rights in general, or it may be that greater support among adults for equal political status for women may be reflected both in the election and appointment of more women to governmental posts and in increased support for women's rights among adolescents.

Attitudinal Patterns in the United States and Ireland—Government Support Countries at Population IV

The second grouping of countries includes the United States and Ireland. New Zealand also shows some similarity to this pattern (especially in high Support for the National Government) but is also like the Netherlands, with which it will be compared later in detail. Pre-university students in Ireland and the United States are below the mean for all countries on Support for Democratic Values and above the mean for all countries on Support for the National Government. Although this represents the major outline of their national attitudinal profiles, Ireland was below and the United States above the mean for all countries on Civic Interest/Participation.

The relatively low Democratic Values support is due in the United States and Ireland to scores below the mean for all countries on all components of that dimension—Anti-Authoritarianism, Tolerance and civil liberties, Support for women's rights, and Support for equality. These pre-university students were likely to agree with items such as the following from the Anti-Authoritarianism scale: "people of certain races or religions should be kept out of important positions in our nation" and "war is sometimes the only way a nation can save its self-respect" and unlikely to agree that "talking things over with another nation is better than fighting."

The minimal amount of Support for women's rights—lowest among Population IV students in the United States and next to lowest in New Zealand—has already been commented upon as well as related to the relatively small proportion of women in public life in

Table 9.7. *Percentage of Students Who Would Grant Differing Rights and Freedoms to Selected Social Groups by Country (Population IV)*

	Religious leaders			Colored people			Communists			Leaders of big business			Tramps		
	More	Same	Fewer	More	Same	Fewer	More	Same	Fewer	More	Same	Fewer	More	Same	Fewer
FRG	3.0	94.0	3.0	1.0	95.5	3.5	1.7	89.3	9.0	2.7	92.5	4.8			
Finland	1.9	95.1	3.1	0.4	96.1	3.5	1.1	87.1	11.8	3.6	92.9	3.5	1.3	92.6	6.0
Ireland	15.8	82.2	2.0	0.4	95.5	4.0	0.3	66.9	32.8	4.0	92.8	3.2	1.7	91.9	6.4
Netherlands	3.6	94.3	2.1	0.6	96.4	3.0	0.7	89.2	10.1	4.1	93.0	2.9	0.9	97.2	11.9
New Zealand	3.1	95.1	1.7	0.5	96.6	3.0	0.4	76.0	23.6	1.7	96.8	1.5	0.8	93.1	6.1
Sweden	0.5	96.6	2.9	0.4	86.3	13.3	0.4	88.4	11.2	1.8	95.7	2.6	1.5	92.2	6.2
United States	3.9	94.4	1.7	1.1	93.4	5.5	1.2	47.1	51.7	3.1	94.8	2.0	1.1	86.5	12.4

	Military leaders			People with anti-mother country views			Doctors			Sum of weights
	More	Same	Fewer	More	Same	Fewer	More	Same	Fewer	
FRG	2.3	92.4	11.3							1 188
Finland	6.4	87.6	5.7	0.2	80.2	19.7	8.3	91.2	0.5	2 357
Ireland	14.2	83.7	2.1	1.2	71.9	26.9	17.1	82.4	0.6	802
Netherlands	5.3	89.5	5.2	0.8	84.2	15.0	11.8	87.0	1.2	1 315
New Zealand	5.6	92.1	2.2	0.6	81.5	17.9	8.2	91.4	0.4	1 696
Sweden	3.4	90.1	6.5	0.9	92.6	6.4	6.2	93.0	0.8	1 867
United States	10.9	86.2	2.9	1.1	65.2	33.7	7.8	91.8	0.9	3 045

Notes: The Federal Republic of Germany is omitted from this table for some items because an omission of one item from their questionnaire led to realignment of subsequent columns. Support for equality score has been corrected for this omission.

those nations. These students would not deprive women of the right to vote, but many fewer of them wish to accord women other rights equal to men or full participation in political life including holding political office.

The relatively low Support for equality scores among the Population IV students in Ireland and the United States may be attributed to the prescription by these students of fewer rights for "Communists" and "persons with anti-Mother country views" and somewhat enhanced rights for military leaders (see Table 9.7). Again, as at Population II, the countries sharing this pattern perceived a state which must protect itself from threat.

In fact, in many respects the data on Democratic Values from the United States for pre-university students appear to be further intensifications of patterns of civic attitudes seen at the 14-year-old level. The same is true for National Government Support, where the students in the United States have the most positive scores (especially on Evaluation and Responsiveness). Those scores in Ireland are in the same positive direction but are more moderate. The high National government evaluations in the United States and Ireland (and also on many items in the Federal Republic of Germany where this sub-dimension was also high) are accounted for by perceptions of the national government as more "friendly," "warm-hearted," "popular," and "caring more about me and my family."

Popularity of the national government and perceptions of relatively less conflict in the system are apt characterizations of the opinions of pre-university students in the United States and Ireland (and in some cases New Zealand). Students in these countries are more likely than others to say that newspapers and Parliament (Congress) agree, that middle and working class people agree, that radio or T.V. commentators and Parliament (Congress) agree, and that poor people and well-to-do people agree about political matters. Population IV students in the United States and New Zealand (but not in Ireland) also are more likely to believe that people of different religions agree on such matters. These are also countries where the leader of the government—the Prime Minister or President—is seen as having an especially important role in determining laws.

In some cases these students are accurately reporting on social and political conditions which have ramifications throughout the pattern of civic attitudes displayed. Some real national differences in social and political realities are reflected both in normative statements (who should have equal rights) and concrete beliefs (who has an influence on laws). To give some examples, religious leaders are important and visible in Ireland; students know this and in some cases will believe that they should have extra rights or privileges. The visibility of women holding political roles which may increase support for women's rights is also relevant. National differences like this are in some respects self-perpetuating in a system reflecting past political history, current national conditions, Civic Education practices, and adult public opinion which children learn about as they read the newspaper or talk with their parents. This also provides a cumulative attitudinal base; future political events may have an impact on this base but its fundamental character is not likely to be drastically changed by alterations in Civic Educational practices independent of alterations in political structure, critical political events, or adult public opinion.

Even the student responses give a clue to this. Given a list of nine possible sources of influence upon their impressions of political life, more students chose mass media presentations—televised discussions or seeing an actual event on television—than any other source. Unlike many other subject areas, the content of political socialization is constantly changing, reacting to events in the world outside the school.

The IEA questionnaire contained relatively few items in the area of political behavior. This is due in part to the age of the respondents and in part to the sensitive nature of questions dealing with voting, party preference, and the like in some of the nations where IEA wished to test. It was ascertained, however, that Civic Interest/ Participation was very high among pre-university students in the United States. This was due especially to moderately high frequency of reported discussion with parents and friends and more such activity with teachers than was reported by the students in any other country. Population IV students in the United States also reported considerably participation in other civic activities. Irish students ranked slightly below the mean for all countries on the Civic Interest/Participation dimension primarily due to less frequent reports of engagement in discussion of political issues.

The critical nature of the active dimension of political involvement leads to the final comparison of country differences at Population IV which in itself reflects complexity in the organization of political attitudes and interest among pre-university students.

Some of the characteristics of the pre-university students in these two nations have been described when the Values Support Countries and the National Government Support Countries were considered. Both New Zealand and the Netherlands have scores on the Support for Democratic Values dimension which are at or slightly below the mean for all countries; scores on the Support for National Government dimension are quite high in New Zealand and about at the country mean in the Netherlands; these countries have the two lowest scores on Civic Interest/Participation at Population IV.

The pattern of the component scales in both countries includes scores slightly below the mean on Anti-Authoritarianism, a little further below the mean on Support for women's rights, and slightly above the mean on Support for equality. Even the particular groups to be given enhanced or lessened rights were somewhat similar in these two countries.

It is on the scales which comprise the Support for the National Government dimension (and the ratings of local government on similar scales) that these countries seem most alike and most differentiated from the other nations. General evaluation of the national government is low in both. However, the Sense of Political efficacy in New Zealand is the highest of all the Population IV nations; the Netherlands has the second highest score on this scale. These scores reflect strong disagreement with statements like these: "there are some big powerful men in the government who are running the whole country, and they do not care about the opinions of ordinary people," "the government does not try to understand ordinary people, most politicians are too selfish to care about ordinary people" and strong agreement that "the government is doing its best to find out what ordinary people want." These items inquire about an extension of one's perception of the government, not an extension of one's perceptions of oneself as an active citizen. There is also some evidence that the high sense of governmental responsiveness among students in these countries is a reflection of their view of the local government (town council) as especially responsive to citizens. The Population IV students in New Zealand and the Netherlands (and also in Ireland) were especially likely to rate the local council high on "pays attention to complaints," "can have their decisions changed by ordinary people," and "run by people just like ourselves." In these countries the sense of political responsiveness may be rooted in the perception of the local rather than the national level of government.

Summary of Population IV Patterns
There is considerable complexity in the attitudinal structure of the older students, particularly with respect to their civic interest and participation. However, the general continuity of the between-country differences from the age of 10 to the end of secondary school is striking. Countries which succeed in fostering strong attachment to the national government are less successful in fostering a strong level of support for democratic values, and vice versa. The civic attitudes of students in each of the countries tested bear the imprint of the real political world—past and present. The comments made about the influence of various classroom practices on the attitudes of 14-year-olds apply almost without exception at the pre-university level.

No discussion of political attitude development can be complete, however, without a consideration of the agents of socialization—parents, peers, teachers, mass media and so forth. It is not possible to speak of fully separable or completely independent sources of socialization in the family, school or peers. In some countries it seems that these agents have a relatively congruent effect; in other countries their interaction is very complex. Political and social reality has an impact upon attitudes and beliefs mediated through schools in their organization and curricular statements, through teachers in their practices with both intended and unintended effects, through parents in the child's accurate or inaccurate perception of their political leanings, through peer groups where politics is of some concern, through the student's background of factual information and misinformation. The process is complex for any given child or country, and a survey such as this can only indicate the important and patterned differences which must be further explored and explained with studies using more fine-grained methods.

CONCLUSIONS

In this chapter and the previous one several conclusions have been drawn. First, the outcomes of Civic Education are multidimensional; there is, in other words, not a single good-citizen type which is a product of any of the Civic Education systems surveyed. However, when one analyzes scale interrelations at the between-student level, the three major dimensions of civic attitudes seem to be the same in all the countries tested—Support for Democratic Values, Support for the National Government, and Civic Interest/Participation. Second, the questionnaire used gives meaningful and reliable group measures of these factors. Third, if one looks at between-country differences in the data related to these three dimensions, one would conclude that meaningful differences exist even when 10-year-olds are compared, that they reflect aspects of the real political world even more clearly among 14-year-olds, and that they exhibit additional complexity at the pre-university level. It is, in fact, possible to classify countries into two major patterns—one including countries where Support for Democratic Values is relatively low and Support for the National Government relatively high and the other including countries where Support for Democratic Values is relatively high and National Government Support is low. It may be concluded that the factors of the educational and political systems which contribute to a high level of support for the national government fail to inculcate a high level of support for democratic values.

Because the data at the national level are in some cases incomplete and because there are at most eight nations which could be compared at a given age level, it is not possible to draw more than tentative conclusions concerning causes of these specific attitudinal pattern differences. These tentative conclusions may be further confirmed from the regression analysis of attitudinal outcomes—of Anti-Authoritarianism (a component of Support for Democratic Values) and Participation in discussion (a component of Civic Interest/Participation)—in the next chapter.

It does seem clear from the analysis completed to this point, that as a political animal the 18-, 14-, or 10-year-old student in the United States and Israel is remarkably different from the comparable student in Finland or the Federal Republic of Germany. Some of the particularities of the differences would be heartily endorsed by some teachers and educational specialists in each country as being adaptive to the particular political system. These specialists would be ill-advised, however, to take too much credit for having inculcated the qualities they endorse. Some of the practices which they may credit with positive outcomes may have unintended consequences which are less positive. Particular topics stressed by teachers seem to have relatively little effect upon civic attitudes, at least when one is considering an entire country as the

253

unit of analysis. Visible and relatively unchanging aspects of the political system and the political culture seem to exert considerable influence.

The recommendations that can be made from these analyses of between-country differences do not include the homogenization of Civic Education programs in the various nations or the construction of a program in country X that will make its attitudinal profile correspond to that of country Y. This would probably be impossible as well as undesirable. Rather, Civic Education decision-makers should become more sensitive to the variety of influences upon civic attitudes, the way they interact with each other, and the unintended as well as the intended consequences of practices. Materials and programs should be provided to allow students to interpret future events, to feel comfortable in discussing political choices with teachers, to be able to recognize creative political conflict, to have free access to the information needed to make political decisions, and to be motivated to act in politics.

Chapter 10

Predictors of Between-Student Differences in Civic Attitudes

The profiles summarizing the mean level on each attitudinal dimension presented in the previous chapter reflect the average response of students in each country to a given set of attitudinal statements. In every country there is variation or variance around these means. For example, although the average level of Support for women's rights is low in the United States, there are some students in the United States who support these rights strongly. And although students in the Federal Republic of Germany tend to have high Anti-Authoritarianism scores, there are also students there who have low scores on this scale. The primary purpose of this chapter's analysis of regressions on the attitudinal variables is to ascertain which independent or predictor variables, particularly home and school factors, are related to variations in students' attitudes within a given country.

There are three major attitudinal factors of the outcomes of Civic Education—Support for Democratic Values, Support for the National Government, and Civic Interest/Participation (see Chapter 8). It was possible in chapter 9 to compare the profiles of countries on these attitudinal outcomes and to identify certain characteristics of the countries which accompanied relatively high or relatively low country mean scores on these variables. These were characteristics such as participation in Patriotic rituals (which tended to be high in countries with low scores on support for democratic values), percentage of women holding high political office (which tended to be high in countries where Support for women's rights was high), and traditional classroom approaches to Civic Education (which tended to be high in some countries with low Support for Democratic Values).

There are several other ways to examine the relationships between variables. In the IEA there were three possible levels at which to operate: aggregation to the country level to examine between-country differences (see Chapter 9), aggregation to the school level (used for school and teacher independent variables in this chapter) and unaggregated student responses. In this chapter between-student differences within countries are analysed utilizing as predictors both school and teacher variables aggregated to the school level. It is also possible to distinguish between two stages of this analysis—a zero-order correlational analysis which takes the simple relationship between variables ignoring the influence of possibly confounding variables, and multiple regression, which orders the predictor variables and partials out the effect of some in order to examine the independent effects of others.

The attitudinal regression analysis presented in this chapter is intended to answer several questions:

1. How much between-student variance in the attitudinal outcomes can be predicted in comparison to prediction of the cognitive outcomes of Civic Education?

2. What is the relative importance of home and school variables in predicting attitudinal outcomes in students? Previous speculation and some research suggests that home factors, generally thought to be important in a variety of types of affective school outcomes, ought also to be preponderant in explaining between-student differences in the attitudinal outcomes of Civic Education.

3. Are the same learning conditions within school important in fostering both cognitive and affective achievement in civics? Would a change in school policy or curriculum which might be expected to increase civics knowledge take place at the expense of desirable attitudes?

4. Are the same independent variables which distinguish countries with different attitudinal and interest patterns in the between-country analysis also related to between-student differences within countries?

The regression analysis to predict attitudinal outcomes can be compared closely to the regression analysis of the cognitive outcomes reported in Chapter 6. The attitudinal regressions were performed by a similar method, using the same predictor variables and weighting procedures. The same analogy of height and weight indicated in Chapter 6 is also useful as a guide for the analysis in this chapter.

After a brief discussion of the choice of predictor variables and the dependent or predicted variables, the description of the results of the attitudinal regressions will be presented in three parts. First, a description of the predictability of civic attitudinal and interest out-comes will be given (corresponding to question 1 above). Second, the power of different blocks or combinations of variables will be examined (question 2). Finally questions 3 and 4 will be addressed by examining the specific variables representing home and school characteristics which add significantly to the prediction of attitudes and interest/participation.

From the beginning of the project the intention was to do a com-plete set of regressions to predict between-student variance in the Civics Education cognitive score. This was the dependent variable which most closely corresponded to the IEA analysis in other sub-ject areas (e.g., total achievement in Science). The affective variables to be included for regression analysis, in contrast, had to be selected from a large number of promising possibilities. The aim was to choose attitudinal outcomes of general importance. For example, given the choice between support for an important democratic value and an idealized perception of the citizen's role the former would be chosen. To put it another way, there was some tendency to favor for further analysis attitudinal variables reflecting major *factors* of Civic Education outcomes. At the time when the outcome variables had to be chosen, the factor analysis reported in Chapter 8 had not yet been completed. But fortunately the procedure which was em-ployed led to the choice of two variables for regression analysis— Anti-Authoritarianism and Participation in Political Discussion— which in fact were found to load on two different factors when that analysis had been completed.

The following procedure was used to choose the two attitudinal outcome variables and a manageable number of specific predictor variables from the hundreds of student, school and teacher characteristics which had been gathered. First, the symmetrical zero-order correlation matrices (approximately 60×60) were pro-duced for each country and population on the major outcomes being considered, plus other important variables available from students. Examination of these matrices and the scale reliabilities of the at-titudinal measures narrowed the field of candidates for the depend-ent attitudinal variables to nine.

These nine outcomes were studied in relation to some 160 pre-dictors (including student variables, teacher variables aggregated to the school level, and school variables). Each of the correlations be-tween the nine outcomes and the 160 predictors was "scrubbed;" that is, a family-background composite of Father's occupation,

Father's education, Mother's education and Number of books in the home was partialled out. What was left was the relationship between the 160 predictors and each of the nine outcomes, controlling for socio-economic background. With this information it was possible to pick two attitudinal criteria, largely uncorrelated with one another, both of which showed a promising pattern of relationships with the independent variables and to choose the approximately 40 school, teacher and student characteristics which were to be included as predictors.

One attitudinal outcome selected was Anti-Authoritarianism, a scale based on student disagreement with items like the following: "People should not criticize the government, it only interrupts the government's work," and agreement with "Talking things over with another nation is better than fighting." In the countries studied this scale represents one objective of the civics curriculum, and in the factor analysis of attitudinal outcomes it loaded on Support for Democratic Values. The other scale selected, Participation in political discussion, was less ideological in character. This scale, which measured the frequency of discussion of political or international issues with friends, parents, and teachers, loaded on the Civic Interest/Participation factor.

In order to allow for as much comparability as possible, IEA had developed a standard plan for regression analysis which is described in greater detail in Chapter 6. The predictors are grouped in blocks. One block consists of the attributes which the student brings to school: a Home Background composite (occupation and education of both parents, number of books in the home), Use of a Dictionary in the home, Size of Family, and the Age and Sex of the student. The second block is made up of only two variables, the Type of school and the Type of program (or track) in which the student was enrolled. As such it is intended as a proxy for the student's previous academic success. The third block contains the specific attributes of the schools and teachers which are expected to have some influence on the outcomes. In the Civic Education regressions (both cognitive and attitudinal) this block includes variables such as the following: the Grade in which social studies instruction is begun in school, Number of hours teachers prepare, Frequency of use of printed drills, Amount of teachers' training in Civic Education and related subjects, Teachers' acceptance of in-class discussion of issues (all aggreated to the school level), students' reports of the Encouragement of independence of opinion in the classroom, and students' report of Stress on patriotic rituals in the classroom. Block 3, the Learning conditions block, was to be compared with the home in explaining variations in attitude. A fourth (Kindred) block consists of additional questionnaire variables, including student aspirations, interests, and activities. To be included in the Learning conditions block or the Kindred variables block for regression analysis in civics, a predictor had to be related to one of the outcomes, controlling for Home background, in at least two countries. It also had to be relatively independent of the other predictors in these two blocks.

The standard IEA order for entering the blocks is intended to be a chronological one so that the joint variance among variables is attributed predominantly to early events in the student's life rather than to later ones. Thus, the Home background variables, representing the earliest point, became Block 1. Block 2 was Type of school and Type of program in their role as proxies for earlier achievement in school. Learning conditions (block 3), which represent the student's most recent experience, was entered third.

At this point the chronological ordering breaks down and the additional or Kindred variables (Block 4) entered, to see if they account for additional variance. Likewise, a vocabulary test score (Word Knowledge), which can be seen either as a measure of intelligence or of general school achievement, was entered as Block 5. Then, in a final attempt to add to the prediction, the Civic Education Cognitive total score was entered as Block 6 in both attitudinal regressions.

THE OVERALL PREDICTABILITY OF ANTI-AUTHORITARIANISM AND PARTICIPATION IN POLITICAL DISCUSSION AT POPULATIONS II AND IV

Tables 10.1 and 10.2 report for each population the total percentage of between-student variance in Anti-Authoritarianism explained by Blocks 1 through 6. The increase in R^2 (the multiple correlation) for each block is calculated following its entry into the regression given the entry of all preceding blocks.

The total percentage of variance accounted for by Blocks 1 through 6 is less in all countries for the attitudinal variable and the participation variable than for the Civic Education cognitive total (see Table 6.3). In the discussion which follows the range of variance

Table 10.1. *Partitioning of Variance Accounted for in the Regression of Anti-Authoritarianism on Six Blocks of Variables*

	Population	Block 1		2	3	4	5	6	Total
		Home background (%)	Age and sex (%)	Type/school Type/progr. (%)	Learning conditions (%)	Kindred variables (%)	Word knowledge (%)	Civics cognitive (%)	
FRG	II	10.5	1.0	1.9	11.4	8.0	3.7	3.7	40.2
	IV	–	0.1	–	11.1	6.7	–	1.3	19.2
Finland	II	9.4	2.0	6.5	5.3	8.0	4.1	5.6	40.9
	IV	0.1	0.1	0.2	1.8	9.1	0.7	3.1	15.1
Ireland	II	14.5	1.8	1.0	8.3	3.6	3.9	8.7	41.8
	IV	1.6	–	–	8.3	3.5	3.3	1.6	18.3
Israel	II	12.1	1.6	1.0	5.6	10.1	4.0	4.0	38.4
Italy	II	5.3	–	4.7	6.9	8.1	5.6	5.6	36.2
Netherlands	II	6.4	1.0	8.6	5.5	4.8	1.3	5.1	32.7
	IV	0.3	0.8	–	4.5	6.7	2.1	1.6	16.0
New Zealand	II	5.9	3.9	4.3	6.2	2.4	2.5	3.3	28.5
	IV	1.1	4.0	0.7	4.6	4.5	1.0	0.3	16.2
Sweden	IV	2.5	3.4	1.3	11.9	5.8	1.6	0.3	26.8
United States	II	10.6	3.3	3.2	3.8	6.3	4.3	3.9	35.4
	IV	5.8	3.5	3.4	3.5	6.1	3.0	3.8	29.1

Table 10.2. *Partitioning of Variance Accounted for in the Regression of Participation in Political Discussion on Six Blocks of Variables*

		Block								
		1		2	3	4	5	6		
	Popula-tion	Home background (%)	Age and sex (%)	Type/school Type/progr. (%)	Learning conditions (%)	Kindred variables (%)	Word knowledge (%)	Civics cognitive knowledge (%)	Total	
FRG	II	3.1	–	0.2	12.0	17.6	–	–	32.9	
	IV	2.3	1.4	0.6	3.7	23.4	–	–		31.4
Finland	II	2.3	0.5	0.2	13.0	19.6	0.1	0.1	35.8	
	IV	2.3	4.4	–	2.1	26.2	0.1	0.5		35.6
Ireland	II	3.9	–	0.9	1.1	18.8	–	0.4	25.1	
	IV	2.5	–	–	6.6	19.6	–	–		28.7
Italy	II	2.3	3.9	–	7.4	13.6	0.2	–	27.4	
Netherlands	II	1.2	0.4	–	9.6	17.2	–	–	28.4	
	IV	2.0	0.8	0.3	6.7	20.7	0.2	0.3		31.0
New Zealand	II	2.5	0.3	0.4	7.1	16.0	0.1	0.1	26.5	
	IV	1.8	1.1	1.3	4.9	23.6	0.1	1.1		33.9
Sweden	IV	5.0	0.3	2.3	3.3	23.0	0.7	0.4		35.0
United States	II	4.5	0.9	0.2	7.9	19.7	0.2	0.2	33.6	
	IV	4.0	1.2	0.9	3.0	18.5	–	–		27.6

accounted for and the medians are computed without considering Israel. All of the Block 3 teacher variables were missing in that country, making comparisons impossible. The range in total amount of variance in Anti-Authoritarianism accounted for at Population II was from 28.5 % in New Zealand to 41.8 % in Ireland. Ireland was also the country in which the largest proportion of variance in Civic Education cognitive achievement was accounted for but it was a considerably larger proportion (62.2 %). At Population IV the percentage of variance in Anti-Authoritarianism accounted for by all blocks was still smaller, ranging from 15.1 % in Finland to 29.1 % in the United States. In contrast, 56.7 % of the variance in Civic Education cognitive achievement was predictable in the United States at Population IV.

In the regression analysis for predicting Participation in Political Discussion at Population II, smaller percentages of variance were accounted for by Blocks 1 through 6 than for Anti-Authoritarianism. Among the 14-year-olds the proportion ranges from 25.1 % in Ireland to 35.8 % in Finland. Cognitive Civic Education outcomes are more predictable among these early adolescents than attitudinal Civic Education outcomes, which in turn are more predictable than interest in civic participation.

A slightly different pattern obtained at the pre-university level. In the majority of countries there was only a slight decline in the total variance in Participation in Discussion accounted for between Population II and IV (not nearly the magnitude of the decline in variance on prediction of Anti-Authoritarianism). At Population IV the proportion of variance in Participation in Political Discussion explainable by Blocks 1 through 6 ranges from 27.6 % in the United States to 35.6 % in Finland. In all countries where pre-university students were tested, with the exception of the United States, the percentage of variance in Participation in Political Discussion accounted for was higher than for Anti-Authoritarianism. Cognitive Civic Education outcomes are more predictable among late adolescents than interest in civic participation, which in turn is more predictable than an attitudinal outcome (Anti-Authoritarianism). This is further evidence that civic participation is more salient to older than to younger adolescents (see also Chapter 9).

THE CONTRIBUTION OF BLOCK 1 (HOME BACKGROUND) TO THE PREDICTION OF ANTI-AUTHORITARIANISM AND PARTICIPATION IN DISCUSSION AT POPULATIONS II AND IV

The percentage of variance accounted for specifically by the characteristics the student brings to school (limited in the study to indices of family socio-economic status, Age, and Sex) was lower for Anti-Authoritarianism than for cognitive Civic Education at Population II. The Block 1 figures for this attitudinal variable ranged from 5.3 % in Italy to 16.3 % in Ireland, with a median of 11.4 % (see Table 10.3). This may be compared with a maximum of 20.4 % for cognitive Civic Education accounted for by Home background at Population II in the United States.

At Population IV the influence of Block 1 variables upon Anti-Authoritarianism was very slight, ranging from 0.1 % in the Federal Republic of Germany to 9.3 % in the United States, with a median of 1.6 % (see Table 10.4). Generally in more selective school systems (e.g. Federal Republic of Germany) less variance was accounted for by these socio-economic status variables.

The proportion of variance in Participation in Political Discussion which may be attributed to Home background, Age and Sex was quite small at Population II—a median of 3.1 % with a maximum of 6.2 % in Italy and a minimum of 1.6 % in the Netherlands (Table 10.5). Italy was the country which was somewhat unique in this respect, showing a contribution of Home background, Age and Sex which was stronger for predicting Discussion Participation than it was for predicting Anti-Authoritarianism.

At Population IV figures for the contribution of Block I variables to Participation in Discussion are generally low. The variance attributable ranges from 2.8 % in the Netherlands to 6.7 % in Finland with a median of 3.7 %. At both Population II and IV Home background, Age and Sex are less important predictors for the attitudinal outcome and the participation outcome than for the cognitive outcome in civics (compare Tables 10.3 through 10.6 with Table 6.3).

It may be concluded that among 14-year-olds the characteristics which the student brings to school tend to account for relatively small amounts of the variance in Anti-Authoritarianism and for very small amounts of variance in Participation in Political Discussion. Among

Table 10.3. *Incremental Variance by Blocks (Anti-Authoritarianism, Population II)*

	Blocks											
	1		2		3		4		5		6	
	Med.	Dev.	Med.	Dev.	Med.	Dev.	Med.	Dev.	Med.	Dev.	Med.	Dev.
FRG		+0.1		−2.4		+5.2		+1.7		−0.2		−1.4
Finland	**11.4**			+2.2		−0.9		+1.7		+0.2		+0.5
Ireland		+4.9		−3.3		+2.1		−2.7	**3.9**			+3.6
Italy		−6.1		+0.4		+0.7		+1.8		+1.7		+0.5
Netherlands		−4.0		+4.3		−0.7		−1.5		−2.6	**5.1**	
New Zealand		−1.6	**4.3**		**6.2**			−3.9		−1.4		−1.8
United States		+2.5		−1.1		−2.4	**6.3**			+0.4		−1.2

Table 10.4. *Incremental Variance by Blocks (Anti-Authoritarianism, Population IV)*

	Blocks											
	1		2		3		4		5		6	
	Med.	Dev.	Med.	Dev.	Med.	Dev.	Med.	Dev.	Med.	Dev.	Med.	Dev.
FRG		−1.5		−0.2		+6.5		+0.6		−1.6		−0.5
Finland		−1.4	**0.2**			−2.8		+3.0		−0.9		+1.5
Ireland	**1.6**			−0.2		+3.7		−2.6		+1.7	**1.6**	
Netherlands		−0.5		−0.2		−0.1		+0.6		+0.5	**1.6**	
New Zealand		+3.5		+0.5	**4.6**			−1.6		−0.6		−1.5
Sweden		+4.3		+1.1		+7.3		−0.3	**1.6**			−1.3
United States		+7.7		+3.2		−1.1	**6.1**			+1.4		+2.9

pre-university students these factors account for very small amounts of variance in both attitude and participation. Although there are some variations by country, these tend not to be very systematic except for the lessened importance of Home background (presumably due to lessened variation in social status) among the students still enrolled at the pre-university level in selective school systems. These are important comparisons because of interest in assessing the general potency of Home background, Age, and Sex as indices of the preconditions of learning. It is clear that variations in democratic values and civic discussion participation are not

Table 10.5. *Incremental Variance by Blocks (Participation in Political Discussion, Population II)*

	1 Med.	1 Dev.	2 Med.	2 Dev.	3 Med.	3 Dev.	4 Med.	4 Dev.	5 Med.	5 Dev.	6 Med.	6 Dev.
RG	**3.1**		**0.2**		+4.1		**17.6**		−0.1		−0.1	
Finland		−0.3		**0.2**		+5.1		+3.0		**0.1**		**0.1**
Ireland		+0.8		+0.7		−6.8		+1.2		−0.1		+0.3
Italy		+3.1		−0.2		−0.5		−4.0		+0.1		−0.1
Netherlands		−1.5		−0.2		+1.7		−0.4		−0.1		−0.1
New Zealand		−0.3		+0.2		−0.8		−1.6		**0.1**		**0.1**
United States		+2.3		**0.2**		**7.9**		+2.1		+0.1		+0.1

Table 10.6. *Incremental Variance by Blocks (Participation in Political Discussion, Population IV)*

	1 Med.	1 Dev.	2 Med.	2 Dev.	3 Med.	3 Dev.	4 Med.	4 Dev.	5 Med.	5 Dev.	6 Med.	6 Dev.
RG	**3.7**		**0.6**		**3.7**		+0.4		−0.1		−0.4	
Finland		+3.0		−0.6		−1.6		+3.2		**0.1**		+0.1
Ireland		−1.2		−0.6		+2.9		−3.4		−0.1		−0.4
Netherlands		−0.9		−0.3		+3.0		−2.3		+0.1		−0.1
New Zealand		−0.8		+0.7		+1.2		+0.6		**0.1**		+0.7
Sweden		+1.6		+1.7		−0.4		**23.0**		+0.6		**0.4**
United States		+1.5		+0.3		−0.7		−4.5		−0.1		−0.4

primarily determined by the characteristics the student brings to school from home or by characteristics such as age or sex (the latter, of course, has a learned role associated with it). In fact, the child's achievement of cognitive civic objectives is more dependent upon these home factors than are attitudinal and participation objectives! This demonstrates on a cross-national basis that the parental socio-economic differences which are often associated with partisan political attitudes are only weakly related to Support for Democratic Values or to Participation in Political Discussion.

A school which has as its objective to teach cognitive material about civics to students may be handicapped somewhat if they come from working class homes. The school will be somewhat less handicapped by this background in attempting to inculcate democratic values or encourage participation in political discussion (and other types of active participation).

THE CONTRIBUTIONS OF SCHOOL VARIABLES (BLOCKS 2 AND 3) TO THE PREDICTION OF ANTI-AUTHORITARIANISM AND PARTICIPATION IN POLITICAL DISCUSSION AT POPULATIONS II AND IV

There are two blocks of variables representing school inputs to the development of civic attitudes and participation. In Block 2 the Type of school (obtained from the stratification categories criterion scored) and the Type of program in which the students are enrolled are included. They may be thought of either as measures of the quality of the students' previous schooling or as general indices of the quality of schooling currently being received. Block 3 includes many specific Learning conditions each of which may be expected to have a small but appreciable effect on student learning and the acquisition of attitudes.

Type of school/Type of program accounted for 1 % of the variance in Anti-Authoritarianism in Ireland and 8.6 % of the variance in the Netherlands (with a median of 4.3 %) at Population II (see Tables 10.1 and 10.3). The more specific learning conditions in Block 3 accounted for about 3.8 % in the United States and 11.4 % of the variance in the Federal Republic of Germany (median of 6.2 %). With the exception of the United States these are all lower than the comparable percentages of variance in cognitive Civic Education accounted for by Blocks 2 and 3. The effect which specific learning conditions have on civic educational outcomes in the United States was very small, and even smaller for cognitive than for attitudinal outcomes.

Among pre-university students, Block 2 becomes of minimal importance accounting for a median of 0.2 % of the variance in Anti-Authoritarianism. In contrast to Home factors which are less important in the United States, Block 2 reached its high of 3.4 % in that country. The specific learning conditions in Block 3, on the other hand, still made some small contribution at Population IV with a median of 4.6 %, ranging from 1.8 % in Finland to 11.9 % in Sweden (Tables 10.1 and 10.4).

The influence of Learning conditions and Type of school and program upon Participation in political discussion showed a very mixed pattern. At Population II and Population IV the percentage of variance accounted for by Type of school (Block 2) is negligible (less than 1 % in every country except Sweden). Specific Learning conditions, on the other hand, influence participation in discussion in some countries. At Population II the median variance accounted for is 7.9 % with a range of 1.1 % in Ireland to 13.0 % in Finland (Tables 10.2 and 10.5). At Population IV the median was 3.7 % with a range from 2.1 % in Finland to 6.7 % in the Netherlands (Tables 10.2 and 10.6). At Population II the school (Blocks 2 and 3) accounted for more variance in Participation in Discussion than did the Home background block in every country except Ireland. This was in spite of the fact that Home background variables were entered first in the regression.

Within the relatively small amount of variance which was predictable in Anti-Authoritarianism and Participation in Political Discussion, Type of school or program and specific Learning conditions account for slightly more than do Home background factors. The influence of specific variables and the masking effect which the Type of school block may have exerted on some relationships will be more closely examined in conjunction with the tables to be presented in a subsequent section. The analysis indicated that it would be inaccurate to dismiss the influence of school variables on civic attitudes—though in most countries it appears less pronounced than the influence upon cognitive outcomes. Even with the removal of home background factors, specific characteristics of the school do seem to influence the student's acquisition of democratic values. However, school variables have a very minimal effect upon civic interest and participation.

THE CONTRIBUTION OF KINDRED VARIABLES (BLOCK 4) TO THE PREDICTION OF ANTI-AUTHORITARIANISM AND PARTICIPATION IN POLITICAL DISCUSSION AT POPULATIONS II AND IV

Block 4 was the most diverse, including student reports of activities both political and non-political, information about the home environment for learning, educational expectations, and the like.

The median contribution of this block to predicting Anti-Authoritarianism at Population II was 6.3 %, ranging from 3.6 % in Ireland to 8.1 % in Italy (Tables 10.1 and 10.3). The comparable figures at Population IV were a median of 6.1 % with a range from 3.5 % in Ireland to 9.1 % in Finland (Tables 10.1 and 10.4). Its predictive power in Population II and Population IV was quite similar.

The median contribution of Block 4 variables to explaining between student differences in Participation in Political Discussion at Population II was 17.6 % with a range from 13.6 % in Italy to 19.7 % in the United States (Tables 10.2 and 10.5). The median contribution at Population IV was 23 % with a range from 18.5 % in the United States to 26.2 % in Finland (Tables 10.2 and 10.6). This was the only block of variables which tended to have higher predictive power in most countries among pre-university students than among 14-year-olds. One possible conclusion is that this mixed set of social experiences, expectations, and other kinds of out-of-school civic interests and activities is much more influential for students nearing the end of secondary school than it is for students earlier in their school careers. This was not surprising, given the evidence of many other studies indicating the importance of peer groups in late adolescence. However, interpretations of the meaning of Block 4 must be tempered by the consideration that several variables in this Block may be manifestations of the same underlying factor as the predicted variable (see Chapter 8).

THE CONTRIBUTION OF WORD KNOWLEDGE (BLOCK 5)
TO PREDICTION OF ANTI-AUTHORITARIANISM AND
PARTICIPATION IN POLITICAL DISCUSSION
AT POPULATIONS II AND IV

A general test of Word Knowledge (synonyms and antonyms) forms the single variable in this block. Its median predictive power for Anti-Authoritarianism at Population II is 3.9 % and at Population IV is 1.6 % (Tables 10.1, 10.3 and 10.4). Variation around these figures was relatively minimal. Its median predictive power for Participation in Political Discussion was negligible, never reaching 1 % in any country at either level (Tables 10.2, 10.5 and 10.6). The figures showing the relationship between Word Knowledge and attitudinal and participation measures were very small in contrast to the considerable contribution of Word Knowledge to prediction of achievement on the Civic Education cognitive test—median of 10.9 % at Population II.

The general ability, intelligence, and previous achievement of students were of importance in determining their cognitive achievement in Civic Education. This was a much less important factor in the acquisition of civic attitudes and participation norms.

THE CONTRIBUTION OF CIVIC KNOWLEDGE (BLOCK 6) TO THE PREDICTION OF ANTI-AUTHORITARIANISM AND PARTICIPATION AT POPULATIONS II AND IV

Finally, as the last block for both of the non-cognitive regressions, the score on the Civic Education cognitive test was included. At this point all previous sources of variance had been explored—home, school (to the extent it had been measured), kindred variables, and word knowledge. Civic Education knowledge did explain a small amount of the remaining variance in Anti-Authoritarianism (medians 3.9 % and 1.6 % respectively at Population II and IV). The contribution of Civic Education Knowledge to predicting the political participation variable was negligible (less than 1.2 % in all countries at both ages). It is interesting to note that this represented a considerable reduction in the predictive power of Civic Education knowledge, which accounted for somewhat more variance when no other effects were partialed out.

SUMMARY CONCERNING CONTRIBUTIONS OF VARIOUS BLOCKS

The contributions of the various blocks lead to the conclusion once again that there were distinctive types of citizenship which not only form between-country patterns but also were predicted by different blocks of variables. There was some commonality in the determination of cognitive and attitudinal outcomes in civics. Home factors, Age and Sex were of some importance for predicting Anti-Authoritarianism, but not in any sense did these over-determine civics attitudes. School variables (particularly specific Learning conditions) played a role, but again not to the extent that it would be possible to create a clear shift in the attitudes of students by the alteration of any single variable or even any definable small group of variables within the school context. A student of high socio-economic

269

status and good verbal skills may develop democratic values more easily; these characteristics do not seem to be a necessary prerequisite, however. Jennings and Niemi (1974) on the basis of a regression analysis with United States high school students, attributed influence to both home and school factors in determining a wide range of political attitudes, with more importance attributed to the home. Home influences (even including parental attitudes) were measured in their study in considerable detail. They indicate, however, that their estimates of school effects are probably artificially low.

The IEA study which over nine countries sampled school variables considerably more fully than home variables, attributes importance to both socializing agents in influencing attitudes. The precise balance varies according to the particular dependent variable being predicted and the age group of students. In all groups, however, the contribution of Home background variables to explaining variation in attitudes tended to be higher in the United States than in the other countries tested. This reminds us again of the dangers of generalizing too widely about the relative importance of two socialization agents based on data from a single country or from a study which more effectively samples potential influences in one setting than in the other.

Although the patterns of variance prediction for Civic Education cognitive achievement and Anti-Authoritarianism are somewhat similar, they are both different from the determinants of Participation in discussion. For this variable Kindreds such as participation with peers and families in various activities seem (especially at the pre-university level) to be of primary importance (although this requires cautious interpretation). Whatever educational or out-of-school programs may be found to increase civics cognitive ability and support for democratic values may not have the additional effect of increasing political participation. The attitudinal domain and participant norms seem to be influenced by somewhat different aspects of the student's social environment both in and out of school.

SPECIFIC VARIABLES WITHIN BLOCKS AS PREDICTORS OF ANTI-AUTHORITARIANISM AT POPULATIONS II AND IV

The variables which performed consistently in the regressions in two or more countries are listed in Section A of Tables 10.7 and 10.8 for

Populations II and IV respectively; also included here are variables which received the "?" rating for sign reversal between correlation and regression in *one* country if the signs in other countries were consistent and variables with one "−" as long as there were four or more +'s. This represents a change from the treatment in Chapter 6 of "?" and "−" when outnumbered by "+". Section B includes variables which were predominantly positive or negative in two or more countries (the number of signs in one direction—either positive or negative—had to outnumber the sum of signs in the opposite direction plus question marks). Section C includes inconsistent variables (usually with a number of sign reversals); Section D includes variables showing a relationship in only one country.[1]

All of the variables in Block 1 were either consistent or predominantly in one direction in the Population II predictions of Anti-Authoritarianism (Tables 10.7 and 10.8). The Home background cluster (Father's occupation, Father's education, Mother's education, Number of books in the home) was positively related; the higher the socio-economic status the less authoritarian the student in all countries at Population II and in five out of seven countries at Population IV. Girls were less authoritarian than boys in seven out of eight countries at Population II and in five out of seven countries (one sign reversal) at Population IV. Students who reported the use of a dictionary in their homes were less authoritarian in four countries at Population II (relationship in the opposite direction in

---

[1] Some variables were tried, but did not stay in the regressions. They added so little to the prediction that they failed to pass the F test, a statistical test whose purpose is to exclude variables whose contribution was insignificant. In the IEA regressions the F level for entry (F = 2.0) was, however, low enough to allow in variables whose contribution in any one country might be considered likely to result from sampling variation. The hope, in permitting such variables to enter, was to see which variables came through consistently across countries even though the magnitude of their contribution in any one country might be small. Variables, once entered, were seldom removed. The F-level for removal was set at 0.01, low enough so that when a variable was removed in order to protect the regression matrix, the reduction in variance was negligible. A tolerance check prevented the entry of variables whose own variance was more than 80 per cent accounted for by variables already in the regression. In similar fashion, a variable, once in, was removed if more than 99 per cent of its own variance was explained by other variables also in the regression.

As extended discussion of the methodological and substantive issues posed by these regressions can be found in Gilbert F. Peaker, *An Empirical Study of Education in Twenty-One Countries: A Technical Report.* Stockholm: Almqvist & Wiksell International, 1975.

271

Israel) and in three out of seven countries at Population IV (sign reversal in Sweden). The larger the family the less authoritarian the student in four out of eight countries at Population II. This variable was related to Anti-Authoritarianism in the opposite direction in Sweden at the older age level. Age in months (within population) showed a somewhat inconsistent relationship. The particular variables which were related to Anti-Authoritarianism in Block 1 were very similar to those individual variables related to cognitive achievement in Civic Education (cited in Chapter 6). However, the direction of relationship was different for two variables; boys and those from small families are more knowledgeable about civics but are more authoritarian.

Block 2 (Type of school and program) which has a different meaning in different national educational systems, was also very consistent in its relationship to Anti-Authoritarianism. Students in academic schools and programs were less authoritarian, especially at Population II. At Population IV this was still important in Finland, New Zealand, Sweden, and the United States. Some of the lessened importance of this variable among older students may be due to the increased selectivity in some of the systems.

Block 3 variables which were consistent or predominantly in one direction include the following, common to Population II and IV (Tables 10.7 and 10.8):

1. Students who reported that independence of expression of opinion was encouraged by the teacher were less authoritarian (Population II in seven out of eight countries; Population IV in five out of seven countries with the opposite relationship in Finland).

2. Students who reported infrequent participation in Patriotic rituals were less authoritarian in their attitudes (in all countries at both Population II and IV).

3. Students in some schools where teachers emphasize non-Western cultures were less authoritarian (Population II in Finland and the Netherlands; Population IV in Sweden and the United States with the opposite relationship in Ireland among the older students).

4. Students in schools where teachers reported frequent use of printed drill were more authoritarian in the Federal Republic of Germany, Finland, and Ireland at Population II and in the Netherlands and the United States at Population IV, with the opposite relationship in the Netherlands at Population II.

These were the only variables which were consistent or predom-

272

Table 10.7. *Variables Entering Regression by End of Block 4 and Their Signs* (*Civics Anti-Authoritarianism, Population II*)

Variables by block	Source	FRG	Finland	Ireland	Israel	Italy	Netherlands	New Zealand	United States
A. Variables Entering Consistently in Two or More Countries									
Block 1									
Home Background cluster	Q	+	+	+	+	+	+	+	+
Size of Family	Q	+		+		+		+	
Student Sex	Q		+	+	+	+	+	+	+
Block 2									
Type of School	F	+	+	+	+	+	+	?	+
Type of Student Program	Q					+	?	+	+
Block 3									
Independence of Opinion encouraged in Classroom	Q	+		+	+	+	+	+	+
Grade in School	Q	+	+	+	−		+	+	
Patriotic Rituals practiced in Classroom	Q	−	−	−	−	−	−	−	−
Teachers' Specialization	T	+	+		M				+
Teachers' Emphasis on Non-Western Cultures	T		+		M	+			
Block 4									
Reports making Peer Group Decisions by Voting	Q	+	+	+	+	+	+	+	+
Interest in Public Affairs TV	Q	+	+	+	+	+	+	+	+
Hours Pleasure Reading	Q		+	+	+		+	+	+
Expected Education	Q		+	+	+	+	+		+
Participation in Civic Activities	Q	+				+	+		
Urbanization of Community served by School	S				M	C	+		+

Notes: Source: Q=Student questionnaire, T=Teacher questionnaire, S=School questionnaire, F=Sampling frame.

Sign of 0-order correlation and regression coefficient after block 4: +=Both positive, −=Both negative, ?=Differ in sign.

Blanks indicate that variables were tested but failed to enter step-wise regression equation (F=2.0).

Excluded variables: M=No data or too little data collected, C=Insufficient variation.

Table 10.7. *(Cont.)*

Variables by block	Source	FRG	Finland	Ireland	Israel	Italy	Netherlands	New Zealand	United States
B. *Variables Predominantly Positive or Negative in Two or More Countries*									
Block 1									
Use of Dictionary in Home	Q	+	+	+	−				+
Age	Q	+	+	+	−		+		
Block 3									
Stress on Facts in Civics Class	Q		+	−		−		−	+
Teachers' Use of Printed Drill	T	−	−	−	M	+			
Teachers' Preparation for Lessons: Hours per week	T			−	M	+	+		
Block 4									
Propensity to Engage in Adult-like Activities	Q	+	+			+	?	?	
C. *Inconsistent Variables*									
Block 3									
Teachers' Pre-service Training in Social Sciences	T	?	?	+	M				+
Teachers' Sex	T				M			+	?
Teachers' Years of Full-time Post-Secondary Education	T				M	−	+		
Teachers' Use of Audio visuals	T	?			M			+	
Teachers' Use of Ability Grouping within Class	T	−			M	?			
Teachers' Emphasis on Country History	T		?	+	M				−
Teachers' Emphasis on Non-political Aspects of Citizenship	T			?	M	−			?
Current Enrollment in Civics	Q	+			−				
Block 4									
Student Liking for School	Q	+			?			?	+
Parental Intervention to Further Learning of Language and Arts	Q	?	−				?		?

Table 10.7. *(Cont.)*

Variables by block	Source	FRG	Finland	Ireland	Israel	Italy	Netherlands	New Zealand	United States
D. *Variables Entering in Only One Country*									
Block 3									
Grade at which Social Studies is Begun	S	?		C	M	M			
Use of Entry Examination by School	S	+			M				
Proportion of School's Students belonging to a Minority Group		C	C	M	M	M		–	M
E. *Variables Included but Not Entering in Any Country*									
Teachers' Use of Standardized Tests									
Teachers' Use of Projects, Term Papers in Assessment									
Teachers' Use of Lectures									
Amount of Teachers' Inservice Training in Social Sciences									
Membership in Social Science Teachers' Association									
Teachers' Readiness to Introduce Sensitive Issues									
Frequency of Discussing Politics and International Affairs with Friends, Parents and Teachers									

Table 10.8. *Variables Entering Regression by End of Block IV and Their Signs* (*Civics Anti-Authoritarianism, Population IV*)

Variables by block	Source	FRG	Finland	Ireland	Netherlands	New Zealand	Sweden	United States
A. *Variables Entering Consistently in Two or More Countries*								
Block 1								
Home Background	Q			+	+	+	+	+
Student Sex	Q	+	+		?	+	+	+
Block 2								
Type of School	F					+	+	+
Type of Student Program	Q		+					+

275

Table 10.8. *(Cont.)*

Variables by block	Source	FRG	Finland	Ireland	Netherlands	New Zealand	Sweden	United States
Block 3								
Use of Entry Examination by School	S	+	+		+			+
Patriotic Rituals Practiced in Classroom	Q	−	−	−	−	−	−	−
Current Enrollment in Civics Class	Q						+	+
Teachers' Use of Standardized Test	T						−	−
Teachers' Use of Printed Drill	T				−			−
Block 4								
Interest in Public Affairs TV	Q	+	+	+	+	+	+	+
Reports making Peer Group Decisions by Voting	Q	+	+	+	+		+	+
Participation in Civic Activities	Q	+	+		+	+		+
Propensity to Engage in Activities Usually Reserved to Adults	Q		+	+	+		+	+
Frequency of Discussing Politics and International Affairs with Friends, Parents and Teachers	Q		+	+		+	+	+
Expected Education	Q				+	+		+

B. *Variables Predominantly Positive or Negative in Two or More Countries*

Variables by block	Source	FRG	Finland	Ireland	Netherlands	New Zealand	Sweden	United States
Block 1								
Use of Dictionary in Home	Q		+			+	?	+
Block 3								
Independence of Opinion Encouraged in Classroom	Q	+	−		+	+	+	+
Teachers' Readiness to Discuss Sensitive Issues	T			+	+	+	−	+
Teachers' Sex	T	−	+		+	+		−
Teachers' Emphasis on Non-political Aspects of Citizenship	T	+	−		−			−
Amount of Teachers' Post-Secondary Education in Social Sciences	T		−			−		?
Teachers' Emphasis on Non-western Cultures	T		−				+	+
Block 4								
Hours of Pleasure Reading	Q	+	+		−		+	+
Parental Intervention to Further Learning in Language and Arts	Q	−	−				?	?

Table 10.8. *(Cont.)*

Variables by block	Source	FRG	Finland	Ireland	Netherlands	New Zealand	Sweden	United States
C. Inconsistent Variables								
Block 1								
Age	Q				+		?	−
Block 3								
Proportion of Schools Population belong to Minority Group	S		−	M		+		M
Teachers' Years of Full-time Post-Secondary Education	T					?	−	
Teachers' Use of Ability Groupings within Class	T			−			?	+
Teachers' Emphasis on Country's History	T	−		+				
Block 4								
Student Liking for School	Q	?	−					?
D. Variables Entering in Only One Country								
Block 1								
Size of Family	Q						−	
Block 3								
Teachers' Specialization	T		−					
Teachers' Preparation for Lessons: Hours per week	T				−			
Teachers' Use of Audio-visuals	T				−			
Stress on Facts in Civics Class	Q						−	
Block 4								
Urbanization of Community Served by School	S						−	
E. Variables Not Entering in Any Country								
Grade at which Social Studies Begun								
Teachers' Use of Projects, Term papers in Assessment								
Teachers' Use of Lectures								
Amount of Teachers' Inservice Training in the Social Studies								

Note: For Key to symbols see Table 10.7 notes.

inantly consistent in their relationships to Anti-Authoritarianism at both age levels.

Among the students there were additional relationships (Table 10.7).

1. The higher the students' grade in school the less authoritarian they were (five out of eight countries; opposite in Israel).

2. Students in schools where larger proportions of teachers were specialized to teach civics and social studies were less authoritarian in the Federal Republic of Germany, Finland, and the United States at Population II (opposite relationship in Finland at Population IV).

3. Students who reported that their civics and history classes stress facts and memorization were more authoritarian in Ireland, Italy and New Zealand and less authoritarian in Finland and the United States at Population II. (At Population IV students who reported stress on facts were less authoritarian in Sweden.) Further analysis should make a composite of this student report variable with teachers' reports of the use of printed drill.

4. Students in schools where teachers spent a large number of hours preparing for civics classes were less authoritarian in Italy and the Netherlands and more authoritarian in Ireland at Population II. (They were more authoritarian in the Netherlands at Population IV.)

There were some school variables which were related among the pre-university students but which did not appear consistently at the lower age level (Table 10.8).

1. Students in schools which used an entry examination were less authoritarian in the Federal Republic of Germany, Finland, the Netherlands, and the United States. This variable was also related in the Federal Republic of Germany for the 14-year-olds.

2. Students who reported current enrollment in a civics class were less authoritarian in Sweden and the United States at Population IV. At Population II in the Federal Republic of Germany the same relationship holds; the opposite relationship is true in Israel at Population II.

3. Students in schools where teachers reported frequent use of standardized tests were more authoritarian in Sweden and the United States at Population IV.

4. Students in schools where teachers reported willingness to discuss sensitive political issues were less authoritarian in Ireland, the Netherlands, New Zealand, and the United States and were more authoritarian in Sweden.

278

5. Students in schools where a large proportion of the teachers were female were less authoritarian at Population IV in Ireland, New Zealand, and Sweden; they were more authoritarian in Finland and the United States at Population IV. At Population II they were less authoritarian in New Zealand and show a regression sign reversal in the United States.

6. Students in schools where teachers emphasized the non-political aspects of citizenship were more authoritarian in Finland, the Netherlands, and Sweden; they were less authoritarian in the Federal Republic of Germany at Population IV. The relationship which held at the Population II level was toward greater authoritarianism in Italy and showed sign reversals in Ireland and the United States.

Many of the expectations regarding particular learning conditions were not confirmed. The remainder of the Block 3 specific Learning conditions were so mixed in their patterns of relationship to Anti-Authoritarianism as to defy even this level of summarization at either the Population II or IV level. These include variables indexing the Teachers' level of training, Methods of teaching such as the use of audiovisuals, Frequency of ability groupings, content factors such as reported Stress of country's history, Proportion of the students who belong to a minority group (further complicated because this variable was missing in several countries). There was still a further set of variables which did not reach the significant F-level in any country in the Anti-Authoritarianism regressions. They had been included in the program because of their relationship to cognitive Civic Education. These unrelated variables included Use of projects, lectures, Membership in teachers' association, Grade at which social studies is first taught and some of the teacher training variables. It may be concluded from the absence of significant relationships with these characteristics that variations between students in democratic values depend more on the climate and character of relationships in the classroom than on a particular level of the teacher's training in the subject matter. The characterization of classrooms where children seemed to learn less about civics as stressing "rote and ritual" also seemed to apply to classrooms where they were less likely to acquire democratic values.

Some additional analysis was undertaken to give clearer evidence about particular aspects of the learning conditions which might have been masked in their effects because the more general school effect had been removed. By reversing the order of entry of Blocks 2 and 3 it was possible to determine which variables in the Learning conditions block would explain additional variance when entered in the regression analysis before the entry of the Type of school and program. This analysis is discussed only for Population II predictions of Anti-Authoritarianism since it was this analysis where Block 2 (Type of school and program) accounted for a quantity of variance which made it likely that the effects of specific learning conditions would be masked.

Some learning conditions which were indicated in the original analysis as important predictors of Anti-Authoritarianism were given additional support when they entered as the second block. The Teacher's use of printed drill was negatively related to Anti-Authoritarianism in Italy (as well as in the three countries previously mentioned). The positive relationship between Teacher emphasis on Non-Western cultures and Anti-Authoritarianism also held true in the United States (as well as in Finland and the Netherlands) when Learning conditions variables were entered before Type of school and program. (This relationship was the opposite in Ireland.) Students in schools where a large proportion of the teachers were women were less authoritarian. In the original order of analysis this was true only in New Zealand. When Learning conditions enter before Type of school/program, it was also true in Ireland, Italy and the Netherlands. Likewise the Frequency of use of ability grouping, which previously showed a negative relationship to Anti-Authoritarianism only in the Federal Republic of Germany, when the blocks were reversed was also negatively related in the Netherlands and New Zealand.

The large majority of the Block 4 Kindred variables which were entered appeared as significant predictors. Both Population II and Population IV students in all countries were less authoritarian if they were interested in public affairs, television and reported making decisions in their peer groups by voting. Somewhat less striking but still strong relationships held between low Authoritarianism and reported Participation in civic activities, Hours of pleasure reading, high Levels of expected education, and Propensity to engage in adult activities. In one or two countries the urbanization of the community was important. At Population IV students who reported frequent discussion of politics were less authoritarian. Kindred variables important in other IEA subjects, such as Parental interest in child's school work and students' Liking for school, showed very mixed patterns in predicting Democratic Values.

SUMMARY OF VARIABLES PREDICTING
ANTI-AUTHORITARIANISM

There were many similarities between the specific variables which accounted for variance in Anti-Authoritarianism and those which accounted for cognitive achievement in Civic Education. Patriotic rituals do not seem to foster democratic values or knowledge of civics. Highly structured classroom settings where teachers use printed materials and do not encourage students to express their opinions do not foster these democratic attitudes. In some countries the teacher who is willing to move beyond traditional civics topics to study non-Western cultures shows somewhat greater success in encouraging anti-authoritarian attitudes. Teachers who are specialized to teach social sciences or have special training foster democratic attitudes in some countries and not in others.

With regard to the last two questions posed at the beginning of the chapter, changes in schools which attempt to produce increases in civic knowledge are also likely to foster democratic values. And some of the variables which are related to between-country differences (e.g. Patriotic ritual participation) also seem to be related to between-student differences in democratic values. Likewise, there are some changes in educational policy and practice which could be effected at the national level, others at the school level and still others at the level of the individual teacher. Only a more detailed analysis of educational systems can do justice to the way in which changes at these levels relate to each other. On the whole, however, it appears that aspects of classroom climate and teacher interaction with students are at least as important as substantive content in the fostering of democratic values.

SPECIFIC VARIABLES WITHIN BLOCKS IN PREDICTING
PARTICIPATION IN POLITICAL DISCUSSION
AT POPULATIONS II AND IV

Tables 10.9 and 10.10 present the results for individual predictor variables in the regression analysis for Participation in Political Discussion.

Among Block 1 variables, the relationships of between-student variance to level of the home tended to be less consistent than they were for Anti-Authoritarianism. Sign reversals for the Home background cluster were common in Population II, and there were posi-

Table 10.9. *Variables Entering Regression by End of Block IV and Their Signs (Participation in Political Discussion, Population II)*

Variables by block	Source	FRG	Finland	Ireland	Italy	Netherlands	New Zealand	United States
A. Variables Entering Consistently in Two or More Countries								
Block 1								
Use of Dictionary in Home	Q	+	+	+	+		+	+
Student Sex	Q	–		–	–	–		–
Block 3								
Independence of Opinion encouraged in Classroom	Q	+	+	+	+	+	+	+
Patriotic Rituals Practiced in Classrooms	Q	+	+	+	+	+	+	+
Current Enrollment in Civics	Q		+			+		+
Teachers' Emphasis on Non-Western Culture	T		+				+	
Teachers' Specialization	T	–		–				
Block 4								
Interest in Public Affairs TV	Q	+	+	+	+	+	+	+
Participation in Civic Activities	Q	+	+	+	+	+	+	+
Parental Involvement in Learning of Language and Arts	Q	+	+	+		+	+	+
Hours Pleasure Reading	Q		+	+	+		+	+
Student Liking for School	Q	+		+	+	+		
Propensity to Engage in Activities Usually Reserved to Adults	Q	?			+	+	+	+
B. Variables Predominantly Positive or Negative in Two or More Countries								
Block 1								
Size of Family	Q	–					–	+
Block 2								
Type of Student Program	Q	+					+	–
Block 3								
Teachers' Preparation for Lessons: Hours per week	T	–			+	+		
Teachers' Use of Audio-visuals	T	–	–					+
Teachers' Emphasis on Non-political Aspects of Citizenship	T	–	–					+
Grade	Q	–	+	–				
Stress on Facts in Civics Class	Q	+			+	–		
Block 4								
Expected Education	Q				–	+	+	

Table 10.9. *(Cont.)*

Variables by block	Source	FRG	Finland	Ireland	Italy	Netherlands	New Zealand	United States
C. *Inconsistent Variables*								
Block 1								
Home Background	Q	?				?	?	?
Block 3								
Use of Entry Examination by School	S	?	+			?		+
Teachers's Sex	T	−			+			
Teachers' Use of Standardized Tests	T						−	+
Teachers' Use of Printed Drill	T	−	?			−		?
Amount of Teachers' Post-secondary Education in Social Sciences	T	−					+	
Teachers' emphasis on Country History	T	+		−				
Block 4								
Urbanization of Community	S				?	−		+
D. *Variables Entering in Only One Country*								
Block 2								
Type of School	F			−				
Block 3								
Grade at which Social Studies is Begun	S	−						
Proportion of School's Students Belonging to Minority Group	S				M	M	+	M
Teachers' Use of Ability Grouping Within Classes	T	−						
Teachers' Readiness to Discuss Sensitive Issues	T					+		
Block 4								
Reports making Peer Group Decisions by Voting	Q	−						
E. *Variables Included but not Entering in Any Country*								
Age								
Teachers' Use of Projects, Term Papers in Assessment								
Teachers' Use of Lectures								
Amount of Teacher Inservice Training in Social Sciences								
Membership in Social Science Teachers Association								

Table 10.10. *Variables Entering Regression by End of Block IV and Their Signs* (*Participation in Political Discussion, Population IV*)

Variables by blocks	Source	FRG	Finland	Ireland	Netherlands	New Zealand	Sweden	United States
A. *Variables Entering Consistently in Two or More Countries*								
Block 1								
Home Background	Q	+	+		+	+	?	
Use of Dictionary in Home	Q	+	+		+	+	+	+
Student Sex	Q	−	−		−	−	−	−
Block 3								
Independence of Opinion Encouraged in Classroom	Q	+	+	+	+	+	+	+
Patriotic Rituals Practiced in Classroom	Q	+	+	+	+	+		+
Current Enrollment in Civics	Q		+	+	+	+	+	+
Teachers' Use of Audio-visuals	T			−	−			−
Teachers' Emphasis on Non-Western Culture	T	+						+
Stress on Facts in Civics	T		+				+	
Block 4								
Interest in Public Affairs TV	Q	+	+	+	+	+	+	+
Participation in Civic Activities	Q	+	+	+	+	+	+	+
Hours Pleasure Reading	Q	+	+	+	+	+	+	+
Parental Involvement in Learning of Language and Arts	Q	+	+	+	+		+	+
Propensity to Engage in Activities Usually Reserved to Adults	Q	+	+	+	+	+	+	
Expected Education	Q	+	+					+
B. *Variables Predominantly Positive or Negative in Two or More Countries*								
Block 2								
Type of Student Program	Q				−	−		+
Block 3								
Teachers' Specialization	T	−			+	+		
Teachers' Readiness to Discuss Sensitive Issues	T				+	−		+
Teachers' Emphasis on Non-political Aspects of Citizenship	T				−	?	−	
C. *Inconsistent Variables*								
Block 1								
Age	Q	−	+				?	−
Block 2								
Type of School	F	−				+		

284

Table 10.10. *(Cont.)*

Variables by blocks	Source	FRG	Finland	Ireland	Netherlands	New Zealand	Sweden	United States
Block 3								
Teachers' Use of Standardized Tests	T		+	−				
Teachers' Use of Printed Drill	T	+		−				
Teachers' Emphasis on Country's History	T					+		−
D. *Variables Entering in Only One Country*								
Block 1								
Size of Family	Q					+		
Block 3								
Grade Social Studies Begun	S		−					
Use of Entry Examination by School	S							+
Proportion of School's Students Belonging to Minority Group	S				M	+		M
Teachers' Sex	T					+		
Teachers' Years of Full-time Post-Secondary Education	T	+						
Teachers' Preparation for Lessons: Hours per week	T			−				
Block 4								
Urbanization of Community Served by School	S					−		
E. *Variables Included but Not Entering in Any Country*								
Teachers' Use of Projects, Term Papers in Assessment								
Teachers' Use of Lectures								
Teachers' Use of Ability Grouping								
Amount of Teachers' Post-Secondary Education in Social Sciences								
Amount of Teachers' In-service Training in Social Sciences								
Membership in Social Science Teachers' Association								
Student Liking for School								
Reports making Peer Group Decisions by Voting								

tive relationships at Population IV in only four countries. Dictionary usage in the home seemed to be a much better predictor of discussion participation than the more general composite of socio-economic status; this single variable showed positive relationships in six out of seven countries at Population II and six out of seven at Population IV. The reason for this is not clear. Age (within grade) showed a mixed pattern of relationships to discussion participation within countries.

There was a clear cut sex difference, girls reported less discussion participation in five out of seven countries at Population II and six out of seven countries at Population IV.

Type of school and Type of program were also more inconsistent in their relationship to Participation in Discussion than for Anti-Authoritarianism; a very small amount of variance in participation was explained by the students' enrollment in an academic, vocational, or general school or program.

The following relationships held between Block 3 Learning conditions and Political Discussion Participation at both populations in a relatively consistent fashion (see Tables 10.9 and 10.10):

1. The more expression of student opinion was encouraged by the teacher the more students reported participation in both in-school and out-of-school political discussion. This was true at both levels in all countries and was congruent with the results for Anti-Authoritarianism.

2. Students who reported frequent participation in Patriotic rituals also reported more Participation in Political Discussion (in all countries at Population II and six out of seven countries at Population IV). It may be recalled that patriotic ritual emphasis was related to low Civic Education cognitive scores and low democratic value support. Perhaps the most reasonable explanation is that a country with a strong and unified nationalistic thrust (indexed by stress on patriotism) is likely to present a situation which stimulates issue discussion but puts far less stress on ideology or democratic values.

3. Students in schools where teachers emphasized non-Western studies were more participant in Finland and New Zealand at Population II and in the Federal Republic of Germany and the United States at Population IV. This finding in Finland and the United States was congruent in direction with the results for Anti-Authoritarianism discussed in the previous chapter. The teacher who considers the less traditional subjects important may be stimulating participation as well as democratic value support.

4. Students who reported that they were currently enrolled in civics classes reported more frequent discussion in three out of seven countries at Population II and five out of seven countries at Population IV. It is probable that this relationship reflects the fact that part of the discussion reported by students actually occurs in these classes.

5. Students in schools where teachers reported the frequent use of

audio-visual aids participated less in political discussion at Population II in Finland and Ireland and at Population IV in Ireland, the Netherlands, and the United States. This relationship was reversed in the United States at Population II. In some countries apparently audio-visual aids are time fillers rather than stimulants of discussion.

6. Students who reported that facts and memorization were stressed in their civics classes reported more discussion participation in Finland and Italy at Population II and in Finland and Sweden at Population IV. This relationship was reversed in the Netherlands at Population II. Students were asked about factual stress only if they were enrolled in civics classes; this relationship may be an artifact of the relationship between enrollment in civics classes and political discussion.

7. Students in schools where teachers reported emphasizing the non-political aspects of citizenship participated less in discussion at Population II in Finland and the Federal Republic of Germany and at Population IV in the Netherlands and Sweden. In the United States at Population II and in New Zealand at the older level these relationships were reversed.

8. Students in schools where teachers were specialized to teach civics or social studies were less participant in discussion in Finland and Italy at the lower age level. They were more participant at Population IV in the Netherlands and New Zealand; they continue to be less participant in Finland.

9. Students in schools where teachers reported readiness to discuss sensitive or controversial political issues reported more in and out of school political discussion at Population II in the Netherlands and at Population IV in the Netherlands and the United States. The opposite relationship holds in New Zealand.

There tended to be relatively inconsistent relationships varying in sign at the two levels and in different countries between such school variables as student Grade, Number of hours teachers prepare, various teacher training variables, Methods used by teachers (printed drills, standardized tests), and various social science content (emphasis on country history), Use of entry examination by the school and Sex ratio of teachers. Some variables appeared in only one country as important, such as Grade in which social studies are first taught and Proportion of students belonging to minority group. Still another set of variables was included in the potential regression predictors because they were related to cognitive Civic Education. They did not predict discussion participation in any country (Teacher use of lectures, Teacher use of projects, ability grouping, some teacher training variables and Teacher membership in subject matter association).

In general Block 4 or Kindred variables were the most powerful predictors of discussion participation. In all countries at both age levels students who reported participating in discussion also reported more interest in public affairs television and more participation in civic activities. Report of engaging in adult-like activities was also related in five out of seven countries at Population II and six out of seven in Population IV. Unlike the finding with regards to Anti-Authoritarianism, parental involvement or interest in the child's schoolwork was positively related to participation in political schoolwork in six out of seven countries at both age levels. At Population II Liking for school was important in half of the countries and at both levels Hours spent in pleasure reading related positively to political discussion participation in four out of seven countries at Population II and in all Population IV countries. At Population II Expected education was positively related in two countries and in three countries at Population IV. There was one opposite relationship. Report that peer group decisions are made by voting was not important in predicting discussion (unlike the Anti-Authoritarianism predictions earlier discussed).

SUMMARY OF VARIABLES PREDICTING DISCUSSION PARTICIPATION

Participation in Political Discussion was a somewhat different kind of outcome than either Anti-Authoritarianism or cognitive achievement in Civic Education. The student who is interested and motivated whatever the socio-economic level will tend to participate; the male student will participate more than the female; the student who is enrolled in civics and whose teacher encourages independence of opinion and discusses controversial issues will participate more. The student who participates in patriotic ritual will tend to participate more in discussion as will the student who is involved in a variety of other in and out of school activities. It appears that in many respects political activity is an extension of a generally active approach to life.

Yet, as with the case of predicting Anti-Authoritarianism, many of the expectations about the important contributions of particular variables were not confirmed by the data.

The between-country differences indicated that no country within the sample can be characterized simultaneously as high in democratic values *and* high in civic interest and participation. The within-country, between-student analysis reported in this chapter indicates that some but by no means all of the predictors of democratic values support are related in the same direction to interest/participation.

To phrase this in terms of the questions set out of the beginning of this chapter, the school-related characteristics which foster cognitive achievement in Civic Education and support for democratic values are not identical with the characteristics which foster discussion, though there is some overlap. A more fine grained analysis of the reasons that the knowledgeable citizen who strongly supports democratic values may not be an active participant in the political process is clearly required.

CONCLUSIONS

The major conclusions from the attempt to predict individual student variation in Anti-Authoritarianism and Participation in Political Discussion may be summarized as follows. Variations in these affective outcomes can be explained less fully by variations in home, school and individual inputs than can the cognitive outcomes. There is evidence for the importance of school as well as home factors in the acquisition of these attitudes and interests, however, changes in school practices (such as patriotic rituals) and teacher orientation to the students as well as to the subject matter (including less stress on drill and rote learning and more stress on fostering independent thought) appear likely to increase democratic value support. No single or piecemeal alteration in a course of study is likely to have a profound impact however, as the contributions of single variables to predicting attitudes are relatively small.

Although there are some differences in the attitudes and participation related to characteristics such as socio-economic status, sex, and previous level of academic success, these are not in any country so overwhelming that school Civic Education efforts are doomed to failure with any group.

The affective aspect of Civic Education is a complex process requiring a balance between various models and methods of education. Drilling students on the "proper" attitudes seems a course of little profit. Attitudes seem not to be acquired in such simple units. Giving students role experience in democratically run classrooms and in situations which foster high levels of general participation seems a more fruitful course. Of all the models proposed for understanding the development of attitudes, Role Transfer seems to be the most adequate. Changes toward more effective education in the attitudinal domain of civics are set within complex national political and educational systems, within a school context and system, and influenced by the interplay of a variety of individual characteristics.

Chapter 11

Students' Perceptions
of the Political System

The patterns of attitudes which characterize adolescents have many implications for understanding the Civic Education process. Children's perceptions of social institutions and the important societal values with which they are associated are relevant topics for study in their own right; they also help to link the affective and the cognitive aspects of political socialization. The "How Society Works" instrument was designed to explore these links and percepts; its construction has been described in Chapter 7. Ten institutions were listed, each accompanied by a list of 12 values. The respondent was asked to indicate the effect which each institution had on the realization of each value. A variety of different scores are possible using the data from this instrument. This chapter describes the patterns in the perceptions of social institutions, the perceptions of values and various summary perceptual scores. Comparisons are made between students in different countries and between those of different ages. A tentative theory is proposed concerning the stages through which children pass in their understanding of social institutions.

COUNTRY PROFILES FOR EACH INSTITUTION

The How Society Works instrument generated data which can be analyzed from a variety of points of view: comparing institutions, comparing age levels, comparing countries, comparing values (items), etc., as well as calculating various summary scores. The basic data themselves can be expressed in different ways: as percentage distributions, as percentage distributions excluding the Don't Know and Omitted categories, as means and standard deviations using weights 4−3−2−1 for the answer categories (Almost Always to Almost Never). They could be displayed as histograms or various other graphics, or in tabular form, selectively or *in extenso*. Even using a crude summary statistic such as the mean (based on the above weights), there are 120 scores per child, distributed over 10 institutions of 12 value-items each, for ten different countries and several age-groups.

To make these results more manageable, means rather than percentage distributions were used. The means were calculated as follows:

Almost always=4
Fairly often=3
Sometimes=2
Almost Never=1

The base for the calculations for any sub-group consisted of the total number giving any of these four responses; omitted and Don't Know responses were excluded.

When inspecting and presenting these results, the country profiles for each institution are dealt with first; these profiles will show what, according to the children, each institution actually does and how its functions are perceived. Where there are differences between countries, it may be possible to suggest explanations for these, and likewise to comment on similarities; there is no concern with "right" or "wrong" answers.

The differences between Populations within each country are also noted. These differences are of particular interest because they may throw light on the developmental process in children's political percepts. However, there are problems here. Ideally it would have been desirable to have had data for Populations I, II and IV in every participating country—and even then it would not have been easy to interpret any age differences, since they might be due to intellectual development, wider experience, different teaching, greater access to the mass media, and so forth. The pupils still at school at the Population IV level are far from being a representative sample of the age-group, so that any differences between Population II and Population IV might, in addition, be due to selective factors. In actual fact, data exist for Populations I, II and IV for only two countries: the Federal Republic of Germany and the Netherlands; here comparisons can be made all the way through. In Israel (judgment sample only) and in Italy Population I data as well as results for Population II are available but none for Population IV. For Sweden there are only Population IV results. For the remaining five countries (Finland, Iran, Ireland, New Zealand and the United States) data for

Populations II and IV are available though the Irish data are weakened by a 50 % omission rate.

In studying Population differences for each institutional profile within a given country the following patterns were examined:

1. no differences, profiles identical;
2. same pattern, but sharper, more articulated profile in the older age-group;
3. same pattern, but vaguer, less articulated profile in the older age-group;
4. same pattern plus new items in the older age-group (widening profile);
5. same pattern but fewer items in the older age-group (narrowing profile);
6. vague, undifferentiated profile throughout;
7. quite different profile, different items, in older age-group.

The results, in any particular case, will be due to a subtle blending of changes in attitudes and understanding. Some institutions are virtually unknown to 10-year-olds, and so it is probable that at that age level a vague profile, with many Don't Know responses, would result; in Population II, however, a clearer profile might well be obtained, and a similar but still more articulated one in Population IV. But other institutions might be well-known even to Population I respondents; here, very similar profiles for Populations I and II might be found, but respondents in Population IV might be more knowledgeable or more critical and so they might be inclined to de-emphasize the earlier profile and, instead, to stress certain more discordant or more power-orientated items. These, and other possible findings, will also differ between countries; for example, Labor Unions may be given very different profiles in different countries. It is also necessary to bear in mind that the study is essentially cross-sectional, and that it is not strictly correct to describe Population differences as "developmental" changes, especially considering the differences in the selectivity of secondary schools in different countries.

There is one further point to be made before presenting the results: evidence was found of a response bias in two items: "Makes sure there are fair shares for everyone" and "Creates a better understanding so that people can live and work together". Both these items tended to attact exceptionally high endorsement rates, especially when a particular profile was weak or vague; these two items imply something fairly positive which could be true of almost any institution, and so the students appear to have checked these options when they felt uncertain. In addition, the fair shares item attracted endorsement because it was always printed first on the list; ideally, randomizing the order of presentation would have been preferred but this was ruled out on practical grounds.

Laws

The Law was one of the most clearly perceived institutions in the How Society Works instrument. It was generally said to perform five functions:

> Make sure there are fair shares for everyone
> Settle arguments and disagreements
> Create better understanding so that people can live and work together
> Force people to obey the rules
> Prevent people from harming others

On the whole, between-country differences were few, and the profiles of Populations II and IV were very similar. It seems that by the age of 14 the image of the rule of law is clear and thereafter becomes neither more articulated nor weakened by cynicism or distrust. The few countries for which Population I data are available show much the same profile, though in somewhat weaker form.

Obedience was stressed in every country—consistently more so in the Federal Republic of Germany, and least in Israel and Italy: so was the preventive aspect of lawfulness—most of all in Israel and in New Zealand. Table 11.1 shows some of the trends for these two items. Compared to other institutions, the rule of law is an institution which is already fairly well understood by children at the age of 10 or 11, and which thereafter does not markedly change its image with increasing age; between-country differences are also relatively slight. Only the institution of the Police shows a similarly clear-cut and early establishment—the remaining institutions in our questionnaire showed rather vaguer results among the younger age-groups

Police

Like Laws, the image of the Police was already well-established by the age of 10 or 11 and thereafter changed but little. In most countries the profile consisted mainly of three items:

294

Table 11.1. *Mean Ratings from "How Society Works" to Describe functions of Laws by Country and Population*

	Population I		Population II		Population IV	
	Force obedience	Prevent harm	Force obedience	Prevent harm	Force obedience	Prevent harm
FRG	3.0	2.7	3.5	3.2	3.8	3.0
Netherlands	2.9	2.6	3.2	3.1	3.5	3.0
Israel	2.8	3.2	2.5	3.4	–	–
Italy	2.9	2.5	2.7	2.8	–	–
Finland	–	–	3.2	3.1	3.6	3.3
Ireland	–	–	3.1	3.4	3.2	3.3
New Zealand	–	–	3.1	3.5	3.4	3.4
United States	–	–	3.2	3.1	3.2	3.0
Sweden	–	–	–	–	3.6	3.1

Note: Figures represent Means (possible range 1.0–4.0). High scores=endorsement of Always or Often.

Table 11.2. *Mean Ratings from "How Society Works"—Country Profiles for the Police as an Institution*

	Population II							
	FRG	Israel	Italy	Netherlands	Finland	Ireland	New Zealand	United States
Fair shares	1.5	2.4	2.3	2.3	2.1	3.0	2.8	2.7
Settle arguments	3.3	2.5	3.3	3.6	3.0	3.4	3.4	3.2
Help the rich	1.4	1.4	1.4	1.3	1.6	2.0	1.9	2.3
Show who is strongest	1.9	1.5	1.7	2.6	2.2	2.4	2.4	2.4
Better understanding	2.5	2.6	2.9	2.5	2.7	3.1	3.0	2.9
Force to obey	3.2	3.2	2.9	3.4	3.2	3.3	3.3	3.4
Create disagreements	1.9	1.4	1.3	2.0	2.1	1.8	1.7	2.3
Chance to speak	2.0	1.8	2.3	2.1	2.1	2.3	2.3	2.4
Make own decisions	1.7	1.8	2.2	1.8	2.0	2.1	2.3	2.4
Afraid to speak	1.6	1.6	1.5	1.8	2.0	1.8	1.7	1.9
Prevent harming others	3.4	3.4	3.0	3.5	3.4	3.6	3.7	3.4
Prices up	1.1	1.2	1.1	1.1	1.2	1.2	1.1	1.4

Prevent people from harming others
Force people to obey the rules
Create better understanding so that people can live and work together

To this preventive/enforcement role, two other values were added in some countries:

Make sure there are fair shares for everyone
Settle arguments and disagreements

This adjudicative role received striking endorsement among Population II in the United States, New Zealand and Ireland as well as some support among both the older and younger age-groups. However, preventive/enforcement was the stronger role component throughout (see Table 11.2).

It would be interesting to follow up these results, to learn why even 17–18 year olds believe that the police settle arguments and disagreements.

Were the police sometimes seen in a discordant or oppressive role? "Make people afraid to say what they think" attracted some slight endorsement in Israel (Population I); "Give help to rich people" was lightly endorsed in the United States (Populations II and IV); "Create disagreements" was endorsed lightly in Germany and in the United States (Population IV); while "Show who is the strongest" obtained a fair amount of endorsement in the Netherlands, Ireland, New Zealand and in the United States (all for Populations II and IV), and well as in Germany and in Sweden (Population IV).

In general, therefore, the image of the Police is established early and thereafter remains consistently favorable, with but minor indications of negative percepts among the older students.

Elections

Generalizing across all 10 countries and all age-groups, the functions of Elections were said to be to ensure fair shares, to give people a chance to write or say what they think, and to help people take part in important decisions about their own lives—with varying degrees of emphasis. (This profile was most clear-cut in Italy and the United States.)

To this "classical" pattern the students in Population IV tended to add endorsement of "Show who is the strongest" and, in some countries (Federal Republic of Germany and the United States),

Table 11.3. *Mean Ratings from "How Society Works"—Elections (Federal Republic of Germany Responses)*

	Population I	Population II	Population IV
Fair shares	2.1	1.8	1.4
Better understanding	2.4	2.2	1.6
Chance to speak	2.6	2.9	2.9
Show who is strongest	2.7	3.2	3.2
Create disagreements	2.6	2.9	3.2

"Create Disagreements," while de-emphasizing fairness and understanding. In other words, the older children are more realistic, even in some cases to the point of cynicism, and have become aware of the divisive aspects of elections (Table 11.3).

The profiles of Population I were fairly similar but less articulated—though even at this early age the West German children showed signs of the general disillusionment with their political system which tended to characterize their responses throughout. For example, of all the countries they were least likely to say that elections create fair shares or create better understanding, and more likely to suggest that elections are trials of strength and create disagreements—and these trends became accentuated up the age range.

Parliament (Congress, Bundestag, etc.)

Generally, the functions of the legislature showed a very weakly defined pattern in all countries and age-groups; the same applies to "Political Parties" (see below). It is possible that our items were somehow less appropriate to these two institutions than to most others, though it is difficult to see why the same argument might not apply to perceptions of the "Democratic System of Government" or the "United Nations." Certainly, from the teaching point of view, these results suggest that there is a good deal of room for improvement in the clarity of these social perceptions: these youngsters showed little understanding of the impact of the legislature on the life of the ordinary citizen. This is not to say that the respondents did not know the "correct" answers, nor did they give many Don't Know responses (except for Ireland, the percentage Don't Know was almost everywhere below 10%); rather, when asked "What does it

297

actually do and what effects does it *really* have?" most children ticked either "Sometimes" or "Almost never" to most items. A generally low level of capability seems to be implied: the legislature does not do or influence anything very much, from the point of view of these students.

Under these conditions, it is not surprising that responses tended to cluster somewhat around the two "escape" items, which could be true of almost any institution:

> Make sure there are fair shares for everyone
> Create better understanding so that people can live and work together.

To a lesser extent, two other items tended to emerge:

> Settle arguments and disagreements
> Give people a chance to write or say what they think

In Italy and the Netherlands, a third item was also endorsed:

> Help people to take part in important decisions about their own lives.

In this general tendency to vagueness or scepticism, the responses from the Federal Republic of Germany stood out: the results of even the Population I students showed little endorsement of any item; Populations II and IV endorsed even fewer while there was a growing tendency to endorse divisive items such as:

> Show who is the strongest
> Create disagreements

One other trend should be noted: unlike the findings for most other institutions, the image of the legislature became *less* articulated with increasing age: the older the children, the less they thought the legislature does much of anything—and in the Federal Republic of Germany the older children more often saw the Bundestag as having divisive functions.

The Democratic System of Government

In terms of content, the image children have of the Democratic system is similar to the one they have of the Legislature: it was said to ensure fair shares, to create better understanding, to give people a chance to speak (especially endorsed in Population IV), and to help them to make their own decisions. However, in terms of articulation the image of the Democratic system was somewhat sharper, and it tended to get clearer (rather than vaguer) with increasing age.

As in the case of the Legislature (above), the results from the Federal Republic of Germany departed somewhat from this general pattern. Again a tendency was noted in Population IV to endorse divisive items: show who is the strongest, create disagreements, force people to obey the rules—though the strongest endorsement went to "Give people a chance to write or say what they think." Clearly the West German children view the Democratic system with mixed feelings as they grow older—though not as sceptically as they perceive the Bundestag.

The United Nations

Perhaps not surprisingly the UN had one of the vaguest profiles of any institution in the How Society Works instrument. "Create better understanding" was the one attribute that was universally endorsed; next to this, there was frequent endorsement of:

Make sure there are fair shares for everyone
Settle arguments and disagreements
Prevent people from harming others

In some countries, there was a slight tendency for the image to broaden with age, for example, by including also "Give people a chance to write or say what they think" (Italy and New Zealand).

In three countries there was a tendency for the UN profile to become vaguer with increasing age: the Federal Republic of Germany, Israel, and the United States. This tendency towards growing doubt or scepticism concerning the roles and functions of the UN may have different explanations in each of these countries: for example, the UN had been widely distrusted in Israel after the Six Day War; in West Germany, the response may be part of a general tendency to scepticism towards political institutions (e.g., the Legislature, the Democratic system).

It is interesting that discordant items (such as give help to rich people, show who is the strongest, create disagreements, make people afraid to say what they think) received hardly any support when applied to the UN. In the perception of these children the UN may not do much of a positive nature, but neither is it perceived as divisive.

Political Parties

One might have expected that the children's perception of political parties would be influenced by their country's party structure. For example, the United States, New Zealand and Sweden have few large political parties, while the Netherlands, Israel, Italy, and to a lesser extent, the Federal Republic of Germany, tend to have numerous political parties and usually have coalition governments. However, there is no evidence in the results to indicate any systematic relationship between degree of articulation of the perceptual profile of Political Parties and a given country's party structure. For example, Italian children might well have come to regard political parties as relatively ineffectual, yet they had one of the most clear-cut percepts, even in Population I:

> Make sure there are fair shares for everyone
> Create better understanding so that people can live and work together
> Give people a chance to write or say what they think
> Help people to take part in important decisions about their own lives.

Virtually the same profile was produced in Italy by Population II. A similar pattern of results for Population II was obtained in Israel (including also "Settle arguments and disagreements"), but in the Federal Republic of Germany and the Netherlands vagueness predominated, with a tendency among the older children to include some discordant items (create disagreements, show who is the stronger).

Welfare Agencies

A number of institutions (the welfare agencies, labor unions, and large business organizations) are less directly "political". Of these, the role of the welfare agencies could be expected to differ quite markedly among the countries represented in the samples.

First of all it should be stated that the term "Welfare Agencies" may have been too broad to allow for generalized responses. It also produced some translation problems. In Ireland it was made to read "Social Services (old age pensions, health services, children's allowances)," in the Federal Republic of Germany it was reproduced as "*Wohlfahrts-Verbände,*" in Sweden as "*Socialvård,*" while in Finland it was translated as "*Social Relief Organizations.*" Perhaps, in making

300

their responses, different children were thinking, therefore, of different agencies or functions.

Reviewing first the results for the wealthier countries it was found there was a striking degree of vagueness or non-endorsement in Sweden, in Finland, in the Federal Republic of Germany and in the United States (though in the latter "Make sure there are fair shares for everyone" was checked). It could be argued from this that the role of the welfare agencies is least visible to children in the richest countries; however, the children in another relatively rich country (the Netherlands) did produce a somewhat dubious profile (fair shares, better understanding, a chance to speak, prevent harm to others) and the same applied to the children in New Zealand (where, in addition, another item was endorsed: "Help people to take part in important decisions about their own lives"). Similar, though vaguer profiles were obtained from children in less wealthy countries such as Ireland, Israel and Italy indicating that, in these countries, the role of the welfare agencies *is* perceived (even by 10-year olds), and tends to include not only ensuring fair shares and creating better understanding, but also helping with important decisions.

Perhaps an analysis within countries by social class would show whether awareness of the role of the welfare services is related to parental status or wealth. There is evidence in some countries that the Population IV results are narrower and less clear-cut than those of Population II—it will be recalled that Population IV children are a class-biased sub-sample of their age group.

Further exploration might also show that inclusion of certain other items might have produced less vagueness and could have allowed the children to express their percepts more adequately.

Labor Unions

In most countries, the results showed a pattern that became clearer and more articulate with increasing age—though not necessarily more favorable! The four main values endorsed by the younger children were:

> Make sure there are fair shares for everyone
> Create better understanding so that people can live and work together
> Help people to take part in important decisions about their own lives
> Give people a chance to write or say what they think.

301

Another item, "Settle arguments and disagreements" attracted some endorsement in Italy and Israel.

In Population II these five items emerged in most countries, but in the United States "Create disagreements" also was part of the profile. In Population IV this latter item received endorsement in several other countries as well as in the United States (including the Federal Republic of Germany, the Netherlands, Finland, Ireland and especially New Zealand). Altogether, the profile at this age level became broader and more articulated; in some countries it included both cohesive and divisive items, while in others only cohesive items were endorsed. For example, in Ireland the Unions' role was seen mainly as cohesive: ensuring fair shares, creating better understanding, giving people a chance to speak, helping them to make their own decisions, and settling disagreements—but there was also a tendency to endorse "Show who is the stronger," "Create disagreements" and "Make prices go up." More discordant items were also endorsed in the United States and New Zealand.

It seems reasonable to conclude from these results that the children's percepts are increasingly affected by influences from outside the school at the higher age-levels, influences which differ from country to country, and possibly by socio-economic background as well.

Large Business Organizations

Compared to most other instutitions, and in particular compared to Labor Unions, the children's profiles of Large Business Organizations were rather vague, and did not really become clear until the age level of Population IV. By then the Big Business image is, in some countries, rather discordant.

In the United States, for example, the following were the items chiefly emphasized:

> Give help to rich people
> Show who is the strongest
> Create disagreements
> Make prices go up.

Almost the same items were also endorsed in Ireland, in Sweden, in the Netherlands, and in New Zealand. In most of these countries the profiles became somewhat more articulated from Population II to Population IV.

However, in the four countries (Federal Republic of Germany,

Table 11.4. *Mean Ratings from "How Society Works"—Large Business Organizations (The Netherlands Responses)*

	Population I	Population II	Population IV
Make sure there are fair shares for all	2.8	2.1	1.5
Create better understanding so that people can live and work together	2.6	1.8	1.4
Give people a chance to write or say what they think	2.4	1.9	1.6
Help people to take part in important decisions about their own lives	2.4	1.9	1.4
Make prices go up	2.4	2.7	2.7
Give help to rich people	2.0	2.3	2.9
Show who is the strongest	1.9	2.3	2.7
Create disagreements	2.1	2.2	2.4

the Netherlands, Israel and Italy) for which Population I data are available the profiles of Business Organizations were almost totally vague, with endorsement mostly for "Fair shares" and "Better understanding" except in the Federal Republic of Germany, where "Make prices go up" was endorsed. In Israel and Italy this vaguely cohesive image also showed up in Population II.

The results for the Netherlands showed an interesting change from cohesive to discordant values across the three age levels (Table 11.4). In summary, the cohesive items showed a decline with age, while the discordant ones increased in endorsement rate. A similar trend can be shown in the Federal Republic of Germany results.

As with Labor Unions so here, too, the results suggested increasing impact of non-scholastic influences at the higher age-levels, influences which differ from country to country, and may also—with further analysis—be shown to differ according to socio-economic background.

PROFILES OF SOCIAL PROCESSES AND VALUE REALIZATION

In the preceding section of this chapter the children's perceptions of 10 different institutions in their countries have been explored. By looking at the same data from a different angle it is possible to obtain the children's percepts of different social values and processes, in terms of the social institutions which serve them. For example, children may be unaware of certain social processes (such as disagreements or conflict between groups of adults) when they are young, and it may be possible to trace their political socialization and growing awareness of conflict with increasing age, experience and education. But other social values (such as authority) may have become part of the child's awareness much earlier, and become linked directly to certain social institutions, such as the Law or the Police. However, of some values or processes it may be found that there is but scant awareness in the youngest age-group; clear awareness, and a link with certain institutions, among the intermediate age-group; and vagueness or uncertainty among the older students, who have learned to see social processes in terms which are more complex.

As in the previous section, the data will consist of the means obtained from the How Society Works instrument, calculated by giving weights to the frequency categories.

The How Society Works instrument allows the consideration of 12 values or processes. First, consideration is given to those which have become established at an early age, and subsequently to those that reflect later and more complex patterns of social-perceptual development.

Force People to Obey the Rules

This social process showed a clear and almost uniform pattern in every country and from the earliest age-group onwards. In the children's view, authority is enforced by just two institutions: Laws, and the Police. Older children accentuated these two institutions still further than younger ones, but the pattern was well-established even by the age of 10 years (Table 11.5).

However, some of the students in Population IV showed a wider conceptualization of authority; for example, in the Federal Republic of Germany (and to some extent also in the United States) they included the "democratic system of government" as a source of authority.

Basically, however, this is an example of a social process which is clearly recognized even by 10-year-olds, and linked closely to two specific institutions at every age-level—though there is some awareness of greater complexity among some of the older students. Some of the data from the Federal Republic of Germany have been given as an example (Table 11.6).

Table 11.5. *Mean Ratings from "How Society Works"—Country profiles for a Social Process (Population II)*
Item: "Force people to obey the rules"

	FRG	Israel	Italy	Netherlands	Finland	Ireland	New Zealand	United States
Elections	2.2	1.9	2.1	1.8	2.0	2.1	2.1	1.9
Laws	3.5	2.5	2.7	3.2	3.2	3.1	3.1	3.0
Parliament	2.3	1.9	2.1	1.8	2.1	2.3	2.2	2.2
Democratic System of Government	2.5	1.8	2.2	2.1	2.2	2.2	2.1	2.5
UN	2.2	1.8	1.9	2.0	2.0	2.2	1.9	2.0
Political Parties	2.1	1.6	1.9	1.8	1.9	2.0	2.0	1.7
Welfare Agencies	1.4	1.4	1.5	1.3	1.7	1.5	1.9	1.6
Labor Unions	1.9	1.5	1.8	1.8	2.0	2.1	1.8	2.1
Big Business	1.7	1.5	1.6	1.8	2.1	1.9	1.8	1.9
Police	3.2	3.2	2.9	3.4	3.2	3.3	3.3	3.4

Table 11.6. *Mean Ratings from "How Society Works"—Force People to Obey the Rules (Federal Republic of Germany Responses)*

	Population I	Population II	Population IV
Laws	3.0	3.5	3.8
The Police	2.9	3.2	3.5
Democratic System of Government	2.4	2.5	3.1

Note: Figures represent means. Possible range 1.0–4.0. High scores=endorsement of Always or Often.

Settle Arguments and Disagreements

The profile for this social process was somewhat less clearly established than the preceding one for authority, but the two had one aspect in common: the Police. In almost every country and in virtually every age-group there was strong endorsement for the Police as a primary agent of conflict settlement. In Population I, at which age there is little awareness of adult conflict, the profile was relatively weak in the Federal Republic of Germany; in Israel the UN, the Legislature, and Political parties were mentioned more frequently than the Police as agents for settling disputes, but in the

Netherlands the emphasis on the Police was very strong (and in Italy only slightly less so).

In Population II there was generally a broader profile: after the Police, there was mention of Laws, of the Legislature, of the UN, of the Democratic system, and sometimes of Labor unions. These latter institutions tended to remain part of the profile in Population IV (though in several countries the emphasis on the Legislature, on the Labor Unions, and on the UN was reduced. The role of the Police in conflict settlement remained prominent.

Give People a Chance to Write or Say What They Think

Freedom of speech and expression is another value which is founded fairly early in life.

The institutions most commonly perceived as securing freedom of expression were Elections and the Democratic system of government, together with a number of institutions such as the Legislature, Political parties, and the Welfare agencies, which varied from country to country; in Population II, students produced a sharper, simpler profile mostly confined to Elections and the Democratic System—but this was followed by a widening of the profile at Population IV level in several countries, to include Political parties, the Laws, Labor unions and the UN. It may well be that a wide, somewhat diffuse profile in Population I was due to ignorance or uncertainty, while a wide profile in Population IV could be due to greater knowledge and sophistication. In the United States, the Population II data already showed the inclusion of numerous institutions (Elections, Congress, the Democratic system, Political parties, and the UN) to which Labor unions were added in Population IV.

Make People Afraid to Say What They Think

This is the opposite value to free speech (above). It showed almost *nil* attachment to any institution in any country at any age-level, confirming that the children considered freedom of speech to be well-secured.

There were, however, slight indications that the Police make people afraid *sometimes* to say what they think. These indications came from Israel (Population I), Finland (Population II and IV), and the United States (Population IV). No other institutions were seen as a possible threat to freedom of expression.

Make Prices Go Up

This is the first of two economic items (the other, "give help to rich people" follows) of which children become aware at a rather later age than the items considered so far. Neither of these items produced any kind of a profile in Population I, and the Population II profiles were often quite weak.

"Large Business Organizations" emerged as the main cause of rising prices in Population II in the Netherlands, Finland, Ireland, and New Zealand, though the Legislature was also blamed in the latter three countries. In Population IV, Big Business was again seen as the main cause of inflation in those four countries, and also in the Federal Republic of Germany and the United States, but hardly at all in Sweden. Besides the Legislature, Labor unions were seen as a cause of rising prices, too, in New Zealand and in the United States, and to some extent in Ireland. The profile for price rises was most widely distributed in Ireland, where Elections were also blamed (in both Population II and Population IV)—suggesting, perhaps, the impact of a specific political campaign.

Give Help to Rich People

This item, like the preceding one, deals with awareness of economic issues and likewise showed virtually no profile at all in Population I, and only a very slight one, here and there, in Population II.

In Population IV, Large Business Organization were mentioned in every country. To some extent these results were foreshadowed in the Population II data in Finland, Ireland, and the United States.

The United States results were different from those of other countries in that there were indications in the Population IV data that other institutions besides Big business sometimes help the rich: the Police, Political parties, Elections and the Laws were perceived as having some degree of class bias. In the West German data there were similar slight indications of a perceived class bias in Political parties, Laws and the Democratic System as a whole.

Make Sure There are Fair Shares for Everyone

This was the first item on the questionnaire and for that reason may have attracted relatively high endorsement. Certainly the profiles were very broad: to a greater or lesser degree *all* social institutions mentioned in the How Society Works instrument were said to help ensure fair shares for all. Usually the profiles in Population I were

Table 11.7. *Mean Ratings from "How Society Works"—Fair Shares for Everyone* (*Population II*)

	Italy	Ireland	New Zealand
Elections	3.3	2.9	2.9
Laws	3.1	3.2	3.0
Parliament	3.0	3.0	2.9
Democratic System	3.4	3.2	3.1
UN	3.0	3.1	3.2
Political Parties	3.1	2.8	2.6
Welfare Agencies	2.4	3.4	3.0
Labor Unions	3.0	3.2	3.0
Big Business	2.4	2.2	2.2
Police	2.3	3.0	2.8

widest, but became progressively narrower with increasing age, certain institutions (such as Big business, and Political parties) being omitted; in some countries, Population IV students indicated that there is little fair sharing by *any* institution (e.g., Sweden, the Federal Republic of Germany), while in other countries the Population IV profile was still very wide (e.g., Ireland). In most countries, the Welfare agencies, the Democratic system, the Labor unions and sometimes Elections were mentioned as the institutions which ensured fair sharing.

Some countries showed a tendency towards a particularly wide profile (e.g., Italy, New Zealand, Ireland) and included even such institutions as the Police, Big Business, and the Law (Table 11.7).

By contrast, Israel and Finland produced a rather narrow profile, the former seeing only the Democratic system, the Laws and the Labor unions as agents of fairness, while the latter confined themselves to Elections, the Democratic system and the Labor unions (Population II data).

In one country, students at every age-level denied consistently that there was any fair sharing by *any* institution; that country was the Federal Republic of Germany, and these findings are in line with our earlier findings of greater realism or scepticism among West German students.

Create Better Understanding so that People Can Live and Work Together

This item, like "Fair shares," tended to attract a high response rate whenever the children felt uncertain, since almost any institution can be said to promote better understanding in some respects.

In many ways, the profiles followed similar lines to the ones for "Fair shares." In Population I this value item had very wide, rather vague profiles covering almost every institution. With increasing age, the profiles became narrower and certain institutions tended to drop out (e.g., Big business, Political parties). In Population IV strong indications of cynicism/realism were found in the Federal Republic of Germany and in the Netherlands—in both these countries only the Police were said to create better understanding. Other countries continued to show very wide profiles (e.g., Ireland, New Zealand, the United States), with considerable emphasis on the role of the Police, and of the UN.

Help People to Take Part in Important Decisions about Their Own Lives

As was seen with the preceding two harmonizing items, in the present case there was a tendency towards wide, rather unarticulated profiles, which at times became narrower and sharper with increasing age. Elections, the Democratic system and (among the older children) Labor unions were checked most often; Welfare agencies, mentioned by Population I, tended to drop out later.

The Federal Republic of Germany responses showed consistently for all three age-groups that *none* of these institutions were seen as promoting participation; negative tendencies were also shown in the data from Ireland and New Zealand.

Prevent People from Harming Others

This item tended to show universally narrow and distinctive profiles, with little change between age-groups: in every country the responses showed that preventing people from harming others is done by the Police, by the Laws and—at the international level—by the UN.

Show Who is the Strongest

This and the next item ("Create disagreements") were intended to explore social conflict. As has already been shown younger children tended to be relatively unaware of adult conflict. It is therefore not surprising to find hardly any endorsement for either of these two items in Population I: institutionalized trials of strength or social strife are not yet perceived at this age except, to a slight extent, by the West German children (who made some mention of Elections, the Legislature and Political parties).

In Israel, Italy and Finland the same could be said for the children in Population II; in the remaining countries—while the profiles were very weak—there was some mention of Elections, the Legislature, Political parties, and the Police. In Finland and in the United States, Big Business was also included in the profile to some extent.

The profiles, though still not very strong—became considerably wider in Population IV. In New Zealand and in Ireland the Labor unions were included, while in the Federal Republic of Germany the Democratic system was mentioned.

There was not much stress on the possibly conflictual roles of the Police, Big Business or the Labor unions.

Create Disagreements

This and the preceding item ("Show who is the strongest") were intended to explore the children's perceptions of social conflict. It has been noted before that younger children tended to be unaware of conflict between groups of adults; an almost total unawareness of adult conflict was observed in Population I, in both these items, and the same could be said—with the possible exceptions of the Federal Republic of Germany, the Netherlands, Finland and the United States—in respect of Population II. In these four countries the beginnings of a very weak profile showed up, mentioning Elections and Political parties.

As in the proceding item, the profiles became considerably wider in Population IV, including not only additional institutions such as the Legislature and the Democratic system, but also—in some countries—economic institutions such as Big Business (Finland, Sweden) or the Labor unions (Federal Republic of Germany, the Netherlands, United States and especially New Zealand). It was evident from these responses that in Population IV the students recognized that the same institutions can have both cohesive and divisive potentials.

POLITICAL CONFLICT PERCEPTION

A Political Conflict Perception score as described in Chapter 7 was calculated for each student on the basis of responses to three items concerning the settlement or creation of disagreements by Elections, the Legislature, and Political parties. Among other things this score reflects, as does the individual analysis of these items in this chapter, the extent to which students in the Federal Republic of Germany perceive conflict in their domestic political system.

DIFFERENTIATION SCORES

The comparisons which the child makes between institutions was assessed by the differentiation scores, the signed difference between perceptions of different institutions (also detailed in Chapter 7).

The results showed the following trends:

Democratic System/Big Business: In Population I there were virtually no perceived differences, but the scores increasingly favored the Democratic System as the institution which gives people a right to say what they think and to take part in important decisions with rising age.

Democratic System/Police: The same trends as above.

Democratic System/Welfare Agencies: Some slight increase in differences with age but on the whole there was more perceived similarity here than between the preceding two pairs.

Democratic System/Labor Unions: Again, relatively slight differences between the two institutions, and slight increase with age.

The above findings refer, not to the percept of each institution as a whole, but *only* to the two items on which comparisons were made.

Obviously, a large number of such detailed, scored comparisons could have been constructed but the large drop-out rate and the considerable effort and cost in computer-time was a deterent. It may be concluded that, at least with respect to those values which are particularly related on an *a priori* basis to the Democratic System, the older students in fact perceived some differentiation from other institutions.

The decision was made to compare *group means* between institutions. While it was known they would produce under-estimates of "different-ness," at least each institution's entire profile would be used and there was a far smaller drop-out rate.

Five pairs of institutions were singled out for examination, using only the grouped means for the entire 12-item profile—despite their disadvantages. Out of 45 possible paired comparisons the following were chosen:

> Labor Unions/Big Business
> Labor Unions/Welfare Agencies
> Labor Unions/Police
> Police/Democratic System
> Legislature/UN.

Detailed inspection of these mean differences for different countries and age-levels showed that there was a general tendency for differentiation to increase with rising age, often more so between Population I and II than between Population II and IV (Table 11.8). The size of the difference depended on the age at which the children develop a clear image of a given institution, or the age at which the image changes (e.g., becomes more cynical/realistic), and such age-points differed from country to country and between different institutions.

SOME FREE RESPONSES

Checks in boxes made by tens of thousands of children and subjected to computer analysis and interpretation acquire, after a while, an air of unreality which makes one wonder about their validity.

For each institution in the How Society Works instrument an optional question was introduced to which the child could give a free, unstructured response: "What else do Elections (Laws, Political parties, the Police, etc.) *really* do?" Unfortunately, no participating country took up this optional question, and so it was not possible to "flesh out" the statistical results with the children's own responses. However, some free responses were obtained during the pilot work, in answer to the same question—though some of the institutions were different.

Here, for example, is the response of a 10-year-old child in the United States to "Taxes" at the time of the Viet Nam war:

> "Taxes can help keep our country safe by buying tanks and guns and bombs, but I don't think that is keeping other people safe, and it doesn't help us stop a war but keeps it going. That isn't safe for anyone."

Here are some further Population I quotations, this time from England:

312

Table 11.8. *Mean Ratings from "How Society Works"—Example of Increased Perceptual Differentiation with Age*

Country: The Netherlands

	Population I		Population II		Population IV	
	Labor unions	Big Business	Labor Unions	Big Business	Labor Unions	Big Business
Make sure there are fair shares for everyone	2.8	2.8	3.1	2.1	3.1	1.5
Settle arguments and disagreements	2.1	2.0	2.2	1.4	2.6	1.3
Give help to rich people	1.9	2.0	1.4	2.3	1.3	2.9
Show who is the strongest	1.9	1.9	2.0	2.3	2.3	2.7
Create a better understanding so that people can live and work together	2.7	2.6	2.6	1.8	2.3	1.4
Force people to obey the rules	2.1	2.1	1.8	1.8	1.9	1.9
Create disagreements	2.2	2.1	2.3	2.2	2.6	2.4
Give people a chance to write or say what they think	2.5	2.4	2.8	1.9	2.5	1.4
Help people to take part in important decisions about their own lives	2.6	2.4	2.7	1.9	2.6	1.4
Make people afraid to say what they think	1.7	1.7	1.3	1.6	1.3	1.7
Prevent people from harming others	2.1	2.0	2.0	1.5	1.8	1.3
Make prices go up	2.2	2.4	1.8	2.7	2.2	2.7

Elections: "There is another reason for having an election and that is they have a chance for the people to vote for another government."

"To choose an M.P. who will do his best for the people in his area."

"I don't think there is any reason for elections."

"We have elections to stop people having war."

313

"To try to bring taxes and mortgages etc. down."

"To have someone to tell us what to do."

"To let people choose themselves a leader."

"It gives different parties a chance to make the living better."

The following are some responses by Italian Population I children:

Elections: "In order to choose one's delegates to the government."

"To improve our political and economical situation and let us live in a free and democratic climate and to guarantee an autonomous state."

"We have Elections so that in a democratic climate any citizen is responsible for his choice, but in my opinion only the ones paying taxes should vote, because they are the most responsible, as they are more mature in giving their opinions on the various parties."

"To elect the ruling class, which will get us in touch with other nations and this helps to spend the money of the State."

"For the good of society even if sometimes good is not always done."

"We have to substitute a person for not behaving honestly."

Some of the older children showed a more critical attitude in their responses. Here are some Population IV responses from England:

Elections: "To keep the present system in control. It certainly isn't a democratic or representative method of running the country. Thus elections cause dissatisfaction for a lot of minority groups whose dissatisfaction could quite easily be remedied by proper representation without necessarily offending the majority (the sleeping, mindless, unaware, silent majority)."

"So that the general public can have a say in running the country. Although an MP does not convey the thoughts of his own constituency to the House on all occasions."

"Elections, but of what? Who are we voting for, against what and for whom? None of these primary questions are answered by the cardboard replicas of actors they call politicians. It is about time that someone with sense enough to see the situation from both sides came down on one side rather than always in the middle, i.e., never pleasing either side."

"If you think this is a democratic system, you must go around with your eyes shut."

314

The following are some critical responses from Italy (Population IV):

Elections: "According to me, elections are held first of all to be in authority and afterwards to take advantage of us and take our money by increasing taxes."
"I think elections are no longer important, they are accepted by the people from force of habit and without a realization of their true importance."
"Through the democratic form of government we can freely express our opinions and our rights. But to live well it is necessary for people to be civilised."

The children in the middle age-group (Population II) sometimes showed a refreshingly novel outlook. Here are some responses from the Netherlands (Population II):

Elections: "Elections are held to see whether or not people are interested in politics" (voting is not compulsory).
"For me, elections are not necessary and neither is a Queen."
"Modernization, leisure activities, recreation."
Laws: "To bring discipline to the people."
"To keep peace in our country."
"To teach neatness and hygiene to the people."
"To make things as easy as possible for people."
"In theory, laws should be superfluous."
The UN: "Because we cannot withdraw from it."
"The UN does nothing (they only talk)."
"We are a member of the UN to improve our defence and so as to be able to import more goods at lower prices."
"They set our country free so we must remain friends with them."
"It is another form of self-defence."

It is hoped that these few selected quotations will give the reader an insight into the quality of understanding which children of different ages bring to political issues.

SUMMARY AND CONCLUSIONS

The How Society Works instrument has shown itself in many ways to be a successful technique, providing subtle yet quantifiable data on the children's perceptions of political institutions and social processes, comparable across 10 different countries and for age-levels

315

between 10 and 19 years. The instrument is capable of expansion and adaptation to a variety of purposes. It effectively fills a gap between attitudinal and cognitive measures of political socialization, with both of which it shows modest correlations.

In many ways the instrument provides evidence for the importance to the child of percepts obtained *outside* the school. It also shows in some detail how a child's political outlook and awareness are linked with the stages of his social and intellectual development, as well as with his country's political and social institutions.

Country Profiles for Each Institution

Some institutions showed a clear-cut profile even among the youngest children in our samples (the Police, Elections, Laws), other institutions reflected a clearer profile among the older children (Democratic system, Labor unions, Big Business Organizations), while still others remained predominantly vague and unstructured (the Legislature, Political parties, Welfare agencies, the UN) throughout the age-range. There are important implications here for possible changes in curricula and in the teaching processes, if young people are to understand the functions of these institutions, and to become less sceptical.

In general, profiles for the older children tended to include more conflictual items. As students become more sophisticated and realistic, two processes seem to take place: they see more precisely what an institution actually does, and they learn to accept multiple and even contradictory functions for it, e.g., Labor unions can both help to settle arguments and to create disagreements.

This developmental process is *most* evident among the children from the Federal Republic of Germany. Their outlook becomes realistic or even cynical quite early on.

From among the multiplicity of findings some specific ones may be mentioned. The image of the Legislature is generally weak and the older the children are, the *less* they think that Parliament (Congress, the Bundestag, etc.) does much of anything. The image of the UN is generally weak too, but more favorable and less divisive—with interesting differences among the children in the Federal Republic of Germany, Israel and the United States. The image of Political parties does not seem to depend on the party structure in each country. The perception of the Welfare agencies was particularly vague among children in some of the countries with high per capita incomes, while in less wealthy countries settling disagreements and helping with important life decisions were included in the profile. The images of the two economic institutions—Business and Labor unions —tended to emerge comparatively late, and included some discordant items. The Police profiles were generally very clear and included two main functions: a law enforcement and harm prevention role and an adjudicative, conflict resolution role (ensure fair shares, settle disagreements). Only in some countries were there minor indications of an oppressive role.

Profiles of Values and Social Processes

As with specific institutions, here it was also found that some value realization processes are established very early, others later in adolescence and some later still. This is partly because children only gradually become aware of certain problems, such as conflicts between groups of adults (e.g., Political parties), but also because they do not learn the functions of some institutions until later.

Among *early established* values are the following:

- obey the rules (Authority), ensured by the laws and by the police, according to most children;
- settling arguments and disagreements, also done by the police, and by the laws and the legislature, and sometimes by the labor unions;
- freedom of expression, ensured by elections and the democratic system generally;
- prevention of harm from others, through the medium of the law and the police and, in a wider context, the UN.

Among the perceptions of values which emerge *later in adolescence* are:

- rising prices, said to be caused by big business and, to some extent, by the labor unions;
- helping the rich, primarily by big business but in the Federal Republic of Germany and the United States also by the political system;
- helping people to participate in important decisions, through the democratic system and elections, and to some extent through the labor unions—but the Federal Republic of Germany respondents consistently denied that *any* institution promoted participation.

Among the values which became articulated *later still* are:

317

- show who is the strongest, through the functions of elections, political parties, and sometimes the police;
- create disagreements, through elections, political parties, and to some extent by big business and labor unions, according to our respondents.

These trends may be summed up by saying that the "harmonizing" values become established first, while discordant and conflict-regulating processes do not enter the children's awareness until the later part of adolescence, after age 14.

Two values showed very wide and general profiles: ensuring fair shares, and creating better understanding. To some extent these two items suffered from response set, but the West German children consistently denied that *any* institution made sure that there were fair shares for everyone.

This developmental process may be interpreted as a change from a "sheltered" to a "sophisticated" or realistic view of society: The *sheltered view* includes firmly established patterns of authority and obedience, public safety and crime prevention, freedom of expression, fair shares, improved understanding, and a lack of awareness of social conflict and trials of strength; the *sophisticated view* of society includes both cohesive and divisive functions of institutions, economic conflict and class bias, less fairness and understanding, low participation, and low general efficacy of institutions. In between these two stages children gradually learn to distinguish and articulate the role of institutions more sharply and with greater subtlety, and to tolerate multiple functions; above all, they become aware of broad conflicts and opposing forces in society, and the need to in-stitutionalize these processes.

A speculative approach might suggest that there are probably not two or three but perhaps five *stages of political socialization:*

Stage 1: Very vague, inarticulate notions, with emergent images of one or two institutions, e.g., the police.

Stage 2: What may be called the "sheltered" view, in which pri-marily the harmonizing values and processes become established.

Stage 3: An intermediate stage of growing awareness of social con-flict, of economic forces, of the UN, of multiple institutional roles, etc. but essentially still with a sheltered orientation.

Stage 4: What has been called the sophisticated or realistic view above, with less stress on fairmindedness and understanding, clear awareness of both the cohesive and divisive functions of many institutions, of overlap between institutional functions, of social bias, low participation, oppressive potential, etc.

Stage 5: Scepticism, a general contempt for institutions and lack of belief in their efficacy, an emphasis on discordant functions, unfairness and class bias, denial of participation and of improved understanding.

Obviously, a cross-sectional study such as this cannot demonstrate that children grow from one stage to the next; that would require a long-term developmental follow-up. Nor is it implied that all children must necessarily go through these five stages—further research will no doubt show various patterns.

To what extent is there justification for regarding these scores, which show children's capacity to form distinctive percepts for different institutions, as an index of their political socialization? This is an issue on which there is a need first of all to re-examine the underlying assumptions of this research and those of Civic Education teachers generally, since clearly the results are but partly due to classroom teaching, and depend substantially on the political system in a given country, on the child's attitudes and awareness through extra-scholastic sources, and on his cognitive and social development with increasing age. What kind of understanding do we seek to develop in young people? Must it pass from vagueness and ignorance towards articulation and distinction, or is there a further stage, where the distinctiveness of institutions becomes blurred again through the realization that many social values or processes can be generated by a variety of institutions, as well as by broader social and political factors? Do we welcome awareness of adult social conflict, and of the discordant functions of some institutions—or do we label this as "cynicism" and seek, in our teaching, to counteract it? Up to what age do we seek to "shelter" the child from a realistic understanding of political processes? Do we aim at uniformity in political socialization, or do we prefer to see each child develop his own differentiated perceptions of values and institutions? Do the IEA results suggest that there is a "double standard" in this field of socialization (as perhaps in others, e.g., marriage), teaching idealized versions at school and hoping that the child will find out the more realistic aspects from other sources and, in all probability, at a later age? If so, how will this reflect on the credibility of the educational process?

These problems may be illustrated by quoting from the Report of

319

the National Civic Education Committee of the Federal Republic of Germany (1967):

> "Taken as a whole, civic education in Germany has up to now presented an over-harmonious picture of the problems of state and society and developed a model of democratic society which is far too peaceful and free from conflict."

> "In civic education teaching in Germany, practical political thinking and a purified national conscience, which are the foundations of the political functioning of a democratic society, are scarcely touched upon. And yet on the other hand there prevails a belief, contrary to science, in the realisation of a conflict-free society, in which assertion of power is regarded as evil and the existence of conflicts as sinful. For this reason, power and strife, in spite of their being eminent political categories, and the conflict of powers and the great ideologists and foreign policy occupy only a very unsatisfactory position in the curricula for civic education in Germany."

These quotations highlight the dilemma indicated by the IEA results, a dilemma which many other countries have yet to face.

Chapter 12

Conclusions and Implications

The outcomes of civic education programs, as displayed in the knowledge and attitudes of more than 30 000 adolescents and pre-adolescents in 10 nations are part of interdependent systems where diverse elements—political structures, policy decisions, teachers' educational methods—all exert an influence. The fact that this study of Civic Education was conducted under the auspices of a comparative education organization is in itself an indication of educators' increasing interest in the development of political and social attitudes and the increasing realization that the school shares great influence with the home and the parents in the acquisition by children of political knowledge and attitudes.

All of those who planned and participated in the IEA Civic Education Survey realized early that the domain of Civic Education was different from other school subjects and that it presented a special challenge because of its serious emphasis upon attitudinal or affective outcomes as well as upon cognitive ones. Schools play an important role in teaching children values and attitudes as well as the factual knowledge and skills they are traditionally expected to impart. The teaching of respect for authority and for property, norms of cooperative interaction, principles of decision making on an individual and group basis, loyalty to one's group (school class as well as country), respect for the rights of others, and the importance of active participation in social life are all parts of the educative process. Occasionally teachers or educational authorities may deny that they engage in the transmission of values or that they have an impact on political attitudes, arguing that it is the school's obligation to uphold norms of objectivity. However, the finding of this study is that Civic Education programs are generally an exception to the norm of detachment. In response to the International Civic Education Committee's requests for information about textbooks, syllabuses and examinations in this field, returns from every country surveyed stressed the great importance of inculcating such values as good citizenship, tolerance, support for civil rights and democratic practices. In several of the participating nations the role of schools in teaching these patriotic and democratic values is formalized in the national constitution or in laws concerning the educational system.

In spite of the fact that the transmission of civic values and attitudes (as well as the appropriate knowledge) was seen a suitable task of the school by those participating in the study, the process by which this transmission actually takes place was not clear. The methods used by the schools often seemed simply to be derived from established educational practices in the cognitive domain rather than from a thorough understanding of attitude formation grounded in socialization theory or social psychology. Some schools endeavor to teach these values by holding up famous national figures as models or requiring participation in patriotic ceremonials; some by holding mock elections or debates on public issues; others by fiat, telling the students what the approved values are; a few by discussing contemporary issues in the classroom; some by attempting to create a school atmosphere perceived as conducive to tolerance and democracy; and some by a combination of these methods. Beyond these efforts of the school, which are to a considerable extent conscious and deliberate, there are other factors which work in a less systematic or less intentional way. These include some school practices as well as the extremely varied and important influences of the home, of leisure activities, and of the mass media.

It must be stated at the outset of this section that action by socialization agents (as well as some unintended effects of these actions) interacts not merely with the child's overall cognitive development but with the development of percepts and knowledge about civic matters, with the student's intelligence, and with values and attitudes in related areas. All this is a subtle and highly complex process. Thus, an attempt to teach or transmit certain values directly may not be successful while some aspect of the associated classroom atmosphere may have an unintended effect upon attitudes. Nor is the direction of causality or influence obvious in all cases. Knowledge may generate interest; interest may generate a search for further knowledge; and added knowledge may stimulate interest still further. Especially in younger children, where all of these processes are themselves incomplete, it is difficult to look at them separately. Even at the level of the political system itself it is a difficult matter to untangle the causal pattern. For example, do students support women's rights because they see women in prominent governmental roles or is the presence of women in such roles the result of a prevailing opinion shared by adults and adolescents alike concerning the appropriateness of female political participation?

In this chapter several issues will be addressed. The first concerns the implications of the study for the methodology of attitudinal research with children and adolescents. The second section is a report on the status of knowledge of civics, of support for democratic values, of support for the government, and of predispositions toward citizen participation in the countries surveyed. The third issue concerns the relative impact of school and home (and tangentially of other factors) on the acquisition of civic knowledge and attitudes. This is the familiar question of the role of socializing agents. The fourth issue is of particular interest to teachers and educational decision makers and has to do with particular characteristics of schools and of political systems which are related to specific levels of cognitive and affective achievement in Civic Education. Here teachers' practices and selectivity of the school system will be inspected. What evidence is there that alterations in Civic Education programs could have a desirable effect upon civic knowledge or attitudes? Finally, an attempt will be made to consider the place of a comparative study of Civic Education such as this in the growing field of political socialization research.

METHODOLOGICAL IMPLICATIONS
OF THE CIVIC EDUCATION SURVEY

This survey demonstrated clear and interpretable differences between countries in the cognitive and affective achievement levels of students. There was considerable range among countries in the mean cognitive scores at each age/population level. Variation in performance levels by age/population group was also apparent. That is, students in some countries performed much better than those in other countries at one age level but not at another (see Chapter 5). There was also considerable variation by country in responses to single items on the attitudinal scales and to items from the instrument How Society Works; this was reflected in summary scores which showed different levels of attitudinal factors in different countries (see Chapters 8 and 11). In particular these differences in responses to attitudinal scales allowed the classification of the average 14-year-old students in any given country as belonging to one pattern (high Support for Democratic Values, low Support for the

National Government, and low Civic Interest/Participation) or to the opposite pattern (low Support for Democratic Values, high Support for the National Government, high Civic Interest/Participation). When Civic Education cognitive achievement is considered along with Support for Democratic Values, Support for the National Government, and Civic Interest/Participation, an even more complex pattern of outcomes can be observed.

Even given these striking differences in levels of response to cognitive as well as to affective items, however, the findings between countries are in a number of respects more striking for their similarity than for their disparity. Cognitive and affective scale reliabilities were of similar magnitude in different countries (reflecting similar patterns of correlations between items within scales); the factor structure of the attitudinal outcomes, producing three similar factors (listed above), was obtained in each country even when no attempt was made to rotate these factors to a common structure (reflecting similar patterns of correlations between scales). The amount of variance in cognitive and affective outcomes accounted for by different blocks of predictors was quite similar in different countries, for a given dependent predicted variable within a given age population. With a few exceptions the teachers of different countries were similar in the kinds of topics they thought important for students to learn and in the methods they reported using.

These between-country similarities were somewhat unexpected, especially since cross-national research is often geared toward explaining between-country differences. Bearing in mind the problems of translation, of differences in the questionnaire layout, of different school systems and teaching practices, of differences in regimes and in the mass media, it seems remarkable to find so many similarities in patterns of association in data on political information and attitudes among the varied populations of children and adolescents included in the survey.

How is it possible to account for this between-country *consistency in association* between variables and *difference in level* of performance or response? First, it could be argued that the reason there were so few between-country differences in relationships or associations lies in the insensitivity of questionnaires to the content area. But against this interpretation there is the evidence of widespread and meaningful between-country differences in level of response on individual items, and the attitudinal scale score patterns reported.

Second, it might be argued that the between-country similarity is due to response set. Response sets have two things in common: in the first place they give the data greater apparent uniformity than is justified; in addition they introduce a spurious or unwanted element into the scales, which makes them less valid (except, of course, where the nature of the response set is correlated with the attitude in question). The attitudinal instrument constructed in the IEA Civic Education Survey meets reasonable criteria of multi-method measurement without obvious response-set bias. The factor analysis reported in Chapter 8 indicates that among 14-year-olds and pre-university students the Civic Education outcomes which factored or clustered together on the basis of their correlations did not represent a single response format but rather a common content area.

Third, it might be suggested that the basic similarity of political structures in the 10 countries tested is responsible. In spite of wide differences in forms of government (monarchy, republic, federation) these countries are all democracies. If this were a sufficient explanation of similarities in patterns of relationship, however, one would also expect similarity in item- and scale-response levels. This was not the case.

Fourth, it is conceivable that the measuring instruments are ideologically biased. There is certain to be bias of one kind or another in instruments of this kind. The important question is whether such biases account for relationships between items or scales within one country which are very similar to the relationships between items or scales in other countries. The question can be posed in a more subtle way: is it possible that in the course of civics teaching a set of assumptions is conveyed to the students which does not reflect the real political world but rather an ideological point of view? There is evidence that there is a somewhat uniform ideology in the nations included in this study. At the most, however, such a common set of expectations could account for similarity at the content level; at that level, between-country differences are in fact more common than similarities. It is difficult to see how the transmission of an ideological bias could by itself account for the stability of first and higher order coefficients of correlation and regression.

Finally, it might be argued that the similarity is caused by common cognitive development and distributions of socio-economic status among the respondents in all the countries included. This argument would suggest that the scores on the affective as well as the cognitive tests are primarily determined by intelligence, home social background, and the stage of cognitive development the student has reached. The assumption would be that children are children everywhere and that there is between-country similarity because any given age/population group is likely to be at a similar developmental stage. Cognitive and intellectual development as well as the education level of the home are important. The regression analysis demonstrates that these particular predictive factors have much more importance in determining the achievement of cognitive (as contrasted with affective) outcomes in civics, however. The Home background factors in Block 1 and Word Knowledge (Block 5) made considerably more contribution to predicting the variance in Civic Education cognitive achievement than to either of the affective civics outcomes. Similarities between countries in cognitive development and socio-economic distribution of the population studied cannot be discounted, therefore, but do not provide an adequate explanation for the particular similarities observed.

No doubt other arguments could be developed which would explain these between-country similarities in patterns of correlation as reflected in factor structures and in regressions. As against these explanations, however, there are many factors which would tend to generate differences rather than similarities: different regimes, inequivalences of language and translation (even when carefully-checked), differences in questionnaire layout, and differences in school organization. All of these militate against similarity of the results at any level. Although considerable difference in level of Civic Education cognitive performance and level of civic-attitude support were found, the *patterns* of relationship within countries were very similar. The conclusion is therefore that although between-country differences may have many possible explanations, consistency and similarity have only one—namely that the measures are valid. This conclusion may lead to placing less emphasis on apparent or superficial differences in the socialization of political attitudes in different countries and more emphasis on the generally fairly uniform processes of socialization involved. It also permits greater confidence in the cross-national stability of measures of this kind. It is still relatively uncommon to find cross-national studies of attitudes among adults; such studies are even more rare with children.

Only too frequently the numerous differences which are found in other studies could be accounted for by poor instrumentation or sampling. The IEA results may be interpreted to suggest that if enough care is taken during initial phases of instrument development, remarkably stable cross-national measures can be obtained which will be sensitive enough to indicate differences in the level of knowledge and attitudinal support. (Oppenheim and Torney, 1974.)

These conclusions about methodology are of course limited to the development of dependent measures of cognitive and affective outcomes of civic education and to the measurement of school inputs as reflected in the responses of students, teachers and principals or headmasters, in the IEA study. For financial and political reasons it was not possible to carry out parent interviews or to collect home-based data, other than those which could be obtained from the student. Such data might well have shown more between-country differences in patterns of relationship as well as helping to account for the considerable amount of unexplained variance in student attitudes.

The Civic Education study as part of the IEA Six Subject survey has retained the basic methodology of step-wise blocked multiple regression. Since Civic Education is recognizably different in several ways from such school subjects as Science or Foreign Languages, since many of its goals are affective rather than cognitive, and since many of its inputs come from outside the school, there are plans to reanalyze some of the data in the future using different statistical models which may be more informative about such matters as, for example, the developmental aspects of political attitudes.

THE STATUS OF CIVIC KNOWLEDGE AND ATTITUDES AMONG PRE-ADOLESCENTS AND ADOLESCENTS IN NINE NATIONS

The results of this survey will be somewhat disappointing to the planners or practitioners of Civic Education in many of the countries studied. In no country did students score above average on all four of the major Civic Education outcome measures: Knowledge of Civic Education, Support for Democratic Values, Support for the National Government, and Civic Interest/Participation. For example, 14-year-olds in the Netherlands had higher Civic Education cognitive scores than the students in any other country; their support for Democratic Values was also very high, but their Interest in Political Discussion and Participation was low as was their Support for the National Government. In contrast, students in Israel, who expressed great Interest in Participation and high Government Support, had low scores on Democratic Values and only a moderate level of Civic

Education cognitive achievement. Students in Ireland had the lowest cognitive scores in civics, a moderately high level of participatory interest, and relatively low support for Democratic Values. In fact, in every country where student support for Democratic Values was above the mean for all countries, Support for the National Government was below the mean for all countries (and vice versa).

There are several possible explanations for patterns like these. It might be concluded that the time and effort which schools presently devote to Civic Education is insufficient to foster all four of the cognitive and affective civic outcomes scrutinized. The school programs which effectively teach students knowledge of civic processes perhaps have insufficient time remaining to foster democratic values or to encourage civic interest. In partial support of this interpretation is the information that although teachers and experts on civics curriculum in these countries rated many potential topics in Civic Education as important for students to learn, the relatively small amount of school time actually devoted to Civic Education was insufficient to cover in depth all the topics which these educators thought were important. A more effective approach might consist of programs of Civic Education which, instead of attempting to cover so many topics, would more sharply focus upon bringing students to a necessary minimum level of knowledge of governmental structure and process and to a sufficient understanding of human rights and democratic values upon which to base a critical evaluation of their own government. This, in turn, might stimulate political activity. Even this is a large order, and to do it well would require careful identification of the most effective techniques and topics necessary to achieve each of the desired outcomes.

The data on specific topics indicate that including a study of non-Western cultures fosters democratic values and knowledge in some nations. A very traditional approach to Civic Education, where facts and memorization are stressed, was shown to be less productive. This is not to say that a return to very traditional approaches to Civic Education should be encouraged, but rather that the most effective methods and most important topics (international as well as intranational) need to be identified. The greatest need in Civic Education, if this argument is accepted, is for materials and methods which are carefully tailored to the individual topics identified as important and for sufficient time to put them to productive use.

A second possible explanation for the failure of the students of any given country to demonstrate uniformly high civics achievement is that there may be an actual incompatibility between some of the outcomes. For example, a stress on patriotism and nationalism, which seems to contribute to adolescent support for the national government and active civic participation, may foster those outcomes at the expense of support for democratic values. The patterns of achievement in different countries at both age 14 and the pre-university level support this interpretation. The regression analysis, based on student differences within countries, indicates that participation in patriotic ritual is related to authoritarian attitudes and also to participation in political discussion. The possible incompatibility of positive attitudinal outcomes makes the task of program reform in Civic Education an especially difficult one. In these nine nations, if practices which increase one positively valued civic outcome do so at the expense of another, imaginative new approaches or new practices may be required, ones which will foster intended positive effects and minimize the unintended negative ones.

The only school-based variables that seemed to contribute in what might be called a positive direction to the students' achievement of all three desired outcomes (as evidenced in the regression analysis) were measures of what is often called classroom climate—particularly indications that students are encouraged to express their opinions. This response was characteristic of the students who were more knowledgeable, less authoritarian, and more participant.

If the argument concerning incompatibility of outcome is taken seriously, it becomes important to examine both the intended and the unintended effects of educational practices. From these data it appears that encouragement of student discussion and participation in the classroom is one practice in which both the intended and unintended effects might be called positive; in contrast, other aspects of school input may increase one intended outcome at the expense of another.

There remains another possible explanation for the failure of students in any country to excel on all measured outcomes of Civic Education. It may be that out-of-school rather than in-school factors are the primary determinants of level of achievement. According to this point of view, it is neither that schools devote insufficient time to the subject of Civic Education, nor that the programs lack focus, nor that there is a basic incompatibility between certain positive outcomes; rather, the political system or régime, or its predominant ideology, acts on citizens of all ages (students, parents and teachers) as well as on school structure and classroom climate. In that case, the prevailing influences of the mass media, of parents and of friends would together exert a more decisive effect than in-school factors. However, though out-of-school inputs certainly should not be discounted, the results suggest that at least part of the between- and within-country differences observed result from school factors rather than from those exerted from outside.

Civic Education is a topic of concern to a variety of members of society. The political socialization process, as it creates and influences these orientations at both the ad ilt and pre-adult level, is important for predicting the future course of citizen political action and opinion. Although distinctive patterns of attitudes do exist, in no country (of the nine where full analysis was conducted) does the distribution of such attitudes suggest that the government is about to lose citizen support or that civil liberties are in serious danger. Policy makers in these countries who look to the future can probably rely on young adult public opinion to be much like what they have known in the recent past. In certain countries they may expect a relatively cynical generation of young adult citizens or a generation which is likely to perceive that the suspension of certain civil liberties can be justified. Political circumstances and events in the next decade will, of course, influence future citizen orientations as they have in the past, sometimes in unexpected directions.

It may be that the impact of political issues upon the attitudes of young adults will find expression primarily in the realm of heightened political interest and participation in civic affairs rather than in more passive support for democratic values. Real activism in the political realm may require issue provocation. Socialization or education may only prepare or predispose the individual to take action; any one of several political issues may then provoke a response.

The conversion of generalized support for democratic values into active support for the rights of a particular group (e.g., the rights of women, the rights of a given minority), may be strongly influenced by groups within the society which attempt to raise the public consciousness about the denial of these rights. The effect of these demands for justice may in some cases be a defensive decline in support for democratic values, a backlash effect.

The data reported here were collected with more stress upon predictors from the educational system than upon current political events, mass media, or adult public opinion. A longitudinal replication of parts of the study with greater attention to social indicators of political conflict, to domestic and international political issues, to other system-wide inputs and to parent attitudes would be highly desirable.

To consider the cognitive realm, students at all levels tested in the IEA survey were relatively poorly informed about many aspects of their government and international affairs. As the analysis in Chapter 5 indicated, some of the incorrect alternatives were chosen with disturbingly high frequency, suggesting that students have some basic misconceptions about democracy, about their own government, and about global politics. However, in none of the nine countries in which the data have been fully analyzed, are the majority of students so ignorant about political structures or so lacking in their support for their government or for democratic values, or in their interest in participation that drastic steps need to be taken. In the future, however, since increasing rather than decreasing complexity of both political and social system can be predicted, there is truly a need for more attention to programs of Civic Education.

RELATIVE IMPACT OF AGENTS OF SOCIALIZATION— HOME AND SCHOOL INFLUENCE

To discuss adequately the issue of the relative impact of home and school factors in influencing cognitive and affective civics achievement requires a quite painstaking review of the data collected, particularly the regression analysis. The argument about the relative impact of home and school upon student achievement is a familiar one. It has been studied by sophisticated statistical techniques in a variety of subject areas (including all of those tested by IEA). In most other studies and reviews of political socialization the matter has been approached with somewhat less statistical sophistication (often simply by asking the student where he believes most of his political opinions have originated). The determination of the relative responsibility of various socialization agents obviously poses a number of questions for policy making—ought schools to take on more responsibility for improving Civic Education programs, or is the home influence so strong that schools would be more or less ineffective even if they were to make a concerted effort to improve political education. As the conceptualization of political attitudes and the understanding of processes of socialization have become more sophisticated, the question about agents has also become a less simple one.

Although Home background, Age and Sex are important predictors of knowledge of Civic Education and of Support for Democratic Values, they do not in any sense overdetermine attitudes. Schools whose students come from less privileged home backgrounds do not have insurmountable handicaps in teaching students about their government or in fostering democratic values. School variables, both the general quality or academic orientation of current and earlier schools and current learning conditions (in the form of classroom practices), play a considerable role in determining support for democratic values and knowledge. However, it is clear that these practices and learning conditions are part of a large and interdependent system; the alteration of any single school variable (for example, putting less emphasis on learning facts or including more in-depth material about non-Western cultures) is unlikely to have a discernible impact upon the acquisition of democratic values unless this alteration is supported by other changes in the climate and objectives of civic instruction and takes cognizance of the more general forces operating in the society.

In evaluating all of the data regarding the relative impact of home and school it must be noted that although school factors were more thoroughly sampled than home factors, the order of the regression analysis (which partialed out the effects attributable to home social background first) operated against the overestimation of school effects.

A somewhat unexpected finding in the IEA data was that although the determinants of support for democratic values and of Civic Education cognitive outcomes were relatively similar, they were quite different from the determinants of participation in political discussion. Out-of-school influences were especially important in explaining variations in degree of political interest. Among 14-year-olds, reports of participation often seem to refer to in-school discussion and activities. At 17, civic interest and participation seems to be much more reality-based and more reactive to events in the political world. Of interest also in the analysis of possible meanings of the term "political participation," is the fact that the sense of political efficacy (the belief that citizens can have an influence upon government policy) was found not to be closely related to actual interest in participation. The efficacy measure was found to be more closely tied to positive feelings about the national government. This suggests, as other researchers who have studied adults have indicated, that the sense of efficacy is a characteristic of citizen beliefs about their government, that it frequently accompanies general positive orientations toward the government, and that it is not necessarily the expression of a strong motivation on the part of the individual to stimulate change or have an effect upon government.

A full understanding of the meaning of political participation in the nations studied also requires a recognition that the knowledgeable student will not necessarily be the most active participant in politics. Activity and knowledge do not show a strong correlation, and they are predicted by different factors.

In a study such as this one, which has a fuller representation of in-school learning conditions than out-of-school influences, one would expect to be able to account for greater between-student variation in the cognitive scores than in the affective ones. This is in fact the case. No information was obtained directly from parents (though the students' perceptions of the level of their agreement with parents was included). The students' friends were not questioned; no inquiries were made about actual teacher attitudes except their conception of good citizenship, and it was not possible to do a content analysis of current media programs or to determine which ones the students actually watched. Information about the social status of parents was available and accounted for a considerable portion of the observed variations in cognitive achievement, but much less in affective or attitudinal scores. The failure to account for more between-student variation in the affective realm may be due to the fact that the cognitive test dealt with knowledge which in a sense, even for adolescents, is an end in itself; the measures of attitudes and participation dealt more with anticipatory roles which depend upon future events for their realization in behavior (i.e., speaking in favor of the protection of fundamental rights for groups with unpopular opinions, or voting in an election).

The frequent and lengthy arguments in the literature about the question of socialization agents will not receive a fully satisfactory resolution from this (or perhaps any) study. The best hope for such a resolution is a study in the future which could include home variables (parental political attitudes and socialization practices as well as socio-economic status), teachers' attitudes and practices (including not only self-report but observational data), media exposure, climate of public opinion as well as the students' knowledge of it, social indicators of variations between countries in political events and characteristics, and peer group interactions. Projects like the one reported here and the Jennings and Niemi study (1974) which sampled home variables more effectively than school variables, are likely to confirm the view that the home, the school, the peer group, and the media are all important agents of socialization.

The IEA study indicates that there is considerable similarity within Western European countries in the goals of Civic Education and in some of the practices employed. There are, however, relatively wide variations in the outcomes and in some cases in the relative impact of socialization agents. (The impact of home background and socio-economic status on democratic values tends to be relatively large in the United States, for example.) A data base in more than one country is a necessity before we can generalize widely about the intended or unintended effects of socialization agents. For this purpose, there is certainly some advantage in studying relatively similar systems which nevertheless show theoretically interesting variations (Przeworski and Teune, 1970).

THE INFLUENCE OF SPECIFIC CLASSROOM PRACTICES ON CIVIC OUTCOMES

The particular characteristics of schools and pedagogical practices which are related to between-country differences in outcomes or are related within countries to variations in student attitudes and knowledge about civic matters are of special interest to policy makers as well as to teachers and public officials.

First, it should be noted that the most general characteristics of teacher training did not tend to be related to enhanced achievement in civics; nor did the number of years that social studies were included in the students' curriculum of study appear to have any effect. A nationalistic orientation stressing support of the national government through patriotic rituals seemed to have an impact upon both the acquisition of knowledge and of democratic values. Countries in which there is stress upon patriotic rituals and/or countries where there is a relatively traditional approach to Civic Education are characterized by student performance which indicates a lower level of knowledge and less support for democratic values, but often higher interest in political participation. The clearest example of the relatively nationalistic pattern with moderate knowledge scores and low democratic value scores is Israel; the best example of the traditional pattern of instruction combined with some nationalistic stress associated with low cognitive scores and low support for democratic values is Ireland. The clearest example of the opposite pattern of low nationalistic stress and high cognitive and attitudinal scores are the Netherlands (at least at age 14) and the Federal Republic of Germany. A country which, by contrast, fits neither the nationalistic/traditional nor the anti-nationalistic pattern but shows especially high cognitive scores at the pre-university level and near average scores on all the attitudinal factors is New Zealand.

Looking at both between-country and within-country differences in Civic Education scores we find that students in schools where there is an emphasis on patriotic ritual and on the use of the more traditional methods of instruction (including substantial rote memorization but giving little encouragement to students to develop their own points of view) know less about civics and are less supportive of democratic values. Of course, this interpretation is made more difficult by the problem of defining with exactitude traditional versus non-traditional approaches to civic education. Stress on factual memorization is one measure of a traditional orientation, while interest in the study of non-Western cultures and the encouragement of independent expressions of student opinion may be indices of non-traditional interest. Better indicators are needed, however.

A further question, related to the issue of schooling, is the influence of selective versus comprehensive secondary schools upon civics achievement. This has been a topic of major interest in other subjects of the IEA survey as well. Because most political socialization studies have been formulated by American social scientists, who are generally less concerned with the transition from selective to comprehensive schooling taking place in several European countries, the effects of selectivity have not been extensively investigated in political attitude research.

In fact, when one is comparing the results from pre-university students of different countries on the Civic Education cognitive test, it is vital to keep in mind that while 75 % of this age group were in school in the United States and 45 % in Sweden, only 9 % were in school in the Federal Republic of Germany (and only slightly more in the Netherlands and New Zealand). Those students who are retained past the termination of compulsory schooling are generally the more able students and/or those from higher socio-economic classes. If one is willing to make a series of assumptions about the selection process—including the assumption that those who were still in school in the Federal Republic of Germany at the pre-university level represented the top 9 % of the students of that age with regard to performance in civics—one can adjust the country mean scores for selectivity. This results in a rise in mean for Sweden and the United States, respectively, from ranks of third and sixth (unadjusted) to ranks of first and second (adjusted for selectivity). This suggests that these two systems succeed in educating a mass preadult public while more selective systems are educating a somewhat smaller elite. This conclusion fails to consider whether it is possible that a minimum level of political knowledge, understanding, and attitudes have already been achieved by the age of 14 (before the selection) or, alternatively, that by intensifying and improving programs of Civic Education for students under 14, such a minimum level could be achieved.

In regression analysis where Type of school and program was included as a predictor, the differences between academic and vocational schools and programs were visible for both Civic Education cognitive achievement and Anti-Authoritarianism among 14-year-olds but were negligible at the pre-university level. The differences were also negligible for Political Participation at both age levels.

The selectivity of school systems is, naturally, embedded in a much larger context of within- and out-of-school factors. It is not to be expected that a government committed to such selectivity will abandon it as a result of this study or that countries who have comprehensive schools will reject them. Countries which have moved toward comprehensive schooling since 1971 may, however, find in these data a particularly useful point of comparison. It does appear that educating a larger proportion of students to age 17 or 18 does not dilute educational quality in civics to any great extent.

An attempt such as this to combine the results of between-country differences and within-country analysis of between-student differences requires considerably more effort before it is possible to make more than a tentative prescription. It does appear, however, that care must be exercised in changing Civic Education programs in order to preserve existing strengths at the same time improvements are made. The ideal goal may be a well informed citizenry, supportive of democratic values, basically supportive of and capable of influencing government policy, and interested in participating in civic activities. Our data show that these four aspects of good citizenship not only are independent but are influenced by different practices or in some cases are influenced in different directions by the same practice. The recognition of the interdependence of these systems of socialization is critical to our understanding of the process. Tinkering with a new course here or setting up a new educa-

336

tional requirement for teachers there is unlikely to produce significant movement toward an ideal citizenry in any country.

CONTRIBUTIONS OF THE IEA CIVIC EDUCATION STUDY TO POLITICAL SOCIALIZATION RESEARCH

Many researchers would agree that developing a middle-range *theory* in the area of political socialization is a necessary next step. One important contribution to such a theory would be made by comparative studies which inquire about basically *similar systems* which nevertheless differ in theoretically important characteristics *and* about *systems which differ* more extensively from each other than those included in this survey. Another valuable contribution to such a theory would be studies which attempt to investigate propositions about the socialization process (which have been derived from survey data) using more carefully controlled conditions, observations of classroom interactions, mass media analyses, and student and parent interviews.

Theories or models which can be used to describe and categorize the socialization process were discussed in detail in Chapter 1. It is instructive to examine them in the light of the empirical findings of this study. The Accumulation Model obtains little support from the analysis of the IEA data. In actuality the memorization of facts and other traditional approaches to school subjects seem to have negative rather than positive effects on the acquisition of civic knowledge or attitudes. The Identification Model, which stresses the attitudes and behavior which teachers, peers and parents provide to students for imitation, is deficient in some respects but very powerful in others. In this study there was no measure of parental or teacher attitudes (only educational practices). Though the Identification Model has been most useful in other studies in explaining political party membership, unfortunately no data about students' party preferences or about their parents' preferences were obtained by the IEA survey.

It is very difficult to disentangle the process of identification from that of role transfer in these results. For example, the relationship between a climate of independent discussion in the classroom and both a high standing in knowledge of civics and support for democratic values could result either from students' modeling or identifying with the teachers' attitudes or from students' augmented practice in the role of independent decision making. Also, the Identification and Role Transfer models help one to understand some of the sex differences found in the regression analysis. Girls are less knowledgeable and less participant in discussion in civics, though they are more supportive of democratic values; this corresponds to sex-role patterns previously identified in studies of political attitude as well as of personality development.

The data have also been inadequate to test fully the Cognitive-Developmental Model. After a variety of other predictors of civic cognitive and attitudinal outcomes have been partialed out, general Word Knowledge (the closest approximation to a measure of cognitive ability in the IEA battery) is still a potent predictor of civic knowledge, to a lesser extent predictive of Anti-Authoritarianism, and to a very small extent a predictor of Political Participation. There has been some attempt in this volume to examine aspects of developmental change by comparing Population II and Population IV: there appears to be a more coherent structure of attitudes among older students (noted in the factor analysis), a greater diversity of patterns of between-country differences in attitude and participation among older students, and a heightened awareness of conflict and dissent at the older level. This study has also postulated the existence of five stages in the perception of political and social institutions, from inarticulateness to sophistication or in some cases cynicism. One limitation of this analysis follows from the fact that the pre-university sample tested was chosen as representative of students still in school at that level, not as representative of the 17-, 18-, or 19-year-old age cohort. In very selective school systems, therefore, the comparison of 14-year-olds with pre-university students must be made very cautiously. The United States is the only country where the Population II/Population IV comparison can be made reasonably fairly since Sweden (which has the second most comprehensive system) tested only pre-university students. Because the regression analysis was done separately by population and country, age as a predictor has very little variation (e.g., at Population II between 14 years no months and 14 years 11 months). The Cognitive Developmental Model and its assumptions require considerable further analysis of these data including between-age comparisons of students matched on socio-economic status of the father and school achievement.

Some of the important problems raised by these data are related to developmental issues. Is there a sequence to the formation of attitudes? Is a certain minimum level of knowledge necessary for

338

the development of support for democratic values? Is an individual's belief in the government's responsiveness a necessary prerequisite to political activity? All of these are questions which are most adequately phrased within the developmental psychological perspective.

Even though it does not provide clear answers to all questions about the socialization process, in the domain of comparative studies of socialization the IEA Civic Education survey represents something of an empirical landmark. To use the framework proposed by Przeworski and Teune (1970) this research has investigated a group of relatively similar systems which possess interesting differences in practices, institutional settings and contexts of political socialization and Civic Education. Careful piloting of both cognitive and attitudinal instruments as well as careful sampling of schools, students and teachers has provided a unique base of data. A series of comparisons at the univariate level, showing substantial between-country differences in attitudinal and cognitive patterns have been made; the patterns of relationships within countries have also been explored and considerable similarity noted. Necessary next steps are the comparison of regression analysis between nations in order to substitute the names of particular variables for the names of social systems; the consideration of a variety of models of developmental change by comparing students of different ages partialling out the effects of selectivity of schools; the generation of specific propositions regarding the effects of the contexts provided by schools and community and their testing through classroom observation, student interviews, and experimental programs.

A major question, which has not been addressed in this discussion is the implications of the findings for defining the democratic personality or ideal democratic citizen. Some writers in the past have pointed to a personality or character type which was thought to foster both the emergence of democratic institutions and their preservation. This modal democratic personality was presumably different from the type fostered in un-democratic systems. In fact, it appears that the nine separate and somewhat different democracies studied here are maintained by several different patterns of attitudes at least among their adolescent citizens. Perhaps there are basic variations in the need for citizen support in the various kinds of democratic systems existing in these countries. Since these differences do not appear to be at the level of governmental structure, perhaps they lie in a country's ideology or history. That is a whole realm of analysis for which these data are only a beginning.

References

Abramson, Paul. "The Differential Political Socialization of English Secondary School Students." *Sociology of Education* 40 (1967): 246–269.

Almond, Gabriel, A. and Sidney Verba. *The Civic Culture.* Princeton, N.J.: Princeton University Press, 1963.

Anderson, Bengt-Erik. *Studies in Adolescent Behavior.* Gothenburg, Sweden: Institute of Education, University of Gothenburg, 1969.

Andrain, Charles F. *Children and Civic Awareness.* Columbus, Ohio: Charles E. Merrill, 1971.

Bromsjö, Birger. *Samhällskunskap som skolämne* (Civics Education as a School Subject). Stockholm: Svenska Bokförlaget, 1965.

Campbell, Donald T. and D. W. Fiske. "Convergent and Discriminant Validation by the Multitrait-Multimethod Matrix." *Psychological Bulletin* 56 (1959): 81–105.

Cleary, Robert E. *Political Education in the American Democracy.* Scranton, Pennsylvania: International Textbook Company, 1971.

Comber, L. C. and John P. Keeves. *Science Education in Nineteen Countries. An Empirical Study.* Stockholm: Almqvist & Wiksell and New York: John Wiley, 1973.

Connell, R. W. *The Child's Construction of Politics.* Carlton, Victoria, Australia: Melbourne University Press, 1971.

Dawson: Richard E. and Kenneth Prewitt. *Political Socialization.* Boston: Little, Brown, 1969.

Ehman, Lee H. "An Analysis of the Relationships of Selected Educational Variables with the Political Socialization of High School Students." *American Educational Research Journal* 6 (1969): 559–580.

Farnen, Russell F. and Sixten Marklund. *The Measurement of Civics Cognitive Outcomes in Different Nations.* Stockholm: IEA Manuscript, 1975.

Federal Republic of Germany National Civics Education Committee. *Report.* I.E.A. Civics Education Project, 1967.

Hess, Robert D. and Judith V. Torney. *The Development of Political Attitudes in Children.* Chicago: Aldine Publishing Co., 1967.

Hirsch, Herbert. *Poverty and Politicization.* New York: Macmillian, 1971.

Husén, Torsten (Ed.). *International Study of Achievement in Mathematics,* 2 vols. Stockholm: Almqvist & Wiksell and New York: John Wiley, 1967.

Hyman, Herbert H. *Political Socialization.* Glencoe, Illinois: The Free Press, 1959.

Inkeles, Alex. "Participant Citizenship in Six Developing Countries." *American Political Science Review* 63 (1969): 1120–1141.

Jennings, M. Kent and Richard G. Niemi. *The Political Character of Adolescence.* Princeton, N.J.: Princeton University Press, 1974.

Langton, Kenneth P. *Political Socialization.* New York: Oxford University Press, 1969.

Langton, Kenneth P. and M. Kent Jennings. "Political Socialization and the High School Civics Curriculum in the United States." *American Political Science Review* 62 (1968): 852–867.

Magnusson, David. *Självvärdering och skolmiljö* (Self Evaluation and School Environment). Stockholm: SOU, 1960: 42.

Merriam, Charles E. *The Making of Citizens.* Chicago: The University of Chicago Press, 1931.

Muller, Edward N. "Cross-National Dimensions of Political Competence." *American Political Science Review* 64 (1970): 792–809.

Newton, R. G. and D. J. Spurrell. "A Development of Multiple Regression for the Analysis of Routine Data." *Applied Statistics* XVI (1): 51–64, 1967.

Oppenheim, A. N. and Judith Torney. *The Measurement of Children's Civic Attitudes in Different Nations.* IEA Monograph Studies No. 2. Stockholm: Almqvist & Wiksell International and New York: John Wiley, 1974.

Passow, A. Harry et al. *The National Case Study: An Empirical Comparative Study of Twenty-One Educational Systems.* Stockholm: Almqvist & Wiksell International and New York: John Wiley, 1976.

Peaker, Gilbert F. *An Empirical Study of Education in Twenty-One Countries: A Technical Report.* Stockholm: Almqvist & Wiksell International and New York: John Wiley, 1975.

Purves, Alan C. *Literature Education in Ten Countries. An Empirical Study.* Stockholm: Almqvist & Wiksell and New York: John Wiley, 1973.

Przeworski, Adam and Henry Teune. *The Logic of Comparative Social Inquiry.* New York: John Wiley, 1970.

Raven, John. "Some Results from Pilot Surveys of Attitudes, Values and Perceptions of Socio-Institutional Structures in Ireland." *Economic and Social Review* 4 (1973): 553–588.

Secretary General of the United Nations. *Report on Political Rights of Women, 1968 and 1970.*

Thorndike, Robert L. *Reading Comprehension Education in Fifteen Countries. An Empirical Study.* Almqvist & Wiksell and New York: John Wiley, 1973.

Torney, Judith V. and Donald N. Morris. *Global Dimensions of U.S. Education: The Elementary School.* New York: Center for War/Peace Studies, 1972.

Walberg, Herbert J. and Gary J. Anderson. "Classroom Climate and Individual Learning." *Journal of Educational Psychology* 56 (1968): 414–419.

Weiler, Hans N. "Schools and the Learning of Dissent Norms: A Study of West German Youth." Paper delivered at the 1971 Annual Meeting of the American Political Science Association, Chicago, September 7–11.

Weissberg, Robert. *Political Learning, Political Choice and Democratic Citizenship.* Englewood Cliffs, N.J.: Prentice-Hall, Inc., 1974.